The Rise and Rise of Merit

The Rise and Rise of Meritocracy

Edited by
Geoff Dench

Blackwell Publishing
In association with *The Political Quarterly*

BLACKWELL PUBLISHING
350 Main Street, Malden, MA 02148-5020, USA
9600 Garsington Road, Oxford OX4 2DQ, UK
550 Swanston Street, Carlton, Victoria 3053, Australia

First published 2006 by Blackwell Publishing as a special issue of *The Political Quarterly*

First published 2006 by Blackwell Publishing Ltd
1 2006

Library of Congress Cataloging-in-Publication Data

The rise and rise of meritocracy / edited by Geoff Dench.
     p. cm.
  "First published 2006 by Blackwell Publishing as a special issue of The political
quarterly."
  "Arises out of a conference held at the Institute of Community Studies on 7 May
2004"–Ack.
  Includes bibliographical references and index.
  ISBN-13: 978-1-4051-4719-4 (pbk.: alk. paper)
  ISBN-10: 1-4051-4719-9 (pbk.: alk. paper)
  1. Young, Michael Dunlop, 1915-   Rise of the meritocracy–Congresses.
2. Elite (Social sciences)–Congresses. 3. Social status–Congresses. 4. Merit (Ethics)–
Social aspects–Congresses. 5. Elite (Social sciences)–Great Britain–Congresses.
6. Social status–Great Britain–Congresses. 7. Equality–Great Britain–Congresses.
8. Labour Party (Great Britain)–Congresses. I. Dench, Geoff. II. Political quarterly.

  HM1263.R57 2006
  306.209'04–dc22   2006034425

A catalogue record for this title is available from the British Library

Set in 10.5/12 pt Palatino by Anne Joshua & Associates, Oxford
Printed and bound in the United Kingdom by The Alden Group, Oxford
Production Editor: Rachel Skeet

For further information on Blackwell Publishing, visit our website:
www.blackwellpublishing.com

Contents

Acknowledgements

This collection arises out of a conference held at the Institute of Community Studies on 7 May 2004. The Institute has subsequently been relaunched as The Young Foundation, which in its turn has given valuable help as the conference papers have moved towards publication. The opinions expressed in the finished chapters are, however, the personal views of the authors.

The editor is grateful for all the interest shown in this enterprise by members of the Institute/Foundation—James Cornford in particular—and for the support of the Robert Gavron Charitable Trust, which made it all possible.

Notes on Contributors

Paul Barker is a writer and broadcaster. He is also a senior research fellow of The Young Foundation (and a former trustee and chairman of the Institute of Community Studies). From 1968 to 1986, he was the Editor of the social affairs journal *New Society*.

Lord Asa Briggs was Chancellor of the Open University from 1978 to 1994 and Provost of Worcester College, Oxford, from 1976 to 1991. His many books include *The Age of Improvement, Victorian Cities, A Social History of England*, a five-volume *History of Broadcasting in the United Kingdom* and his biography of Michael—*Michael Young: Social Entrepreneur*.

Belinda Brown is a research fellow of The Young Foundation and University College, London, where she is working on a study of children's social networks. She is author of a number of books and papers, on Polish migrants to London, women's lives and local community; including *The Private Revolution: Women in the Polish Underground Movement*.

Jon Cruddas has been Member of Parliament for Dagenham since 2001. He was political advisor to the Prime Minister from 1997 to 2000.

Jon Davis is Assistant Director of the Mile End Institute, Department of History, Queen Mary, University of London, and is in the final stages of his Cabinet Office sponsored doctoral thesis on 'Prime Ministers and the British Civil Service, 1960–74'. He worked previously in the Cabinet Office, and as an investment banker.

Geoff Dench is a senior research fellow of The Young Foundation, and was formerly head of sociology and social policy at Middlesex University. He has written a number of books on ethnic relations and on family relationships, and edited several collections.

Claire Donovan is a research fellow at the Research Evaluation and Policy Project in the Political Science Program, Research School of Social Sciences, The Australian National University.

Ronald Dore is an Associate of the Centre for Economic Performance at LSE and was formerly Professor of Political Science at MIT. He learned Japanese during the war and has spent most of his life studying Japanese society and economy. Recent books are *Stock Market Capitalism, Welfare Capitalism: Japan and Germany versus the Anglo-Saxons* (OUP) and *Hataraku to iu koto* (Chuokoron, Chuko Shinsho).

Andrew Gamble is Professor of Politics at the University of Sheffield and joint editor of *The Political Quarterly*.

Irving Louis Horowitz is Hannah Arendt University Professor Emeritus at Rutgers, The State University of New Jersey. Among his relevant writings are *Three Worlds of Development: the Theory and Practice of International Stratification* (OUP) and *Behemoth: Main Currents in the History and Theory of Political Sociology* (Transaction).

Takehiko Kariya is Professor of the Sociology of Education at Tokyo University and a leading commentator on the social consequences of school system reform. Recent books published in Japan are *The Educational Crisis of an Increasingly Stratified Japan*, *The Illusions of Educational Reform* and *The Opportunities of Decentralisation: Rebuilding the Curriculum at the Local Level*.

Michelynn Laflèche has studied and worked on social justice issues relating to race and gender in Canada, Germany and the UK. She joined the Runnymede Trust in 1997 and began coordinating the UK Race and Europe Network, as well as managing the Trust's projects relating to European social policy, citizenship and employment. She was appointed Director of Runnymede in February 2001.

Hilary Land is Emeritus Professor of Family Policy at the University of Bristol and an honorary senior research fellow in the School for Policy Studies. She has been an active feminist for over thirty years and is currently a member of the management committee of the Women's Budget Group.

Ruth Lister is Professor of Social Policy at Loughborough University. She was a member of the Fabian Commission on Life Chances and Child Poverty and is author of *Poverty* (Polity Press).

Peter Marris has taught at the University of California, Los Angeles, and Yale University, and is currently affiliated to the Sociology Department at Yale. His most recent book is *The Politics of Uncertainty: Attachment in Private and Public Life*.

Eric Midwinter, social historian, social policy analyst and author, was closely associated with Michael Young for over thirty years, principally with the post-Plowden Educational Priority Area Projects, the Advisory Centre for Education, the National Consumer Council, the Bulk Buy Bureau and the University of the Third Age.

Ferdinand Mount was Editor of the *Times Literary Supplement* from 1991 to 2002 and has worked for numerous papers and journals, including the *Sunday Telegraph*, the *Daily Mail*, *The Times* and *The Spectator*. He has written both novels and non-fiction, notably *The Subversive Family*, *Of Love and Asthma* and *Mind the Gap*.

Jim Ogg is a research fellow of The Young Foundation and is also currently working in Paris at the Caisse Nationale d'Assurance Vieillesse on a number of projects relating to family life and older people. He is co-author of *The Family and Community Life of Older People* and author of *Living Alone in Later Life* and numerous research reports and papers on the life of the elderly.

Rajiv Prabhakar is at the Centre for Philosophy of Natural and Social Sciences at the London School of Economics. He is conducting an Economic and Social Research Council research fellowship on 'The Assets Agenda: principles and policy'.

Yvonne Roberts is an award-winning journalist, writer and broadcaster. She writes regularly for *The Guardian*, the *Independent*, *The Observer*, *Community Care* and the Internet magazine, *The First Post*. She is also the author of four novels, and several non-fiction books on sexual politics, most recently *Where Did Our Love Go?—Reviving a Marriage in 12 Months*, an analysis of marital conflict.

Peter Saunders is currently Social Research Director at the Centre for Independent Studies in Sydney, where he works mainly on tax and welfare reform. Before moving to Australia, he spent twenty-five years at the University of Sussex, where he was Professor of Sociology. He is best known for his work on urban social theory, home ownership, class inequality and social mobility.

Richard Sennett is Professor of Sociology at the London School of Economics and was formerly Director of the New York Institute of the Humanities. His books include *The Fall of Public Man*, *Respect* and *The Corrosion of Character*.

Peter Wilby is former Editor of the *Independent on Sunday* and the *New Statesman*, and was an education correspondent for seventeen years. He is now a columnist for the *New Statesman* and the *Times Educational Supplement*.

David Willetts has been Member of Parliament for Havant since 1992, and has held a number of government and opposition front bench positions, currently as Shadow Secretary of State for Education and Skills. He is a Visiting Fellow at Nuffield College, University of Oxford, and the author of numerous pamphlets and books, such as *Modern Conservatism*, *Civic Conservatism* and *Why Vote Conservative*.

Sir Peregrine Worsthorne saw active service in Phantom during the Second World War and then was leader writer and Foreign Correspondent on *The Times* (1948–53), *The Daily Telegraph* (1953–61) and the *Sunday Telegraph* (1961–85); finally, he was Editor of the *Sunday Telegraph* from 1985 to 1991. He is author of *The Socialist Myth*, *Tricks of Memory* and *Democracy Needs Aristocracy*. He was given a Knighthood on the recommendation of Mrs Thatcher.

Introduction: Reviewing Meritocracy

GEOFF DENCH

Background to the collection

THIS volume arises out of a conference, 'Reviewing Meritocracy', held at the Institute of Community Studies (ICS) in May 2004 to mark its half-centenary. Michael Young had written *The Rise of the Meritocracy* shortly after founding the institute, and the book was first published soon after ICS research reports started appearing. It was immediately successful, won literary prizes and became translated into numerous languages. But, curiously, the ideas he explored within that book were barely incorporated into the work of ICS itself. Our aim in the conference was to end this separation and neglect by giving *Meritocracy* some direct attention, and looking at its relevance to our evolving research programme.

Our main interest was to see whether there was anything in the book that helped to illuminate contemporary British society, by stimulating some longer perspectives on where we stood and where we might be going. There was already a good deal of work taking place nationally on social mobility, some of which called on the idea of meritocracy. But we felt that much of this debate missed out important, and logically prior, questions about the overall structure of society. A discussion organised around the idea of meritocracy itself seemed more likely to flush these out.

The collection now published contains all of the original papers for the conference—some of them subsequently extended—plus a number of contributions from participants who did not present papers on the day. In addition, several further chapters have been included from other colleagues and associates, mainly outside of ICS, who were able to write on issues not already covered. The result is a collective effort that embraces a wide range of questions relating to meritocracy, and does so in a variety of styles fitting the different topics and perspectives.

In our original conference we organised papers into three sessions, dealing respectively with meanings of meritocracy, life experiences of various groups in contemporary Britain, and the implications of both for current political agendas. For this published collection for *Political Quarterly* we have changed the ordering to fit the new mix of chapters. We now have four parts. The first deals with the context in which *Meritocracy* was written, and its reception and interpretation. This part ends with the transcript of a short interview with Michael in 1994—when the third edition of *Meritocracy* was published—looking back on how it was conceived and received, and the influence it has had. (This transcript, made available recently by Gabriel Productions, was not circulated at the conference and has not been seen by other contributors to this volume.)

Published by Blackwell Publishing Ltd, 9600 Garsington Road, Oxford OX4 2DQ, UK and 350 Main Street, Malden, MA 02148, USA 1

The next part then explores the current relevance of the concept in modern Britain, by investigating the perspectives of a number of divergent sectors of the population. In the third part the debate is broadened by evaluations of the wider analytical value of Michael's concept and argument, including within societies outside Britain. We come back to a national focus in the final part in order to consider implications of meritocracy for British public policy agendas and priorities.

Before the chapters themselves start, I will briefly summarise the topics that they cover, and then indicate what I personally feel to be the key issues coming out of this ICS review of *Meritocracy*.

The chapters

Asa Briggs begins the collection, appropriately, by examining Michael's relationship with the Labour Party during the period when *Meritocracy* was taking shape in his mind. It was Michael's growing disenchantment with the party over key aspects of its unfolding mission that prompted him to write the book. This contextual analysis is carried forward by Jon Davis, in his exposition of efforts to introduce meritocratic procedures into the Civil Service since the Northcote–Trevelyan Report. This report was treated in *Meritocracy* as the first modern meritocratic impulse in British public life, and it was influential in Labour Party thinking in the late 1950s and early 1960s.

The early impact of the book itself is then evaluated by Paul Barker, who shows that although many reviewers did not entirely understand it, or even know how to approach it, the issues that it dealt with chimed well with current concerns. It has, moreover, worn surprisingly well, and has continuing relevance and importance. Not all commentators have felt, however, that *Meritocracy* fits their own experience, and Hilary Land argues that Michael was not sufficiently attuned to the problems faced by women in the public realm, and that this reduced the value of the book for many readers right from its first publication.

Because of the satirical style adopted in *Meritocracy*, many readers have simply got hold of the wrong end of the stick. Claire Donovan analyses the content of a sample of political science journal references to it and finds that there are big variations in how it has been understood by different readers. Finally in this introductory part, we include a transcript of a short interview with Michael carried out in the mid-1990s. This confirms that Michael felt himself to have been often misunderstood. It also shows, though, that he did remain ambivalent himself on certain matters, so that it is not surprising that others may have been confused too.

The part dealing with meritocracy in contemporary Britain looks at the experiences of a variety of specific groups. This starts with an analysis by Jim Ogg of data from *British Social Attitudes* surveys, organised according to respondents' levels of education. Those with the highest levels of qualifications are revealed as having a set of attitudes that are consistent with belonging to a secure and confident social elite. This broad pattern contains much variation, though, and Michelynn Laflèche shows that among ethnic minorities there is not a clear sense that promotion actually takes place on the basis of merit and qualifications. While indigenous white Britons may suspect that minorities are treated favourably, minorities for their part fear the opposite.

This conclusion is shared by Yvonne Roberts, in her discussion of the treatment of marginalised young men—who are disproportionately black. Worryingly, she points out that while the experience of exclusion does help to generate alternative, compensatory value systems, and ideological diversity, their content is generally negative and feeds criminal lifestyles. On the other hand, Ferdinand Mount recounts that the cultural autonomy and strength of the old working class has been stripped away in the drive to modernise British society. The people at the bottom have been abandoned and exposed in a way that makes *Meritocracy* as pertinent as it has ever been.

Cutting the cake a slightly different way, Eric Midwinter suggests that as Britain becomes more meritocratic, and socially polarised, it is people at the opposite ends of the life-cycle—children and the elderly—who are losing out most. The new opportunities are effectively confined to the generation in the middle. Peregrine Worsthorne then turns on the new British meritocrats themselves and finds them sadly lacking in general leadership qualities. In their hands, the conduct of national affairs and authority of our national institutions have undergone a serious and possibly terminal decline. It is high time for us to demand something better.

The third part of the book tackles the question of how well the theory contained in *Meritocracy* has stood up, and can be generalised. Writing as an American (and publisher of the edition of the book currently in print), Irving Louis Horowitz notes that it is a complex thesis, and that Michael himself was an ambivalent and complicated theorist. On balance, he feels that Michael's pragmatic (albeit reluctant) acceptance of meritocracy is justified. Takehiko Kariya and Ronald Dore then give us a detailed account of the history of meritocracy in Japan. Modern Japan is a society that has had to modernise itself very rapidly and systematically in order to survive in its contacts with the West. The application of meritocratic procedures has led to a very hierarchical education system, and this has been linked by critics to a sharp and increasing polarisation in Japanese society. The future is unclear, and wide-awake readers will spot that Kariya and Dore's subtitle, 'From here, where?', is the subtitle of the last section in *Meritocracy* itself, shortly before the unspecified but clearly bloody events at Peterloo.

Next, Peter Marris, who was working with Michael at the ICS when *Meritocracy* was written (and who opened the 2004 conference), considers how ideas about social justice have fared subsequently in Britain and America, where he now lives. He finds that the capitalist meritocracy we now share to some extent differs in several ways from the model presented by Michael. Then Richard Sennett discusses how, within the New Economy that has flourished in the United States with globalisation, a restructuring of expectations has taken place as new definitions of skill and value—and above all of career—are laid down. Meritocracy refers to a form of investment in human capital that is rapidly disappearing.

Moving to a different domain, Belinda Brown documents how *Meritocracy* is written on an assumption that families are the enemy of individual merit—and so they have to be undermined in order that meritocracy can be born, and social justice achieved. This neglects the value of families as sources of social and cultural capital, especially for poorer people. Peter Saunders then makes an upbeat appraisal, that Britain now is broadly a meritocratic society, in which those who are talented and work hard can expect to do well. This is, moreover, as in other Western countries, seen as legitimate by a large majority of the population. Michael Young was unduly gloomy when anticipating social dislocation.

Finally, there are some chapters concerned with the unfolding future and what we may need to do about it. Andrew Gamble and Rajiv Prabhakar consider some ways in which greater equality could be promoted through the distribution of assets—which could provide all citizens with economic opportunities. The more widely that valuable assets can be spread, the harder it is for a self-perpetuating elite to take hold of society. Following this, Jon Cruddas notes that New Labour faces growing difficulties in keeping the working-class vote. The party has anticipated that the working class will wither as the Knowledge Economy changes the nature of work and economic interests. But this may not be happening. The largest growth in jobs is in lower-grade service occupations, for which New Labour has shown little concern.

Education is where Labour has traditionally held its main debate on meritocracy, with the introduction of comprehensive schools in the 1960s representing a symbolic rejection of the concept. However, Peter Wilby argues, under New Labour various forms of selective education have been encouraged. Attitudes shown in the debate on the 2006 Education Bill indicate that the future of comprehensives may not be secure. Geoff Dench then suggests that what may be needed is a shift of focus away from personal educational accreditation at the outset of people's careers (educational capitalism) towards help for citizens to acquire skills needed to play useful roles in society. To justify social rewards, effort should embody contribution to the community.

In summarising the case against meritocracy, Ruth Lister reminds us that Michael's main fear was that stress on equal opportunities would increase the overall volume of inequality in society. The idea of merit operates within a very narrow definition of what is valuable to society. While New Labour lawyers may feel that it contains a notion of equal worth, we must remember that this is not how it is experienced in practice. Finally, David Willetts points out that a concern for diversity of moral worth is also a powerful strand in Conservative thinking. But a government has to manage the economy efficiently, and the education system is the key to ensuring that talents are not wasted. Opportunities have expanded greatly, but more still needs to be done for children from modest backgrounds.

Meritocracy reviewed: New Labour's dilemma

An ongoing dialogue

These, then, are the chapters making up the collection. What do they tell us about the value of Michael's idea of meritocracy in contemporary Britain? How much can the concept inform us, or prompt us into asking useful questions about where we are, and where we are going? Here, I will briefly sum up my own reflections following this ICS review—including the discussion at the conference itself. In some ways, my remarks should be part of a conclusion rather than a preface. But to present them as such would, I think, give them greater generality and weight than they deserve. So I will leave them here.

The main point that I want to put forward is that a number of features of Michael's book, and of contemporary British society itself as well, make better sense when we appreciate that Michael's central motivation when writing *Meritocracy* was to influence the Labour Party, and that although he failed to make the impact he wanted he may still have had an effect that he did not intend. The book can be seen as part of a dialogue between Michael and the party, which had started when he was a good deal younger and which perhaps continues even now, after his death. This dialogue was not an equal one, and his relationship with the party was often difficult. He found blind loyalty to it impossible, and there were times when he appeared to lose faith in it altogether, and look for alternative vehicles for his ideas and idealism. As Peter Hennessy has written recently, Michael had an acute historical sense of the perpetual struggles in British political life between merit and patronage, equality and plutocracy, fraternity and efficiency and altruism and greed; and 'Sometimes the Labour Party was, in Young's eyes, the best instrument for levering the right blocks into place, sometimes not.'[1]

This is true. But what is also true is that Michael was not happy when distanced from the Labour body. Sharing in its aspirations, and arguments, gave him the family, and community, of which he had enjoyed rather little in his formative years. Appropriately, his main disagreements with the party centred on how, when it became a party of government, it forgot the importance of family and community in the lives of the ordinary people who voted for it. Had it been willing to listen to him, Britain today might be a very different place. But it was not willing. This limited what Michael felt able to express, and reduced the impact of that which he did.

Meritocracy came to be written during the intense soul-searching in the party that followed 1951 election defeat. Traditional class warriors insisted that the defeat was caused by postwar middle-class sympathisers returning to the Conservatives. Revisionists, however, recognised that it was more a matter of working-class supporters defecting, as a reaction against Attlee's preoccupation with the creation of remote state controls and corporations. Rising figures such as Tony Crosland and Hugh Gaitskell argued that it was no longer safe for Labour to rely so heavily on the working-class vote—or, indeed, to tie the national interest closely to their interests—and that increasing attention had to be given to workers using brain power rather than muscle. The 1944 Education Act was unleashing a wave of social mobility from the old working class, and Labour was anxious to prevent this becoming political mobility too, and benefiting the Tories. By attaching a growing importance to personal cultural capital, in the form of educational qualifications, and linking this to a new vision of open, classless society, the modernising wing of the party was able to hitch its fortunes to this rising young interest group without abandoning its belief in social justice. And this is I think why it subsequently proved so successful, and became the most powerful and formative influence in postwar British society.

Michael found himself in agreement with much of this emerging programme. But he was anxious at the same time that the party should not too readily cut its bonds with traditional working-class solidarities. He was becoming fearful that too much attention to the interests of ambitious young meritocrats might eventually assist the spawning of a new type of ruling class. His pamphlets on the first, more general, point had been routinely ignored by the party hierarchy. *Meritocracy* continued his campaign—and gave it more focus—through movement into the realm of fiction, where it was easier to handle sensitive matters discreetly and, perhaps, examine his own uncertainties.

The format of novel expresses his ambivalence by splitting Michael Young into *two* persons. On the one hand, there is the solemn and callow young narrator, embodying Michael's less critical sentiments. On the other, there is the apparently all-knowing author, sprinkling the text with insights and cautions that pass unnoticed through the unsuspecting narrator. So, while the narrator is possessed of unbounded enthusiasm for meritocracy, the author, although himself conscious of the social improvement that it represents, is also cursed by awareness of where it may be leading—while blessed with a power to reveal and possibly influence this, or at any rate to drop some heavy hints.

Michael adopted this fictional device to help tease out party opinion more publicly and widely than in his earlier pamphlets, but without causing too much offence or revealing himself irretrievably as a rebel. Although he had left its employment, he still saw himself as a loyal party member at this point, and did not want to burn bridges. The pro-meritocracy arguments that the book contains were both close to what many party members felt at the time and also, I believe, not that far away from his own position.

Thus a number of participants in this review have noted how odd it seems, given Michael's well-publicised views since on community, that *Meritocracy* places so much emphasis on the attributes of individuals, such as IQ, and relatively little on social processes and the embedding of human development and character in them. To some extent, the hidden side of the story, running as a critical undercurrent through the sly asides of the author, does hint to the reader that such things were in fact important, merely overlooked by the dumb narrator, and in the end would re-emerge triumphant. But the weight given in the book to this alternative analysis is so muted that this cannot be the whole story. Other processes must have been operating. Michael was clearly giving a nod of assent to those Labour values that portray the public realm—and the direct links between individual citizens and the state—as more real and important than the private realm of intervening groups and interpersonal relationships. It is conceivable that, in spite of the emphasis on kinship and community in his concurrent sociological research, this conformity was not just superficial; that is, Michael *did* still subscribe to a primarily individualistic model of society himself at this stage.

There are some grounds for this interpretation. Although Michael had been lobbying for higher value to be attached to people's family and community ties, he had consistently identified 'fraternalism' as a public rather than private virtue. Even in *Family and Kinship*, Michael did not assert the fundamental and independent nature of family life and processes. In fact, he and Peter often referred to families as 'women's trade unions' through which, as relatively powerless members of society, they could combine to provide mutual support. That is, there was a presumption that family life was not something that followed its own, autonomous imperatives, but that operated in response to conditions in wider society. So, perhaps, in certain circumstances it might prove dispensable? It seems possible, therefore, that in writing *Meritocracy* Michael was testing out a number of unknowns—how far he could believe, himself, that family life had the independent momentum to contain radical social change; what people in the party outside Transport House thought about this; and whether the use of fiction would help him to influence party opinion—satire as subtle persuasion.

However, and as I have noted elsewhere, his writing on such issues (both here and in *Family and Kinship*) did *not* win him the approval that he would have liked in the party and among rising young meritocrats, especially women who were breaking free of family ties at this time.[2] This, I suspect, is why he subsequently concentrated on other matters where he was in tune with more party colleagues—such as education, consumer rights and the use of the voluntary sector and self-help groups to supplement (or contain) the power of the state. For the next twenty to thirty years, he confined himself on family issues mainly to small, sniping comments, before eventually picking up that gauntlet in earnest. It was not until the 1990s, as a community elder, that he finally came out unambiguously in favour of families and against the blight of individualism, and insisted that this had been his firm position all along.

Michael's loyalty to party may therefore have restrained him from pressing his critical case on community as forcefully as he could have done, or even from fully accepting it himself. As a result of this, and damagingly, Labour modernisers who read *Meritocracy* may have been let off the hook and allowed to draw the wrong conclusions from it, such as that the future *would be* meritocratic, and that Labour needed to prepare for this. Predictions such as the following must have been fairly alarming to party strategists: 'The Labour Party could no longer be the force it had been once the classes it represented had lost the intelligent from their ranks. The Party's standing in the country was bound to suffer.'[3] Under Harold Wilson, the party's readiness to embrace an opening up of society quickly ripened into a vigorous courting of the growing numbers of young, educated voters, at the expense of its responsiveness to the voices of ordinary people left behind by them in working-class heartlands.[4] Far from being self-defeating, as he hoped, by warning Labour against meritocracy, Michael's menacing vision may have proved self-fulfilling.

Open and closed models of meritocracy

The most likely reason for this was that the chosen fictional device, of cautionary satirical tale, was too complicated to deliver a clear message, with the result that British society was warned off some lines of social development but not others. Certainly, it has avoided some of the *specific* characteristics used by Michael to mark out the dangers of meritocracy—such as heavy reliance on intelligence testing, and formalised, rigid social and occupational stratification according to educational achievement. And yet in a number of other respects it does seem to have converged remarkably, since the Labour administrations of the 1960s, with the twenty-first-century Britain that Michael portrayed.

Prominent among these are several current ideological emphases that are self-consciously meritocratic—on education as virtually the sole key to valued social participation, on educational opportunity as the main source of social justice and on social mobility as the best index of overall social health. Alongside these, there is corresponding disdain for all private realm activities and satisfactions. Pursuit of this *soi-disant* meritocratic campaign is vested in a centralised state machine that handles the motivation and educational accreditation of useful citizens and the dispensation of personal security to losers. The apparatus is highly responsive to the attitudes and opinions of the educated elite, and contemptuous of the views and values of menial workers and the unemployed, unproductive rump of society, whose consequent political alienation from the state is moderated only by their economic dependence on it. So while British politicians have clearly steered away from the most distinctive (and least acceptable) aspects of Michael's meritocracy, they do not seem to have been deterred from embracing the notion itself and the state interventionist conceptions of social justice associated with it. (And, significantly, it is these features of modern British society that were viewed as most questionable by participants in the ICS review.)

This partiality of British reactions to the idea of meritocracy is surely down to the complexity of the multilevel story, which ensures an interesting read but effectively invites readers to pick and mix what they want. Half the story—the historical and factually grounded bits—is devoted to examining the social injustice (and inefficiency) inherent in the old class-based British social system, where talented individuals born into the lower orders faced enormous obstacles to achieving the positions their personal qualities warranted. The other half then deals with how imagined state intervention in the future progressively breaks down this system and replaces it with selective educational instruments and processes for scientifically matching personal characteristics with jobs, so that no talent is wasted. Running throughout the story there is also the critical undercurrent, periodically surfacing to hint that even the carefully honed procedures for identifying and cultivating merit will in the end founder on new forms of resentment and resistance. But this counterpoint is tentative and speculative. So while some readers will pick up the message that all forms of social closure have drawbacks, it is also quite easy for committed Labour readers to latch on to the idea that state intervention is good, because it solves the problems of class, without being forced to consider the limitations to this point of view.

Such a reading is made even easier by the way in which the story does not explicitly confront the distinction, made by a number of contributors to this present volume, between open, or market-based, meritocracy and closed meritocracy. It seems fairly safe to say that the basic idea of meritocracy is rooted in principles of exchange and reciprocity that lie at the heart of all social systems, and that enjoy high levels of acceptance in all cultures. What you put into society directly determines what you can legitimately take out of it—and within this broad rule, inequality of rewards does not seem to be a problem.[5] Acceptance of inequality is not confined to people at the top of the social hierarchy—as argued by Michael himself in relation to the popularity of the monarchy among the working class.[6] This is not based on servility, but on recognition of the valuable role seen to be played by the royal family in standing up for the country and, more broadly, family values.

More general willingness to embrace inequality is evidenced by the widespread acceptance of the enormous earnings of pop (and also perhaps sporting) stars and celebrities, who form a sort of alternative, people's meritocracy. The field of popular entertainment is a domain that is almost wholly responsive to demand, and provides opportunities for 'ordinary people' to earn fabulous incomes in return for working hard to develop their talents in order to give the public what it wants. Far from being vilified for their success, they are loaded with praise and adulation for providing pleasure and excitement to lighten people's lives; with John Lennon as one of the first to define himself as a 'working class hero', but certainly not the last. The entertainment industry endorses an escapist value system in which stars and humble fans are united in sharing a good time (or in the case of sport, collective glory). It is noteworthy that evaluations of success are highly dependent on public judgement, and remain fiercely immune to political or bureaucratic control (though with some rumbling suspicions of commercial rigging), and also to the views of social superiors. Popular culture in Britain provides a laager where the beleaguered working class has regrouped to resist elitist interference. Equally interesting here is that family inheritance of success and position is not frowned on, and that pop and sporting dynasties are seen as fair so long as they reflect the inheritance of natural talent and not simply the influence of money.

For where differential rewards do become problematic is where there are restrictions on access to highly rewarded social positions; that is, when the market for high social status is closed or rigged. Social class was the most familiar form of closure in 1950s Britain, and so virtually all early readers of *Meritocracy* could be expected to have some sympathy with the book's attack on class stratification, and its account of the freeing up of opportunities. The general notion of meritocracy would have acquired some open connotations through this, with the formula $I + E = M$ coming over as an essentially moral equation.

Michael the author does also try to show that using state political power to overcome economic differentials may not produce the most durable solution to class inequality. But because the book makes the case through the medium of an obtuse story, rather than in an orderly analysis, his point could easily have misfired. He regarded the Conservatives as driving meritocracy, but he also considered that the statist reflexes of Labour social planners might lead them to collaborate with such a programme in order to bring down the old class system. In the book, he shows the Labour Movement playing a technical role of this sort, which assists directly in the evolution of a new meritocratic class. Labour are spent and discarded before this new class is fully formed, and do not endorse it. But I personally believe that he was trying to warn us further, warn the Labour Party, that state intervention does itself entail a form of restriction on the marketplace where social inputs are traded for social rewards. Bureaucratic and political controls themselves constitute, and can promote, new types of closure and class inequality.

However, I can also see the attractions of another reading, which Labour modernisers have presumably found more palatable. This concentrates on a different warning in the story, namely that selection by intelligence facilitates the formation of a new hereditary class, and that when this happens the liberating potential of meritocratic state intervention becomes subverted, and closed. Through this alternative interpretation, proponents of a strong state might well believe, even against Michael's own (often ambivalent) protestations, that he was in fact advocating even stronger forms of state action, managing educational selection *politically*, in order to secure perpetual liberation and social renewal. Among Labour activists who do not regard IQ as significantly determined by genetics, which is most of them, there is great readiness to believe that state control of access to education equates with permanent revolution. A state with the means to promote constant social mobility can head off the formation of a new class, and stay forever a fountain of open, individualistic social justice.

This, I suspect, is what many Labour modernisers have seen *Meritocracy* as being all about, and is why Tony Blair has been so enthralled with it. And it certainly helps to explain the direction that British society has taken under New Labour impulses. But, by the same token, it also suggests to me that many of Britain's contemporary problems, commonly regarded as aspects or products of meritocracy as such, may actually be the consequences of New Labour's own values, priorities and reflexes. In so far as these have been reinforced by a particular reading of *Meritocracy*, then attachment to that concept may now be a millstone around the party's collective neck.

Countdown to Peterloo?

The denouement in Michael's story, mentioned only briefly and obliquely in a final footnote, is a confrontation at Peterloo between the leaders of the meritocratic regime and a rebellious group of 'Populists'. We are led through this to assume that growing social divisions eventually bring down, or at least substantially weaken, the social and political system built around rigid educational and occupational stratification. Fraternalism fights back. And to the extent that contemporary Britain is subject itself to growing polarisation, we may well ask ourselves whether we should anticipate a similar pattern of events here.

My own answer to that question would be that it rather depends on what we mean by similar. As I have indicated above, and argue more fully in my chapter later in the volume, there are significant differences between current British society and the fictional meritocracy set out by Michael. In the book, an increasingly formal and systematic grading of people is established, which produces a gradual weakening of the Labour Movement based on fraternal values. Change in contemporary Britain, on the other hand, is being driven by a Labour Government that long ago abandoned working-class fraternalism in favour of a more individualistic ideology. It now appears to be trying to use state power to create an interventionist meritocracy—through centralised control of education and accreditation, and sponsored social mobility—to head off the formation of a new hereditary class system.

So what we actually seem to have in Britain is not so much a meritocratic class system as such, but middle-class Marxist practices organised around state management of personal social capital and entailing political exploitation of the concept of meritocracy—the 'education mantra'—to conjure up permanent, benign social revolution. On the one hand, this means drawing on the moral appeal of the idea that what is important is 'education, education, education', in order to make citizens desire the certificates controlled by the state. As I point out later, this is something that *was* 'predicted' by Michael. But on the other hand it also involves more direct *political* control over social mobility than the story itself suggests (but as Nicholas Lemann *has* predicted), rather than leaving such crucial processes in the technical hands of educationalists and scientists.[7] This role for the state would be defended by Labour—if it were challenged—as enabling the people to avert the new class closure foreseen by Michael, and thereby to boost the liberative potential of education and to maximise resulting social justice. However, more critical interpretations might see it as confirming the ascendancy of the political realm in modern Britain and the power of the *political* ruling elite—firmly rooted in public-sector offices and living off rent, in the form of state taxes.

Following this interpretation, we could argue that social polarisation in Britain largely stems from failures in New Labour's own social analysis and policies, including its attempts to stage-manage meritocracy. The fundamental mistake lies in the way in which it has cut links with the working class and their interests, and even their role in society. Other countries treat ordinary people as an essential part of the national community. *Pas de paysan; pas de pays.* But New Labour seems to assume that manual and menial workers can be ignored, either because they are disappearing or there is no need to value them or reward them properly in order to get their jobs done. Most non-partisan observers agree that there are now massive problems in motivating workers at the lower end of the job hierarchy, with widespread reluctance to take on that work which is available, especially among (young) men, and a relentless slide instead into criminality and drugs that is tearing apart the lives of many working-class communities. This is not because there is no work to be done. Indeed, New Labour is continually lecturing us on the need to accept (more) immigrants in order to fill vacant jobs. Their inability to understand the importance of valuing such work, along with a state education system that pays little attention to preparing people for real employment, means that they are no longer husbanding the nation's human resources efficiently.

A related mistake lies in the lavish attention paid to social mobility. This has become an anxiously managed tool for balancing the resources and well-being of different sections of the population.[8] But too much emphasis on mobility devalues ordinary work further; and where mobility is obviously assisted from above, it may undermine the value of higher-level work too. Nor does the importance attached to mobility actually reflect or impress popular opinion. Party grandees such as Peter Mandelson talk as though working-class communities are full of people burning with ambition to become High Court judges, and that where mobility is not actually taking place, then this is proof of social closure. The open model of meritocracy has shifted into an imperative form.[9] But it has long been recognised by sociologists that the majority of people do not want to lead lives that take them away from the communities in which they have grown up.[10] What they aspire to is the chance to do well within that context, by finding a reasonably secure job to support their families. A society in which there was a random relationship between position of origin and position by achievement (the mobility-watchers' definition of perfect mobility) would be a bleak and lonely place.[11]

Pushing social mobility is part of the more general failure of Labour to respect the private realm. Mobility is about success in the public domain: but most people's vital satisfactions and motivations are found in personal relationships and activities. By cutting itself off from ordinary people, Labour has deprived itself of this understanding. It has become attuned to the opinions of the high-flying and successful, and no longer listens to (or represents) ordinary folk: it just tells them what to do. The 1960s strategy of broadening the appeal of the party worked so well that Labour soon became the political vehicle of Britain's new elite, and helped to sculpture their evolving social and ideological sensibilities. It is now right at the heart of the new establishment; but it would still like to see itself as the voice of the underprivileged at the same time. The broad political coalition needed to pull this off is proving fragile, though; ordinary people are getting a rough deal and becoming increasingly disgruntled.

This is New Labour's dilemma. By anticipating the rise of meritocracy, and siding *with* this vision, it has left a vacuum in British political life that it does not want to fill itself, but is reluctant to let any other party occupy either. It wants to be everything. However, this may be impossible. In the early days of the Labour Party, its position was easy, and mainly came down to playing a moderating role. Labour was the party of moral values—of fraternity, decency and fairness—which could be wielded to restrain the boss class from behaving too selfishly. It was a secular church rather than a vehicle of government. But with success after the Second World War a new career as ruling party opened up, and with it contradictory imperatives that have compromised the party's original mission.

So are we bound for Peterloo? Perhaps we are, though not quite in the way that Michael imagined, and certainly not yet irreversibly. Michael's story hints that sharpening social and political divisions lead to a renewal of fraternalist values, and formation of a new party of popular resistance, within the moribund Labour Movement. In real life, though, Labour—as it became New Labour—itself adopted a more top-down, bureaucratic set of values in its effort to combine the pursuit of social justice with greater individual opportunities. This was partly a specific response to dangers anticipated in *Meritocracy* itself. But alongside this it was also, to be fair, a consequence of widespread Marxist sympathies during the 1960s, along with Britain's response to decolonisation, which I discuss in my chapter below, which together encouraged the view that state collectivist action was superior to traditional working-class communalism. The social polarisation we now have in Britain seems to me to be more ideological and political—and to do with the failure of this new state machine and political elite to reflect working-class values—than a result of changes in the class and opportunity structure.

New Labour has a choice. It can go on spurning fraternalist values. But if it does so, some other party, such as the BNP, could easily take on the role played in Michael's story by the Populists. For most of what New Labour now dismisses as racism is simply traditional working-class communalism searching for political expression and representation. In meeting this need, the BNP is gradually turning itself into a British Socialist Party, which can compete for Old Labour voters. Alternatively, Labour can revive fraternalism itself, and detach itself from centralised, individualistic definitions of social justice by moving back nearer to Old Labour. I believe that this is what Michael was urging all along, and that his aim in writing *Meritocracy* was not primarily to alert colleagues to new forms of class structure, which is how Labour readers seem to have taken it, but to warn them to beware the temptation to adopt statist solutions. In the event, these tendencies have proved even stronger than he feared. Paradoxically, New Labour may not have avoided the future that Michael predicted, but simply pre-empted it. However if its current leaders can now see this, then there is still time to change.

Origin and Reception

The Labour Party as Crucible

ASA BRIGGS

Facing the future

The Rise of the Meritocracy cannot be fully appreciated without some understanding of Michael Young's relationship with the Labour Party while the book was gestating and, indeed, with his attitude towards political parties then, before and later.[1] It was while he was actually working in the party, and close to the hub of its policy deliberations, that the core issues of *Meritocracy* crystallised in his mind. These reflected some of the divisions in the party, but there were other issues that interested and divided members of the party even more. Disenchanted with Clement Attlee's administration as it became worn down by the realities of postwar reconstruction, Michael both gave inadequate weight to the health problems of its ageing leaders and the extent of popular weariness with 'austerity'.[2] After failing to influence policies as much as he would have liked, he left paid party employment in 1952 in the hope of rediscovering its soul elsewhere. The writing of *The Rise of the Meritocracy* represented a continuation by other means of his argument with the direction that the party was taking during the early 1950s.

Michael had been working with Political and Economic Planning (PEP), a voluntary cross-party think tank, founded in 1931, when he was invited by Morgan Phillips, an ex-miner, who had recently been appointed Secretary of the Labour Party, to leave PEP and join the Research Department at Transport House. His first job was to help to put together the party's general election manifesto, *Let Us Face the Future*, a task that turned out to involve writing large parts of it himself. Fighting the first electoral campaign for ten years gave point to the existing strong rivalries in the party, with both personality and policy divisions between its senior members. Yet these were successfully contained during the campaign itself, not least because the mood of the country seemed so favourable to a party that had become identified with the national solidarity engendered by war. Michael himself was impressed by this solidarity and was confident that it could be turned to party advantage and electoral success. In the light of his own experience during the war, he was keen to use the campaign to tap the enthusiasm of those people who were determined not to return to the 1930s. Much of *Let Us Face the Future* was devoted to spelling out party plans for the future more fully. The mobilisation of such people, he was sure, was the key to the future, just as it had been the key to the winning of 'a people's war'. Servicemen in particular were attracted to an optimistic Labour Party in 1945, and the result of the 1945 election, in which no fewer than 126 successful Labour candidates were ex-servicemen, showed that the attraction was mutual.

© 2006 The Author. Editorial organisation © 2006 The Political Quarterly Publishing Co. Ltd
Published by Blackwell Publishing Ltd, 9600 Garsington Road, Oxford OX4 2DQ, UK and 350 Main Street, Malden, MA 02148, USA

The belief in the need not only to face but to control the future was shared by most senior party figures during the campaign, although few foresaw the scale of an unprecedented electoral victory. Herbert Morrison, wartime Home Secretary, for whom as chairman of the party's Policy Committee Michael worked directly, was optimistic about the future provided that he could widen the party's appeal by attracting 'the small man' and, in particular, the technicians who had played a big part in the war effort. Sir Stafford Cripps and others shared the commitment to this strategy, as had earlier the '1941 Committee' and later in the war Sir Richard Acland's Commonwealth Party. Michael had been one of the people who persuaded Cripps, expelled from the Labour Party before the war, not to join forces with Acland, who himself subsequently rejoined the Labour Party. Much of the flavour of *The Rise of the Meritocracy*, including the designation of his party of fraternity as the 'Technicians' Party', arose directly out of early postwar sentiments. They were driven by a will to win.

In this context, it was understandable that *Let Us Face the Future* should deal very positively with public ownership—the main issue that divided the parties, and potentially (and, indeed, soon) the party itself. Under the heading 'Industry in the service of the nation', the manifesto called ambitiously for industry to be organised so as to enable it to 'yield the best that human knowledge and skill can provide'. 'Only so,' it went on, 'can our people reap the full benefits of this age of discovery and Britain keep her place as a Great Power.' This was Morrisonian language, for it was Morrison, himself no believer in 'wholesale nationalisation', who coordinated nationalisation policy and formulated nationalisation rules.[3]

Campaigning rhetoric was not fully matched by performance after Labour took power with a huge majority in 1945, and by the beginning of 1947, when shortages of food and fuel obliged Transport House to shift to defensive propaganda claiming that things were not so bad as they seemed, Michael was not the only party official to feel increasingly uneasy about the machinery of planning itself.[4] Although he was still close to Morrison, he came to mistrust the Morrisonian pattern of nationalisation, which Morrison never attempted to modify in the light of experience. Little had been done or was being done, Michael felt, to close the gap between 'them' and 'us'.

Coal, about which Michael knew little at first hand, seemed to him a test case. The first chairman of the National Coal Board had spent his life in the coal industry and had long favoured nationalisation. He believed, too, that the welfare of miners should be ensured. But Michael wanted miners not just to be 'well looked after', but to have a greater degree of participation in the running of their industry. He was in sympathy, therefore, with a comment in the *Manchester Guardian* after the fuel crisis of 1947 that the National Coal Board had 'turned out to be little more than another Government Department'. Owners had changed: management had not. And when Grimethorpe miners staged a dramatic and economically devastating unofficial strike in the summer of that year, he sympathised with the rank-and-file rather than with official trade unionism. Arthur Horner, communist secretary of the National Union of Miners, whom Morrison would have liked to join the National Coal Board,[5] and William Lawther, its President, tried in vain to stop the strike, but the Yorkshire miners now attacked the Board as fiercely as in previous generations they would have attacked the owners. Michael, disturbed by what he judged to be the 'remoteness' of the Board from many rank-and-file miners, concluded—although he himself was just as remote from the scene—that the strikers were right.[6]

Michael's sympathies cannot have made life easy for him at Transport House. In a period when 'unofficial' strikes were common, his unconditional statement that the 'brotherhood of man' was expressed in 'working-class solidarity during strikes' did not appeal to most trade union leaders, who called themselves brothers. For Michael, however, his doubts were deepening over whether public ownership really was any better than private. In his book *Labour's Plan for Plenty*, published later in 1947, a very difficult year for the country as well as the party, he showed loyalty to Morrison, who himself set limits to nationalisation, by emphasising that economic difficulties, financial restraints and physical shortages stood in the way of speedy implementation of all aspects of the programme set out in *Let Us Face the Future*, and that 'planning by persuasion is bound to be more complex than planning by coercion'. He also urged, as Morrison was urging, that the 'civil servants of socialism' should be 'drawn from industry and science and should be versed in economics and psychology'.[7] But in his chapter on nationalisation he did depart from Morrison by suggesting that 'for every management function there is an appropriate level', and that 'the lower the level to which authority can be devolved, the better'.[8] And over the next few years this difference in approach intensified as Michael became more interested in psychology (and in sociology) than in economics and as Morrison's range of political pre-occupations and responsibilities broadened.

From the start, Michael was temperamentally attracted to the idea of 'workers' control', a cause that had been advocated years earlier by G. D. H. Cole, whose writings appealed to many young socialists in the postwar years,[9] but the most that Michael could do while at Transport House was to press the case for what was called 'industrial democracy'. And this, too, was a case that was difficult then to propound in the face of considerable trade union opposition. At the heart of it was Ernest Bevin, who in anti-Morrisonian mood in wartime—a not uncommon mood for him—had described as 'almost intolerable' the prospect of the country being governed by 'a series of London Transport Boards' (Morrison's model). But Bevin had no sympathy either with theories of industrial democracy.[10] When Michael wrote a party pamphlet on the subject in 1948, entitled *Industrial Democracy*, the first in a series of pamphlets called *Towards Tomorrow*, it almost got suppressed by both Morrison and Bevin, for once in coalition—as they were to be more often in the years that followed—and the first edition, which in Bevin's view did not give the trade unions their proper place, had to be withdrawn. A second edition met some of the official objections, but the revisions left Michael uneasy.

Growing disenchantment

While still working in the Research Department, where Morgan Phillips achieved increasing independence from Morrison, Michael started an LSE thesis, supervised by Harold Laski, on how the Labour Party (and other parties) operated at the local level. Laski had been chairman of the Labour Party when Michael had joined the Labour Research Department, and the thesis subject emerged directly from Michael's own experience, which was for the party a topic of perennial importance, raising questions both of policy and of 'discipline', the latter a word that the party then used frequently. Studying the subject formally made Michael read more Labour biographies than he had ever read before—they were not in short supply—but they left him dissatisfied. Above all, they did not resolve his own growing problems inside Transport House. Unlike some of his colleagues there—such as Denis Healey, who won East Leeds in 1952, and Michael's successor in the Labour Research Department, Wilfred Fienburgh—he was not looking for a parliamentary constituency, and he had no personal incentives to attach himself to any of the Labour groups who were increasing in numbers if not in influence and pointing ahead to a 'New Left'.

The direction of his own increasingly individual thinking became established clearly in 1948 with the publication of a further *Towards Tomorrow* pamphlet, *Small Man, Big World.*[11] This began with a series of challenging, if disparate, quotations concerning the nature of socialism, from Robert Owen, William Morris, Friedrich Engels and Aneurin Bevan, and ended with a series of highly loaded questions for discussion groups. The first of these was 'Does the individual feel that he matters far less in the big organisation than in the small group, like the family?' and the second 'Do people regard the authorities of one kind and another as remote and impersonal?' They were not the questions that the authors of his own quotations would have chosen. Nor were they questions being asked generally in Transport House or the constituencies.

Michael suggested in the following discussion that communists were too caught up in the intricacies of dialectical materialism to be capable of looking beyond the 'dictatorship of the proletariat' to a genuinely classless society. He had briefly been a member of the Communist Party before the war as an LSE undergraduate, but already he had deviated totally from Marxism in 1945 when helping to draft *Let Us Face the Future*. And now he was clearly thinking on quite different lines, as shown by his choice of final quote from Bevan, 'Bigness is the enemy of humanity.' In another quotation he cited William Temple, the late Archbishop of Canterbury, who had complained during the war that 'while the worst horrors of the early factories' during the industrial revolution had at last been disposed of, 'the wage earners' were still not yet fully recognised as persons.[12] The question that was posed below the surface of *Small Man, Big World* was whether they were being recognised any differently *after* nationalisation. Michael looked across the Atlantic in trying to reach answers, reading the psychologist Elton Mayo with great delight, and meeting and talking to him when he visited Britain in 1948, accompanied by his daughter.

The 'great dilemma of modern society', as Michael set it out in *Small Man, Big World*, was that industrial efficiency, based in the application of science, and on which future productivity and prosperity appeared to depend, seemed to demand bigness, while democracy on the other hand seemed to require smallness. However, as the argument unfolded, Michael insisted that in the longer run, management that was democratic need not be more inefficient, because it would be far better for morale. The modern dilemma could not be solved by going back to a misty past and opting out of modernity, but it could be minimised by developing more respect for workers. For Michael, the value of democracy lay not least in the fact that it gave everyone the opportunity to contribute what he or she could to the welfare of his or her fellows, which was a great antidote to feelings of powerlessness. Thus, 'If the socialists [committed to efficiency were prepared to compromise with idealism, this] need not lead to economic collapse and political disorder but to a society, built on the model of the family, which is not only more comradely but more efficient.'

Perhaps the kernel of Michael's divergence from postwar Labour Party conventions lay in this emphasis on the family as a model. For Michael, the family was the supreme example of a small group in which everyone could have 'an active part in making decisions and carrying them out'. This was the best antidote to alienation and social polarisation: 'The common purposes of the small group are more easily understood; in the large group the people at the top tend to get out of touch with those at the bottom, and the small man to regard those at the top as "they", the impersonal authorities with mysterious power over himself.'

This emphasis rendered Michael far more receptive than senior Labour figures to popular fears about 'nationalisation' and growth in state power. But he was unable to communicate this understanding to them. One of the only ways in which he was actually able to influence the content of the next (1950) election manifesto, *Let Us Win Through Together*, was to suggest that industrial insurance should not be nationalised, a matter of contention within the party, but 'mutualised'. For most of his colleagues this was little more than a change in terminology, but for Michael himself it was far more. He was becoming increasingly attached to the idea of 'mutual aid', and personal and family insurance, the province of large and uncontrolled business, seemed the right place to start. Mutualisation appealed too to the Co-operative Insurance Society, which itself had a substantial stake in the insurance business and was alarmed by the word nationalisation.[13] Subsequently, Michael never changed his views on mutual aid: in 1977 he designated 18 Victoria Park

Square, Bethnal Green, as a Mutual Aid Centre; and two years later he co-authored a book with Marianne Rigg, *Mutual Aid in a Selfish Society*. It was published by the Mutual Aid Press, which he had founded.

That was far ahead. Back in time, in the painful course of analysing the 1950 election result, the evidence that consumer issues interested the electorate was ignored as the Labour Party failed to respond to Michael's line of thinking. Significantly, the reflex among its leaders with regard to its loss of seats in 1950 while it polled more votes than in 1945, was to argue that there had been defections from Labour to Conservative 'among some middle-class voters'. According to Gallup Poll analyses, however, the real problem was a rise in the working-class Conservative vote. This was acknowledged up to a point by Attlee and Morgan Phillips, and it was to become a topic of study among political science professors, whose work Michael seems to have ignored.[14] It was enough for him that the party had lost touch. He said little too about the conclusions of an independent writer with whom he has often been compared, Seebohm Rowntree, making little use of *Poverty and the Welfare State* (1951) by Rowntree and G. R. Lavers which compared poverty in 1941 and in 1951.[15]

Retreat to the East End

Michael did not leave Transport House until 1951. His first instinct in 1950 had been to intensify his efforts to correct the direction of policy, and the party respected his wish by continuing to employ him while he wrote for the party's Policy Committee a longer statement of the ideas originally presented in *Small Man, Big World*. The resulting *For Richer For Poorer* was so long, he claimed later, because he did not have time to make it shorter. While it left no impression on the party's Policy Committee, it stands out in retrospect as a seminal document in Michael's own thinking. By concentrating so heavily on the development of the state, the party, he complained once more, was neglecting the moral heart of socialism, which was grounded in family and local community. The title *For Richer For Poorer* deliberately played on the solemn pledges given in marriage, and the report ended with passages on family and community values. These celebrated civic virtues that were not being given serious attention by any of the major parties at the time: 'The values to preserve and strengthen are the values of the family: words such as "kind", "generous", "gentle", "liberal", all have a common derivation. The values to preserve and strengthen are the values of the community: solidarity, neighbourliness, and mutual aid.'

This conclusion was accompanied by a statement on the limitations of the 'welfare state', which he was now doubting could ever adequately serve the needs of ordinary families: 'The very name [welfare state] is against it recalling the smell of carbolic acid and the tough brown paper of ration books. . . . When the name is so ill-chosen, is there any wonder that many people should find so distasteful the idea that this thing should help the family. The family is small and intimate, real people who sing songs and drink stout together on Christmas Eve: the family is mine. The State belongs to someone else, belongs maybe to itself.' And so did its finance: 'If the national budget is balanced, it will be done at the expense of unbalancing the budget of every poor family in the country.' *For Richer For Poorer* also explored the notion of equality, identifying more directly than Michael was able to do in *The Rise of the Meritocracy* itself the kind of 'classless society' that he wished to see.

'Diversity of values' he placed uppermost:

Socialists have attacked the class system not only because it was difficult to justify existing inequalities by any test of reason or justice, but because it was impossible in a society founded on such simplification to cultivate diversity of values. . . . Were we to evaluate people not only according to their wealth, their occupation, their education and their power, not only according to their intelligence and manual skill, but according to their kindliness, their courage, their imagination, sensitivity, honesty, sympathy and humility, there could be no classes. Who would be able to say that the scientist was superior to the manual worker, the University professor without children superior to the porter with admirable qualities as a father, the Chairman of the Board superior to the lorry-driver with unusual skill at growing roses?

According to Michael, 'Neighbourly socialism could become the core of a Third Force in ideas, a faith free from the materialism of the USA and the tyranny of the USSR.' And he went on to place his vision within a global context, as he was to do increasingly when he dealt with 'mutual aid' in the future, picking up language that was then common in current argument about the Labour Party's views on foreign policy.

'Globalism', a word not then used, provided for the party an exit strategy and for Michael himself a swansong. At the end of 1950 it sent him on a kind of farewell tour of the world, looking for ideas among labour and socialist leaders in Commonwealth countries. In the course of it, he very fittingly enjoyed a family reunion with relatives in Australia, the country where he had lived as a child, and met some family members there for the first time. (Most of them were communists.) It was only after returning from his tour in 1951 that he completed *For Richer For Poorer.* He was disappointed, but hardly surprised, that senior members of the party, which was already descending into civil war as its fortunes declined, did not feel that there was anything of relevance to them in what was effectively his political *magnum opus.* Only Edith Summerskill, author of an autobiography, *A Woman's World,* was impressed by it not as a party report but as a statement of conviction. It was the second rather than the first half of Michael's first sentence that gripped her: 'You can always find out what a man's wife is like by listening to his opinions on women in general and discover people's attitudes to the present by hearing their judgements on the past.' We are already near to *The Rise of the Meritocracy,* which took the form of a historical thesis. There was some straight party politics, however—or, rather, comment on current party organisation—in his report. Michael had been amazed when the secretary of the Australian Labour Party told him that Morgan Phillips was the greatest man he had ever known. And when he had asked Ben Chiffley, the Australian Prime Minister, whose Labour government fell from power two years before Attlee's, why it had been defeated, he had only been able to reply 'God knows'.

Michael's world trip, sponsored and paid for by the Labour Party, was the prelude to a new largely non-party career, although in 1955 he returned briefly to Transport House to help during the election, admitting that part of him was still a politician. His new non-party career had begun earlier than 1951, when he switched his LSE thesis supervisor from Laski to Richard Titmuss and his subject from Labour Party organisation to 'Kinship and Family in East London'. Titmuss was to help Michael when he went on boldly to create the Institute of Community Studies in Bethnal Green, but his role then and later in Michael's life was less formative than that of the American sociologist Edward Shils, who at a crucial time was the major influence on Michael's thought and practice. In Michael's own words, in his LSE seminars Shils made him feel that he was already more of a sociologist than a politician, and he joined Michael in writing an article on the Coronation. He was not, however, the only influence. Between leaving Transport House and founding the ICS, Michael spent a year at the Tavistock Institute, working up his ideas not about sociology or anthropology, but about social psychology and about the importance of family democracy in nurturing healthy personalities. His jottings at the time noted that 'Child can be stifled by love if parents do not respect the child's personality. Family should be democratic group, defined as one in which all members are invited to participate in determining ends and means.' The main aim of government policy should accordingly be 'to help parents to form democratic family groups in which children [are] treated with respect'.

It was in London's East End, when installed within the Institute that he had created as an autonomous vehicle for reconnecting with the 'ordinary people and families', that Michael was able to follow up *For Richer For Poorer* most energetically. The East End had been a stamping ground for generations of social reformers and was a major current Labour heartland. In consequence, therefore, Bethnal Green was a natural location for Michael to carry out groundbreaking research with three main associates—Peter Willmott, eight years younger than himself, who had worked with him at the Labour Research Department, an ex-Bevin boy during the war who had gone on to Ruskin College, Oxford; Peter Townsend, a sociologist, centring his studies on poverty, with an active and distinguished future ahead of him, who arrived in Bethnal Green from PEP; and Peter Marris, writer of a chapter in this volume, whose researches were to span Europe and Africa and Bethnal Green and California. Michael was to join with Willmott in writing *The Symmetrical Family* in 1973.

The Rise of the Meritocracy, however, was very much Michael's own book, a fictional construction that enabled him to explore symbolically his thinking about the relationships between family, class and the state, and to demonstrate his contention that a ruling class that failed to value all its citizens was not 'efficient' in the longer run. The fact that it took the form of an LSE thesis, written by another Michael Young and submitted in 2033, led to its being turned down for publication by many publishers who took it to be a real thesis and not a work of fiction.

In the extracts from *Meritocracy* that were printed in October 1958 in *Encounter*, a journal that was financially dependent on American backing, Michael referred to the 'devitalisation of the two party system' in Britain, with the Labour Party ultimately changing its name to the Technicians Party, 'catering in the broadest possible manner for technicians by head and brain'. There were some people in the Labour Party—all anti-Morrisonian—who were already thinking along the same lines at the end of the 1950s. Morrison referred more than once to 'technicians' as examples of the 'useful people' on whom the economy and society depended, while Hugh Dalton, no admirer of Morrison, records in his *Memoirs* that at an 'inquest' meeting held after the Labour Party's defeat in the general election of 1959, when Douglas Jay suggested loosening the link with the trade unions, changing the name of the party from 'Labour', and perhaps merging with the Liberal Party. Roy Jenkins, who was present at the meeting and who described himself at this time as a 'semi-detached MP', corroborated the account.[16] In the 1980s he was to promote the union of the breakaway Social Democratic Party, launched by himself and others in 1981, with the Liberal Party—a step that Michael, who had joined the new party in a spirit of hope, strongly opposed.

The intimations during the 1950s of the shape of things to come thus reached a climax a generation later. Michael's closest friend in the high politics of Labour in the 1950s and 1960s was Roy Jenkins's closest friend, Anthony Crosland, at whose invitation Michael became Director of the Social Science Research Council in 1965. Such a council figured in *The Rise of the Meritocracy*, as did Crosland by name. A maker of history in *Meritocracy*, he was 'the sort of leader open to new ideas,' Michael recalled in 1971, 'who keeps people like me in and with the Labour Party'. Nevertheless, Michael had some disagreements with Crosland over the goals of socialism. While Michael was most moved by fraternity, Crosland was more disposed to prioritise equality. They shared enough common ground, however, to develop a strong personal friendship and alliance in pursuing educational reform. When Labour came back into power under Harold Wilson in 1964, Michael was very closely involved with Crosland, who became Secretary of State for Education, in research and action to promote comprehensive schools. He was involved, however, in a personal capacity, not through party committees or through the Labour Research Department. Michael never again submitted himself to the requirements of party discipline. Indeed, later in his life, when he joined the breakaway Social Democratic Party (until they merged with the Liberals), he set up within it the 'Tawney Society'—an SDP Fabian Society—in a neatly choreographed manoeuvre to remind everyone that it was Michael, not Labour, who had stayed close to the values that fed the party's enduring soul.

This was not the only time that Michael contemplated political campaigning outside the Labour Party; in 1960 he wrote a pamphlet entitled *The Chipped White Cups of Dover: a Discussion of the Possibility of a New Progressive Party*. The pamphlet was turned down by the Fabian Society, of which Michael was a member. He had refused, with Cole, to put his name to *New Fabian Essays* (1949). Although he rejoined the Labour Party during the last years of his life and saw it return to power as 'New Labour' in 1997 under Tony Blair, after long years of Conservative rule, Michael concluded in 2001 that the party was no more in line with his own approach to politics than it had been in 1951. It must have rung bells in 1995 when Blair wrote a Fabian Tract, No. 571, called *Let Us Face the Future*. Yet the very word 'meritocracy' meant something as different to Blair, as it had done to his Conservative predecessor John Major, from what it had meant and still meant to Michael. He remained an independent spirit. Nevertheless ironically, looking at his life as a whole, it was during the period when he was trying hardest to be a good party member, after 1945, that he made his greatest progress in analysing—on paper—the direction of the development of British society.

Meritocracy in the Civil Service, 1853–1970

JON DAVIS

The model for meritocracy

MICHAEL Young wrote in his hugely influential *The Rise of the Meritocracy* that '[t]he 1870s have been called the beginning of the modern era [with] patronage at last abolished in the civil service and competitive entry made the rule. Merit became the arbiter, attainment the standard, for entry and advancement in a splendid profession, which was all the more an achievement because so many of our great-grandfathers were positively hostile to "competition wallahs" in British government.'[1] The British Civil Service's adherence to the principle of merit came after a hard-fought battle. Essentially, the struggle began in 1853 when Sir Charles Trevelyan, Permanent Secretary to the Treasury, and Sir Stafford Northcote MP were asked by the then Chancellor of the Exchequer, William Gladstone, to conduct an investigation into its recruitment and promotion. The inquiry was swiftly concluded and given to ministers in January 1854. It was published in February 1854.[2]

The Northcote–Trevelyan Report, which has since become synonymous with upholding the almost uniquely unpoliticised nature of the permanent side of British government, was short, pithy and punchy. It was essentially the work of Sir Charles Trevelyan, who was a paragon of the Victorian ideal—high-minded, unbending and often overzealous, certainly to more secular, modern tastes. The report stands as an excoriating critique of the British state's evolution up to the mid-nineteenth century. Trevelyan described what had to change:

It would be natural to expect that so important a profession would attract into its ranks the ablest and most ambitious of the youth of the country; that the keenest emulation would prevail among those who had entered it; and that such as were endowed with superior qualifications would rapidly rise to distinction and public prominence. Such, however, is by no means the case. Admission into the Civil Service is eagerly sought after, but it is for the unambitious, and the indolent or incapable that it is chiefly desired. Those whose abilities do not warrant an expectation that they will succeed in the open professions, where they must encounter the competition of their contemporaries, and those whom indolence of temperament, or physical infirmities unfit for active exertions, are placed in the Civil Service, where they may obtain an honourable livelihood with little labour, and with no risk . . .

The report went on to unambiguously support the principle of competitive examinations for recruitment to the Civil Service, much on the basis of Macaulay's (Trevelyan's brother-in-law) reforms to the Indian Civil Service.[3]

Published by Blackwell Publishing Ltd, 9600 Garsington Road, Oxford OX4 2DQ, UK and 350 Main Street, Malden, MA 02148, USA

The Northcote–Trevelyan Report did not have a smooth ride. The Prime Minister, Lord John Russell, was adamantly against it and successfully postponed its implementation. But the issue would not die and in 1855 it again returned to centre stage—this time, in the House of Commons—on the occasion of the creation, under an Order in Council, of the first Civil Service Commission, a body established to certificate the quality of recruits. The debate in the Commons over this was fascinating, and provided a microcosm of the nineteenth-century debate over merit. Henry Layard, Tory MP for Aylesbury, illuminated the two strands in the argument. He railed against ' . . . obstructions proceeding from party and family influence. That is the chief evil of which we complain', but at the same time defended Russell: 'No doubt the noble Lord at the head of the Government will say this evening, as he has done upon former occasions, that this is a mere attack upon the aristocracy. That accusation is odious to me. The noble Lord is welcome to say that I am attacking an oligarchy, but I utterly deny that I am making any attack upon the aristocracy.'[4] The aristocratic element in the debate again seems odd to twenty-first-century readers, when aristocracy is more akin to celebrity and stories of impoverished peers selling the family silver abound.

Gladstone responded to the charge that competitive merit was an attack on the aristocracy with a defence of the aristocracy, contending that 'aristocracy has been continually recruited from among the very best of the people'[5] and to lament that there was 'a tendency out of doors to mix up the two ideas of corruption and weakness in the public service, and the prevalence of the aristocratic element'.[6] He went on to explain how, for many, 'promotion by merit is not believed in, but is looked upon with distrust, and regarded as a cover for jobbery'.[7]

A Mr Gower, another Tory MP, pursued the point further when he said that he 'would be glad to see an infusion of the middle classes into the Govt of the country, for he entertained a high admiration for the energy, industry, and intelligence of these classes; but there was a tendency in the public mind to look upon men who had no high social position, and who engaged in political life, as mere political adventurers'.[8] Gower's statement is fascinating for two reasons: first, the view that only a blue-blooded birth could lead to a respected life of sacrifice in public duty; and, second, that a powerful impulse in the drive to reform recruitment to the Civil Service was to open the doors to the industry and efficiency of the burgeoning and increasingly powerful middle classes. On the one hand, would the middle-class entrants demonstrate the right 'character', that amorphous but highly influential test of a 'gentleman' in the nineteenth century? As an MP by the name of Fawcett said in another debate on the principle of merit in 1869, some claimed that 'examinations, while they tested intellectual merit, did not test the physical and moral qualities of the candidates? Did the present system test the physical and moral qualities of the candidates?'[9]

The other class-based angle to the debate was directed not upwards but downwards, towards the working classes. This controversial aspect centred on whether Northcote–Trevelyan could be seen as an attempt to provide a bulwark against the also increasingly powerful working classes. It will be remembered that in 1867 the Second Reform Act gave many urban working-class males the vote. It does not require a quantum leap of the imagination to envisage fear in the minds of those in government and, for want of a better word, the 'establishment' that the last thing that was needed was for the uncouth and the uncivilised to be given a stab at running the country. Seen in this light, the push towards giving state employment in effect only to those who had received good degrees from good colleges (a gentleman should study the classics or mathematics at Oxford or Cambridge)—in other words, the upper and middle classes—could be interpreted as a way of keeping the working classes out of the Senior Civil Service altogether (they had always been there fulfilling roles such as messengers, for example).

The nineteenth-century debate was effectively ended in June 1870 when Gladstone, now as Prime Minister, and his Chancellor, Robert Lowe, joined forces to persuade a sceptical Cabinet to support another Order in Council that the Treasury would in future control Civil Service recruitment. This followed a Treasury minute dated 30 November 1868, which stated that 'promotion by merit is the established rule in the Civil Service, and to every young man who becomes the servant of the Crown in the CS, a way is opened to independence and even eminence'.[10] Thus the meritocratic principle was now firmly ingrained in the Whitehall culture (barring the ancient departments of the Home and Foreign Offices, which fought hard to retain patronage on the threatened basis of 'character'). The Civil Service that emerged from the battles of 1850s, 1860s and 1870s was therefore middle-to-upper class, university trained and modelled on the basis of the very ideal of a Victorian—a first-class umpire for what was then a minimal state.

Expansion of the state

It was all to change in the twentieth century. First came the New Liberal agenda, from 1906 until the Great War broke out in 1914. Though not comparable in scale to the social reforms of the mid-twentieth century, the development of state activity pioneered by the Prime Minister, Herbert Asquith, his Chancellor, David Lloyd George, and the President of the Board of Trade, Winston Churchill, meant that, for the first time, the Civil Service needed to be proactive rather than simply regulatory. The first baby-steps for state unemployment benefit, sickness insurance and labour exchanges meant that civil servants had to on occasions get out into the provinces and understand the world they were administering. That Greats and the Classics at Oxbridge produced finely ordered minds and an ability to write an essay *sans pareil* was beyond doubt, but it was significant that in the twentieth century's first British stab at expanding state power, of which there was to be much, outsiders were drafted in. These included William

Beveridge, a young permanent secretary during the Great War, who was to make such a mark during the Second World War.[11]

The truly great example of where the reach of the Northcote–Trevelyan Civil Service was found wanting came first in 1914–18 and then again in 1939–45. For in the early days of the First World War, Lloyd George (Chancellor of the Exchequer) coined the phrase 'business as usual'. This was to become a millstone around the neck of the government, as supply problems to the army turned into a national *cause célèbre*—the 'shell scandal'. But it was not only this. The first total war involving all sections of British society over four and a half years meant that the state had to get involved in areas it had never reached before. This again called for civil servants the like of which had never been seen before. Industrialists, academics, statisticians and economists, amongst many others, were subsumed into the bureaucracy.[12] The same happened during the Second World War, but now the mandarins had learnt what was required and created a database of those who would be needed should war break out again[13]—the delay in the Great War had seen many of the country's young and highly educated, such as the Prime Minister's son, end up as statistics themselves in the mud of the Western Front.[14] The importation of all the country's talents into the Civil Service at the nation's moments of greatest peril led to the British state being the most far-reaching and organised amongst the combatants. One would have thought that success on this scale would have led to the belief that a single kind of merit was unable to deliver effectiveness, especially when the state, which did contract after 1918, actually gained responsibilities during Clement Attlee's 1945–51 governments. Not a bit of it. The years in the Civil Service immediately after 1945 have come to be known as 'the missed opportunity'.[15]

Clement Attlee and other Labour leaders held senior posts in the wartime coalition under Churchill. The aforementioned British development of the most organised state the world had ever seen in both world wars, but most comprehensively in the second, fostered confidence in the Labour leadership that the Civil Service was both efficient and trustworthy.[16] The latter point had been called into significant question by some left-wingers, such as Professor Harold Laski of the London School of Economics, throughout the 1930s and 1940s.[17] But come 1945 it was difficult for any criticism of the Civil Service to hold sway after such a clear-cut triumph throughout the war years. In this moment of supreme confidence lay the seeds of later difficulty. For the undoubted effectiveness of the Civil Service, demonstrated in running the wartime state, encouraged many in the country to support William Beveridge's 1942 report calling for the state not to abandon its wartime involvement once the conflict had ceased.[18] Labour adopted it wholeheartedly. This may have worked seamlessly but for a big problem—the vast majority of those outsiders who had blended with the Civil Service career-lifers to produce such a fine machine immediately left the bureaucracy (the greater complexity of peacetime was another huge issue). There were many reasons for this, with poor pay, the stuffy atmosphere and a desire to return to their own jobs after the wartime emergency chief amongst them.[19] But perhaps the most significant was the overconfidence of the mandarinate, which thought that the pre-1939 Civil Service could cope with the post-1945 world. The lessons of the war had been casually ignored and Attlee's confidence bolstered the senior civil servants' position.

Thus the self-confidence of the Civil Service was at its zenith in the early postwar period. It was not to last very long. Two far-reaching events were to damage it forever. The first was the Suez crisis. While it was undeniable that the chief culprit in the seedy 'collusion' with the French and Israelis over the botched invasion of Egypt was clearly the Prime Minister, Sir Anthony Eden, there were significant question marks over the involvement of senior civil servants in the enterprise. The future Head of the Home Civil Service, Sir William Armstrong, recalled how he was uncomfortable with the adventure, but instead of saying so outright—or even resigning—decided on the almost infantile action of wearing a black tie for a week.[20] Only a handful of officials resigned over Suez.[21]

The end of British supremacy

The folly of Suez is often seen as the death knell for Britain as a superpower—it could no longer launch an armed campaign without the blessing of the United States (though perhaps this was perception catching up with reality, especially after the loss of the one million men that the Indian army had provided up to 1947). It can be seen to mark the acceleration of decolonisation and the turn to Europe. Undoubtedly, the Suez debacle destroyed forever much of the influence Britain had enjoyed in the Middle East. The question for the Civil Service was whether the reliance on merit reduced the amount of backbone, perhaps of that elusive 'character', which could have saved Britain from the Suez mess. While this has not been a clear-cut argument in the criticism of the Civil Service, the issue has simmered continuously.

The over-riding adherence to conformity in the Senior Civil Service was powerfully enhanced in the 1920s and 1930s with the Civil Service leadership of Sir Warren Fisher. Originally backed by Lloyd George, Fisher tried hard to make the Service highly generalist by enforcing a rigid 'musical chairs' policy, whereby nobody stayed in a position or a specialised area long enough to become an expert. This led to a cadre of senior civil servants who all followed a recognised path to the top, usually through the Treasury. Conformity was the watchword, and it was massively supported by the adherence to few recruits brought in after the age of 21 and all by meritorious examination. Conformity reduced the independent character of civil servants. One, Sir Leo Pliatzky, went as far as to question the difference between senior British officials and those in the Nazi bureaucracy.[22] Continuing analysis of the Suez debacle was to cast a shadow over the British Civil Service for many years.

The more damaging event in postwar Britain, certainly for the Civil Service, was the perception of relative and long-term economic decline. From the vantage point of the early twenty-first century, the near-paranoia and obsession that Britain was falling behind her partners and competitors at a rate not seen since the end of the Spanish Empire in the sixteenth century is as much a relic of history as the period itself. For though Britain had the largest economy in the world in 1900, it finished the century in fourth place, hardly justifying Anthony Sampson's 1962 claim that it was 'becoming to the twenty-first century what Spain was to the eighteenth'.[23] But one's perception determines one's reality, and the late 1950s, the 1960s and the 1970s were fretful decades. As economic growth began to be lauded as the key economic indicator, critics pointed to the 7.8 per cent year-on-year growth that Germany was enjoying (between 1950 and 1958), the 5.8 per cent of the Italians and the 4.6 per cent of the French, and they compared it to the 2.6 per cent of Britain throughout the 1950s.[24]

Where was the blame to be apportioned for the seemingly dreadful performance? The majority of it fell on the government, the Civil Service and the Treasury in particular. The government of the day was blamed, as first the Labour Party in the late 1940s and then the Conservative Party in the 1950s accepted that the government had a responsibility to manage the economic cycle. This followed John Maynard Keynes' remedy to the Depression of the 1930s, which saw government as the only protagonist in the economy that could do anything on the required scale. Keynes' theory was made government policy in the *Employment Policy* White Paper of 1944.[25] Thus, when the economy faltered (or appeared to) it became the responsibility of the government and of those who had carried out the government's wishes over many years, the Civil Service, and—within the Service—the Treasury in particular.

Other massive pressures on the British state, and especially on its management of the economy, included the recurring balance-of-payments crises linked to running the world's second reserve currency, maintaining disproportionately large armed forces—thus further hampering the balance of payments—and also the decision to avoid joining the embryonic EEC, which soon proved to be an economic mistake. The Treasury had also scored an own goal in 1961, when it acted appallingly in brutally halting an upswing in the economy when the downswing was already on its way. This glaring example of what was then known as 'stop–go' damaged confidence in the Treasury on the part of the Prime Minister, industrialists and commentators, and—perhaps most importantly—it shook the Treasury's confidence in itself.[26] Many began to question the Treasury's role and who was staffing it. The scene was set for an attack on the Civil Service and its servants, which was to last for decades.

What kind of merit?

The first big critique of the postwar period came in 1959, with Thomas Balogh's *The Apotheosis of the Dilettante*. Balogh was an Hungarian economist and Oxford don, close to the Labour leadership, and to Harold Wilson in particular. He joined Wilson in government in 1964 as Economic Adviser to the Cabinet, but kept a keen eye on all things Civil Service. His analysis was, in its way, as blistering as Trevelyan's had been a century before. Balogh began his attack with a backhanded compliment. The Victorians, he said,

smashed the inefficiency of the old system of state administration based on corruption and nepotism. They conceived the role of the state in purely negative terms but were determined that those 'night-watchman' functions should be ably, efficiently and cheaply performed. There were to be no sinecures or spoils . . . They knew what type of person and qualities they wanted: absence of corruption and favouritism on the one hand, and reticence from bureaucratic pretensions on the other . . . Within the limits of the Victorian social and economic framework, and so long as no positive duties devolved on the state, so long as it was sufficient to keep things basically as they were and not to interfere too much with 'other people's business', no obvious deficiency arose.[27]

Balogh was closely identified with the Labour Party's attempt to build an effective planning apparatus at the very centre of British economic policy machinery. Indeed, he was a chief protagonist in the ill-fated splitting of the Treasury and the creation of the Department of Economic Affairs in 1964.[28] Being forever critical of the Treasury's record, Balogh turned his ire on those manning it. That the Civil Service recruited through merit, he could not deny. But what kind of merit?—'[i]n a planned economy, the crossword-puzzle mind, reared on mathematics at Cambridge or Greats at Oxford, has only a limited outlet'.[29]

Balogh, himself a tutor at Balliol College, Oxford, was highly dismissive of the relevance its education was providing:

The cultivation of tolerant scepticism was obtained by insisting on a formal kind of education, which developed powers of dialectical argument only, rather than a knowledge of the present world and its problems. . . . Classics or mathematics were the way of the chosen: in aristocratic Platonic philosophy and in the total demonstration of the futility of efforts at social betterment by ancient history . . .[30]

How an irrelevantly educated cadre came to form 'a tight new caste of mandarins', 'the crowning of the Victorian reforms', was his true target.[31] He centred his attacks on the examination process.

There had always been two elements to the recruitment examination, a written test and an interview. Balogh wrote that

Already before the last war, in connection with the broadening of the syllabus of the competitive examination (and possibly to counteract the consequences of the increasing democratization of education, the change in the social background of many potentially successful competitors, in consequence of the improvement of higher popular education after the 1902 and 1914 Education Acts), greater weight was given to the interview. Thus the safeguards against class-prejudice and nepotism established by the anonymity of the written examination were considerably weakened.[32]

Balogh was therefore not only criticising the recruitment of, as he saw it, irrelevantly trained youths, but also that these recruits were of a protected elite. 'Formal equality,' he contended, 'could be preserved yet effective choice limited mainly to the well-to-do, by demanding educational and social equality at the universities which ruled out the plebs—apart from a sprinkling of scholars—because of its high cost, without open discrimination: the rich and the poor were both to be permitted to dine at the Ritz.'[33] Balogh also wrote of '[t]he social (rather than intellectual) snobbery and "apartheid" of Oxbridge'.[34] He concluded his attack by commenting about 'Recruitment favouring the smooth, extrovert conformist with good connections and no knowledge of modern problems, or of up-to-date techniques of getting that information.'[35]

The next key publication criticising Civil Service meritocracy was 1964's Fabian Tract, *The Administrators*. The authors were of a very high quality: Balogh was party to it; Robert Neild, Cambridge economist, economic special adviser in 1964 and member of the Fulton Committee's inquiry into the Civil Service during 1966–8, was in the chair; Anthony Crosland, Labour intellectual and future Cabinet Minister, was also a member; as were Shirley Williams, another future Cabinet Minister (and briefly on the Fulton Committee), and five senior civil servants. *The Administrators* began, as Balogh's lone discourse had, with a dissection of the Victorian reforms and the Service they had created. The Fabians also observed virtues of honesty and dispassion in it. As the tract had several serving civil servants as part of its authorship, it was naturally far less incendiary in its analysis. But it was still highly critical, if in measured tones. Though it did mention the reliance on candidates from Oxbridge, it was far more interested in the generalist education and nature of the recruits. The group lamented '[t]he concentration of Oxford and Cambridge graduates with degrees in Arts subjects; the shortage of recruits and difficulty in attracting good people, particularly those with degrees in science or mathematics'.[36]

The Fabians identified four elements of criticism:

(a) The administrator often lives in isolation from industry, local government and other fields of the society which he may administer; his career is not designed to give him experience and first-hand knowledge of the field he administers.

(b) The administrator is still expected to be an omniscient all-rounder capable of formulating policy in any field.

(c) The administrative hierarchy is as closed and protected as a monastic order. A young man enters at 21 or so and is virtually locked in until 60. There is practically no movement of new blood inwards or old blood outwards at any age between the early 20s and 60. In an age when the value of persons with professional training is increasingly acknowledged, the status of the professional in the Civil Service, with a few individual exceptions, is inferior to that of the administrator.

(d) There is no provision for new appointments from outside when governments change. The administrator is supposed to be apolitical, and yet equally good at helping to devise and advocate socialist, liberal or conservative policies and capable of switching wholeheartedly from one to the other at any time of life. (The importance of his being able to do so increases with seniority and age, whereas his ability to do so is likely to decline.)[37]

The Fabian group made clear their technocratic aims with the following criticism:

In the past the service has been slow to adapt itself to political, social and economic changes. This did not seem to matter too much in previous periods. Now, however, it has become necessary to improve the instruments of policy to keep pace with changes in our society; indeed some alteration in the higher civil service may be a pre-requisite to enabling a Labour Government—or any other government—to carry through the modernisation of the country.[38]

For 'modernisation', read 'creation of far-reaching economic planning apparatus'.

That the Northcote–Trevelyan reforms created a meritocracy is beyond doubt. Examination has been the route to the Senior Civil Service since that time. But what came into question in the 1960s was the kind of meritocracy that was in place. Were those being recruited the *right* meritocrats? Was the examination process skewed towards the manner and standards of the public school and Oxbridge? Were these gilded youths of the calibre to steer Britain away from debt and disaster, or were they chiefly responsible for the problems of the postwar world?

The pressure upon the Civil Service in the 1960s led directly to the establishment of the aforementioned Fulton Committee in 1966, to 'examine the structure, recruitment and management, including training, of the Home Civil Service and to make recommendations'.[39] The Fulton Report of 1968 included many recommendations with the aim of broadening the social representation of the Service, whilst moving towards a more specialised regime. The effective end to the pressure came in 1970, when Edward Heath embarked on a wholesale reform of the machine—all the while not touching those working in it. The truce lasted until the advent of the Thatcher administration.

Michael Young was still troubled in 2001 at the way *The Rise of the Meritocracy* was being perceived. He meant it as a satire, but some, including the Prime Minister of the day, Tony Blair, appeared not to appreciate this. Young wanted to warn of the dangers that a purely meritocratic society would bring. He certainly observed dangers that it had brought to the Civil Service. He spoke of the senior staff amongst them being 'quiet meritocrats' and said that 'They didn't seem to have the light of imagination in them . . . They weren't the people who invented ideas, they were good at honing them.'[40] The Victorians hit the nail on the head with their many parliamentary debates on the conflict between merit and character. To rely totally on one was mistaken. A combination of the two, Aristotle's 'golden mean' again, would prove to be the difficult aim in the years after the Civil Service's low points of the 1960s and 1970s.

A Tract for the Times

PAUL BARKER

Introduction

It has never been easy to categorise *The Rise of the Meritocracy*.[1] This may be why it is the best and the most influential of Michael Young's books. In some ways, it is an extended pamphlet. But if that were all, it would have faded into the dust of old disputations. The books that last longest are those that can be read more than one way.

From its first publication, in 1958, it created a puzzle for those who wanted to cram it into one category or another. I was given a copy the following year, as a birthday present, perhaps with ironic intent. But then irony is an essential part of the book itself. The magazine I eventually went on to edit, *New Society* (launched in 1962), was described by Robert Hewison, in his cultural history of those years, as 'a forum for the new intelligentsia'.[2] A less friendly interpretation might be 'a forum for guilty meritocrats'.

I first met Michael Young in 1967, and soon afterwards wrote a profile of him for an American magazine. I described *Meritocracy* as 'his most important and most maverick work'.[3] I hold to that. But what, exactly, was its first impact? What was its practical influence? What is its continuing importance?

First impact

To look back at the reviews it got in 1958 is to enter the world of the assumptions that marked the first period that could really be called 'post-war'.[4] The Attlee years, when Young ran the research (i.e. propaganda) department of the Labour Party, were preoccupied with trying to hold a precarious balance between the disastrous financial implications of the Second World War and the determined enactment of social legislation based on prewar and wartime ideas. R. A. Butler had brought in the 1944 Education Act as education minister in the wartime coalition government. (Young wrote, in his 1947 book, *Labour's Plan for Plenty*, that 'Of all the social services, education is far and away the most important.') But in 1953, as Chancellor of the Exchequer after Churchill's return to office, Butler brought in the first budget since the war's end that didn't put up taxes. Food rationing, once defended as socialism in action, was abolished. Domestically, the 1950s had a golden glow.

Among the first sociology Young published was an article on the meanings of the 1953 Coronation.[5] It was sympathetic to national sentimentality about the young Queen. In *Meritocracy*, the 1950s and 1960s are referred to as the

 Published by Blackwell Publishing Ltd, 9600 Garsington Road, Oxford OX4 2DQ, UK and 350 Main Street, Malden, MA 02148, USA

'Elizabethan' era. In fact, this usage barely outlasted the mid-1950s. After the Suez debacle of 1956, the sun quickly began to set on the British Empire and 'Elizabethanism' alike. In the year the book was published, the Campaign for Nuclear Disarmament held its first Aldermaston march (which started at Trafalgar Square—the order of march was thereafter reversed, for better publicity). It inaugurated a new style of middle-class, often meritocratic, dissidence:

Dr Young has written an admirable tract on latter-day Platonism. He has shown how social inventions, like technological inventions, can turn and bite the inventor. It is not many years since horticulturalists discovered that DDT was not an unmixed blessing . . . Dr Young's fantasy is a discovery that the Education Act [1944], too, was not an unmixed blessing. In saving Britain's intellect, it may destroy Britain's soul.

Thus Sir Eric Ashby, botanist and education grandee, in the books pages of *New Scientist* in December 1958. He took it all with a mandarin calm. Not so, for example, Alan Fox, an Oxford sociologist, writing in *Socialist Commentary* (a magazine of the Labour right). 'Was there ever such a society as ours, one wonders,' he expostulated in the November 1958 issue, 'for projecting nightmare visions of its own future?' He cited Aldous Huxley, George Orwell, Arthur Koestler and, interestingly, James Burnham. In *The Managerial Revolution* (1941), Burnham predicted inexorable dominance by a manager class. His thesis is an acknowledged influence on *Nineteen Eighty-Four*. It is also part of the intellectual undergrowth out of which Young's book sprang.

'Well, here we are still taking punishment,' Fox went on—Young, he said, had produced 'another spectre to make us gasp with anguish.' Fox's anguish was matched by other reviewers. *The Economist* was vitriolic: 'Should we really exalt the saintly moujiks of Tolstoy above, say, Leonardo da Vinci?' The truth was, it said, that 'A "meritocracy" of one sort or another is on the way. Not even the most rigidly comprehensive schooling, so long as it does not flatten superior ability, will keep that ability in the working class.' Nor was the book in any sense positive: 'Mr Young has retreated behind a smokescreen of entertaining jibes.' (Sir Geoffrey Crowther, not long retired from editing *The Economist*, was preparing a government report on the education of 15–18 year olds [15 was then the school-leaving age]. It emphasised how much working-class talent was going to waste.[6] Was he tempted back as a reviewer? As editor, Crowther's advice to his journalists was 'Simplify, then exaggerate.')

The educationist Boris Ford told the readers of *The Spectator* that 'Michael Young is a sociologist not altogether approved of by his fellow-sociologists.' Not only did he take 'too few statistical samples'—the contemporary, and often-repeated, reproach against the Institute of Community Studies' first book, *Family and Kinship in East London* (1957)—but he had also been 'dilatory in shouldering his pole of the banner of Social Mobility'. Ford didn't mind, because Young was confronting 'outstandingly important issues'. The meritocracy the book feared derived, Ford said, from the 'inheritance of wartime assumptions about efficient selection and promotion, reinforced by an LSE sociology intent on demolishing roadblocks in the way of talent', and all 'backed up by the proliferating growth of the power and outlook of the Civil Service'.

In Young's introduction to the new American edition (1994), he said he hawked the book around London publishers for years. It was only by accident that it appeared after *Family and Kinship*. It was also only by accident that it ever appeared at all. He met an old friend, Walter Neurath, on a beach in North Wales. Neurath had just founded the publishers Thames & Hudson. Their speciality was, and remains, art books, but Neurath published the book anyway. 'Fortunately,' Young wrote, 'his kindness was rewarded this side of the pearly gates.' Penguin followed up with a paperback in their Pelican series. It sold many thousands of copies. The Pelican list had an authority in Britain hard to imagine today, when so many paperback series compete.

The re-publication in the United States demonstrated the book's continuing power to provoke. *The Bell Curve: Intelligence and Class Structure in American Life*, by Charles Murray and the late Richard Herrnstein, was also published in 1994.[7] Among Americans, *Meritocracy* has always found itself caught up in the crossfire of the bitter battle between environmental and genetic explanations. (Murray himself is an admirer of the book.)

Reviewing the new edition, *The Atlantic Monthly* attacked it for sneering at the idea of equal opportunities for all.[8] And when it was first published in America, in 1959, *The Wall Street Journal*'s reviewer wrote angrily:

What Mr Young seems to be saying is that society is better off for being a hodge-podge, with some people getting by on ancestry, some on inherited money, some on favouritism or nepotism, and some on brains. From 1946 to 1951 Mr Young, as head of the Labour Party's research department, helped build Britain's welfare state. Since he now evidently holds with Lord Melbourne that it is better to leave things alone, his past hardly explains his present. Or maybe it does explain it; maybe he has 'had enough'.

In Britain, the book was received more often with puzzlement than with hostility. In the *New Statesman*, Peter Shore—who held Young's old Labour Party post between Hugh Gaitskell's failure in the general election of 1959 and Harold Wilson's modified success in 1964—worried away at its 'harsh and pessimistic' vision, though he judged it 'certainly not implausible'. It was, he reckoned, 'a reasonable projection of Mr Butler's Opportunity State'. This was an odd use of 'reasonable'. Perhaps the magazine's literary editor was unwise to mail a satire to a man without much evident sense of humour.

The literary and cultural critics Richard Hoggart and Raymond Williams were especially important reviewers at the time. What they said showed which way the centre-to-left wind was blowing. The heyday of their influence was just beginning. Hoggart's *The Uses of Literacy* was published in 1957;[9] Williams's *Culture and Society* in 1958.[10] Both wrote reviews that walked around *Meritocracy* like hesitant border terriers, rather than confront it directly. Both had risen (from working-class Hunslet and Abergavenny) through the operation of the gospel of equal opportunity, though both in their different ways saw its shortcomings. Williams grew increasingly angry and, over the years, ended up boxed into a semi-Marxist corner. Hoggart portrayed poignantly the way the rising lad (less often, then, lass) had to cut himself off from his own family.

Williams told the readers of the *Manchester Guardian*, rightly, that 'The logic of the future-story is the logic of extending tendencies.' (Nothing 'reasonable' about it.) For him, the best in the genre was Swift's *A Modest Proposal*, which suggested that the way to cure, at a stroke, poverty and overpopulation in Ireland was to fatten up the children of the poor as food for the rich.[11] For Williams, as for Hoggart in his *Observer* review, Young's book, short though it is, was too long for its own good. The theme, Hoggart said, was 'sufficient only for a good short squib'.

Williams used the book as a way to hit contemporary society over the head. (And why not? All books about the future are really critiques of the present.) 'I see no evidence,' he wrote, 'in contemporary England, of *power* being more closely connected with merit, in any definition. The administrators, professional men and technicians are increasingly being selected on educational merit, but the power is still largely elsewhere, "and no damned merit about it".' The meritocrats of 1958, he argued, were no more than a superior servant-class: 'To be an upper servant may be as high, really, as we can raise our heads.'

He thought that Young was extrapolating from some supposed 'cultural decline' of the working class, due to their 'limited intellectual potential'. This was beating the book with the wrong end of the stick. The stick would have fallen more accurately on many pages of *The Uses of Literacy*, with their sentimental view of urban working-class life (another reproach often made, also, against *Family and Kinship*, published the same year). Working-class culture, Hoggart thought, was careering downhill under commercial, and especially American, influence. In 1994, in *Theatres of Memory*, the social historian Raphael Samuel quoted Hoggart's denunciation of milk bars 'as a caution against a too immediate hostility to what is alien and innovatory'.[12] Hoggart had written:

Girls go to some, but most of the customers are boys aged between fifteen and twenty, with drape-suits, picture ties, and an American slouch . . . the 'nickelodeon' is allowed to blare out so that the noise would be sufficient to fill a good-sized ballroom, rather than a converted shop in the high street . . . Compared even with the pub around the corner, this is a peculiarly thin and pallid form of dissipation, a sort of spiritual dry-rot amid the odour of boiled milk.

The first Teddy Boy on record was seen in South London in 1953.[13] The first milk bar reached my West Riding home village about four years later. Anthony Burgess's novel, *A Clockwork Orange*, which opens in a milk bar, was published in 1962.

Appearances barely feature in *Meritocracy*. But the world Hoggart decried was, in fact, an accurate foretaste of the way things would go. For his *Observer* readers he suggested an alternative future to Young's. He imagined 'an unequal society in which "equality", far from being discredited, had *formally* been allowed to rule in fantastically diverse areas of experience; a society so generally prosperous that material differences between people would be exploited only, but intensely, to rouse marginal rivalries'. This sounds very much like the Britain we ended up with (though it supplements meritocracy, rather than supplants it).

Practical influence

When I first read it, the book's science fiction thesis of an IQ-justified hierarchy seemed far-fetched. Re-reading it, the section closest to science fiction—the eventual revolt against that hierarchy—still seems weak. But it was in line with Young's recurrent, admirable recognition of the right of the poor, the bloody-minded and the unintellectual to be the way they want to be, and to have their lives and their preferences respected.

Many of the reviewers also preferred Part One, where Young has a lot of fun with his new idea. In Part Two, we are due to find out more about the attempt to counter it. But the 'Chelsea Manifesto'—supposedly forged in an alliance between revolution-minded 'shaggy young girls from Newnham and Somerville' and 'aged men' who still remember the Labour Party's original ideals—may be radical but is undoubtedly very skimpy. A folk memory is invoked of an even earlier set of ideals. One of the 'vivid' young women leading the revolution is Lady Urania O'Connor. She shares a surname with Fergus O'Connor, the best-remembered Chartist leader. Further irony lurks. Urania was the name of a project, launched by Charles Dickens and the bank heiress Baroness Burdett-Coutts, in the last days of political Chartism, to rescue fallen women. It failed, like other Burdett-Coutts philanthropic projects. One of the few remaining signs of the baroness's well-meant efforts is a luxuriant marble fountain, often vandalised, in Victoria Park, a short walk from the Institute of Community Studies (now The Young Foundation).

The *Times Literary Supplement*'s anonymous reviewer enjoyed the first two-thirds of the book, but found the final revolt 'too sketchily contrived to be convincing'. The sympathetic Boris Ford found that 'positive values are insufficiently explored'. The unsympathetic Alan Fox said that 'Dr Young clearly rests much importance on his concept of "plural values", but to this reviewer it 'fails to provoke cries of "Eureka".'

It is easy to understand reviewers' puzzlement. Irony is a dangerous freight to carry. Like wagons bearing nuclear materials, it should come with a warning for the unwary. The message of the book could be taken in at least two ways, possibly three.

Because of the title, it was often taken as simply the prehistory of a new phenomenon. As the *Oxford English Dictionary* confirms, Young had invented a useful neologism. His new word must have appeared in print millions of times from the pen, typewriter or laptop of writers who have never read the book. As he said in the 1994 American edition, 'the most influential books are always those that are not read'. (*The Origin of Species* is perhaps the most famous example, though *Das Kapital* must once have run it close.)

Alternatively, Young's book can be read as a simple attack on the rampant meritocrats. In this guise, in the 1960s and 1970s, it had its most far-reaching practical influence.

But, third, it can be read—and, I would argue, best read—as sociological analysis in the form of a satire. Whatever its weaknesses, it still beats most sociology. Young is the sole twentieth-century British sociologist I can find in the current edition of *Chambers Biographical Dictionary*.[14] It gives most weight to his consumerist campaigns and educational innovations. *The Rise of the Meritocracy* is his only sociological publication mentioned by name. 'Meritocracy' is the only concept put forward by a British sociologist recently that has attained common currency. To match it you might even have to go back as far as Herbert Spencer, who invented the 'survival of the fittest'—a concept Spencer wasn't in the least ironic about.[15]

One reason for the book's continuing power is that its forecasts have worked at more than one level. Historically, it was an important intellectual propellant behind the educational attack on the eleven-plus, streaming and grammar schools generally. Here, the crucial link is personal. Anthony Crosland is among the varied collection of people listed in the note of acknowledgements. (They range from Margaret Cole and Peter Townsend on the left to Irving Kristol and Edward Shils on the right.) In 1965, Harold Wilson appointed Crosland as Secretary of State for Education.

Under his regime, comprehensive schooling moved from being an ideal, which appeared to have worked well on a small scale, to a doctrine to be imposed everywhere. Even in 1954, after the London County Council decided to put its own money on comprehensive schools, one friendly early critic pleaded for experimentation, rather than homogenisation.[16] Having been at one of the first comprehensive schools, as well as (thanks to the eleven-plus) a local grammar school, I always agreed with this. I thought, and tried to convey through the pages of *New Society*, that what happened inside classrooms was far more important than external systems of administration. Teachers and the curriculum are what deliver, or don't deliver, the goods. But this was Mr Secretary Crosland, as recorded in his wife's published memoir of his life:[17]

'If it's the last thing I do, I'm going to destroy every fucking grammar school in England,' he said. 'And Wales. And Northern Ireland.'

'Why not Scotland?' I asked out of pure curiosity.

'Because their schools come under the Secretary of State for Scotland.' He began to laugh at his own inability to destroy their grammar schools.

Over the next ten years, under a succession of education secretaries and their civil servants, Crosland's anti-meritocratic ambition was almost fulfilled. Yet the flaw in neighbourhood schools had already become clear in the US, home of the original model. They locked children into their background. This was fine if the background was fine; less fine if it wasn't.

This administrative doctrine was laid down by a minister who was educated at public school and who left fee-paying schools untouched. (The Butler Act's most important innovation in secondary education was to abolish fee-paying as a way into grammar schools. This was the point, and the effect, of the eleven-plus examination, IQ test and all.) The public schools were therefore ready to receive an injection of talent from the children of anxious parents. Oddly, it was also Crosland who promulgated a two-tier system of higher education (now abolished): polytechnics on the one hand, and universities on the other. This exactly corresponded to the divide between secondary modern and grammar schools that he was attacking. But perhaps he saw polytechnics as comprehensives and universities as public schools.

What was wrong about Crosland's policy, and his reading of Young's satire, was the rush to ditch something good before you were sure it was being replaced by something better. The supposed groundswell of public support for comprehensives was misleading. One segment consisted of modestly placed parents who were well enough off to pay the pre-Butler grammar school fees, but couldn't afford public schools; their children were now shut out from grace if they failed the eleven-plus. Another, larger segment were voting *against* the secondary modern schools, to which most of the failed went, rather than *for* comprehensives (as the social policy analyst David Donnison pointed out as early as 1967[18]).

Continuing importance

Painfully, the bureaucratic homogenisation is being dissolved. With lengthening hindsight, it becomes clear that the sociology in *Meritocracy* is more enduringly true than any short-term misinterpretation of it. The unstreamed comprehensive schools, with mixed-ability classes, never achieved total dominance. From the mid-1980s, a gradual reversion began, towards a more meritocratic model. The roller-coaster started to loop upwards again, and was soon roaring away. It seemed to be what people wanted.

Thus the Major and Blair governments followed Mrs Thatcher's lead in re-emphasising meritocracy. Tests for pupils have flourished and more specialist schools have been introduced; these have often amounted to selection under another name. Various schemes—beacon schools and city academies, for example—have been copied, as comprehensives had been, from the US. In 2004, with a general election in prospect, Tony Blair was setting out again his vision of 'an opportunity society', though many commentators saw the logical complications in this. *The Economist* noted: 'The government is trying to reconcile its egalitarian belief that all should have prizes with the requirements of a meritocracy.'[19] The Conservative 'One Nation' political writer Ferdinand Mount praised the continuing relevance of Michael Young's work, and argued that 'equality of opportunity is an odd kind of equality. "The opportunity to become unequal"—what kind of justice is that?'[20] But after Labour's victory in the 2005 general election, both Blair and Gordon Brown repeated the commitment to continuing on the meritocratic track.

Young's book correctly foresaw the way higher education would go. In its pages, Eric James, then the High Master of Manchester Grammar School, is regularly cited as the flag-waver of the meritocracy. When James became the first vice-chancellor of the new University of York (founded in 1963), he wanted it to become a grammar school among universities. A generation later, this meritocratic, work-based ideal has lasted better than the 'plural values' of the other new universities of its day; from among them, York is one of the best regarded. Many more new universities have been launched since; often they are former polytechnics or upgraded colleges of further education. But there is usually little doubt where these stand in the academic pecking order, with the elite 'Russell Group' of older-established universities at the top.

In 1958, reviewers thought Young was stretching the limits of probability when he suggested that Oxford and Cambridge might end up purely meritocratic. But with Oxford's acceptance in 1995 that entrance should turn on A-level grades (since supplemented again by special tests), this is what happened. Unfortunately, for the time being, and to the Blair Government's public distress, this has locked Oxbridge colleges even more tightly into taking entrants from fee-paying schools. As Young also predicted, these have become devoted to churning out good grades, rather than good chaps on the rugby field.

The immediate influence of *Meritocracy* was unfortunate. A politician without ideas is a sad sight, but a politician in the grip of an idea can be dangerous. The Thames & Hudson edition went out of print in 1970, and the Penguin edition in 1979. My interpretation is that, in Britain at least, by the end of the 1970s, it was felt that the book's political message had had its day. The task was complete: the meritocracy had been shafted. (Yet this coincided with the apotheosis of our highest-flying postwar meritocrat, Margaret Thatcher.) By contrast, *Family and Kinship* remained in print in Britain for much longer—up to 1990 at least. But this was less, I think, because of such sociological concepts as the 'Demeter tie' between working-class daughters and mothers than because of the book's friendly observation of an apparently bygone era of inner-city life, which readers found as fascinating as similar pages in Henry Mayhew or Charles Booth.

A study should be written of the remarkable group of middle-class Englishmen who, in the mid-1950s, found in the working class an appealing sense of fraternity, an alternative family, that they themselves hadn't known as young children. They are Colin MacInnes (key work, *Absolute Beginners*, 1959),[21] Peter Opie (key work, with Iona Opie, *The Lore and Language of Schoolchildren*, 1959),[22] Michael Young (key work, with Peter Willmott,

Family and Kinship, 1957) and the photographer Roger Mayne, with his extraordinary portrayal of a cluster of mid-1950s streets in Kensal Town and Notting Dale.[23] Photographs by Mayne appeared on the dust jackets of the first editions of MacInnes's novel and the Opies' book, and on the 1961 Penguin edition of Young and Willmott.

In his 1994 introduction, Young said that one publisher who rejected his manuscript suggested he rewrote it as a novel. In principle, this wasn't a bad idea. The most powerful dystopian and utopian books have usually been presented as stories about more or less plausible people. The utopias have always been thinner on the ground; but both Edward Bellamy in his utopian *Looking Backward*, and William Morris in his *News from Nowhere* (written to counter Bellamy's all too accurate prediction of the bureaucratic, even Stalinist, course of much socialism), used the form of a novel. So, among dystopians, did Samuel Butler in *Erewhon*, Aldous Huxley in *Brave New World* and George Orwell in *Nineteen Eighty-Four*.[24] They all crop up in the pages of *The Oxford Companion to English Literature*.[25] But *Meritocracy* does not (or doesn't yet), even though the fact that it is almost a story has probably done it no good among academic sociologists.

In its review, the *Financial Times* regretted that the reader 'waits in vain for the sound of a human voice or a glimpse of earthy people'. The attractive hubbub of such voices is one reason why *Family and Kinship* was so widely read for so much longer. But *Meritocracy* embodies an all-embracing view of the way society might go; and, as it turned out, is going. Even its own influence in causing politicians and administrators to attempt to stem that tide did not, finally, undermine its accuracy. Satirists always fire their best arrows at targets they can see (or once saw) the attraction of. The paradox is that the vigour and wit of Young's onslaught on the meritocracy reinforces the reader's feeling of the power of what he is supposedly attacking. And looking around the shipwreck of much state education in many English cities—Michael Young's beloved East End of London included—it is clear that, of the various choices of evils, the creation of a meritocracy is the least of them.

We Sat Down at the Table of Privilege and Complained about the Food[1]

HILARY LAND

Introduction

MICHAEL Young analyses the rise of the meritocratic society mainly from the perspectives of social class and of men. It is not until the end of the book that he describes the development of serious challenges to such a society half a century later. These challenges are revealed in the rebellious Technical Society's *Chelsea Manifesto*, launched in 2009. Only then does he explicitly discuss the place of women in the meritocratic society he is satirising. He explains why feminists were so prominent among the leaders of those who rejected a meritocratic society's core values and the inequalities they fostered. Their aim was a classless society:

They oppose inequality because it reflects a narrowness of values. They deny that one man is in any fundamental way the superior of another . . . every man is a genius at something, even every woman, they say: it is the function of society to discover and honour it, whether it is genius at making pots, growing daisies, ringing bells, caring for babies, or even (to show their tolerance) genius at inventing radio telescopes.[2]

Their manifesto referred to studies conducted at the end of the twentieth century that particularly concerned feminists. The evidence from these showed:

. . . that society seemed to many women, especially the able ones, in mind men if at heart women, to have been constructed expressly for the convenience of the opposite sex. Are there not, the indignant asked, as many intelligent girls born every year as there are boys? They get as much the same education as any male cadet for meritocracy. But what happens then? They take the post for which they were trained only until they marry. From that moment they are expected, for a few years at least, to devote themselves to their children.[3]

Michael Young described how, by the end of the twentieth century, many women—in particular, intelligent women—had been relieved of the drudgery of housework by the revival of domestic service. The Home Help Corps was staffed by the least intelligent women and men in society (numbering 10 million in 2002) along the lines of the Pioneer Corps in the army.[4] Husbands were also 'helping' their wives more than in previous generations. The care of children, however, was another matter altogether. Mothers could not delegate this because:

They cannot, if they take any notice of the teaching of psychology, entrust the entire care of their offspring to a person of low intelligence . . . she will neglect her

© 2006 The Author. Editorial organisation © 2006 The Political Quarterly Publishing Co. Ltd
Published by Blackwell Publishing Ltd, 9600 Garsington Road, Oxford OX4 2DQ, UK and 350 Main Street, Malden, MA 02148, USA

motherly duties only at the peril of her children, not to speak of the displeasure of her husband.[5]

Here, he was not being satirical. These were his views, which in Britain had a long history and were widely shared. John Bowlby was the best-known British expert, whose concept of 'maternal deprivation'[6] was widely accepted, and used by expert and lay opinion to justify keeping married mothers of young children at home, throughout this period and beyond. Michael Young did not change his mind on the matter. In the 1990 Annual Lecture of the Economic and Social Research Council, he said:

The way things are going, if equality between the parents is attained, the equality could be astride the bodies of their children. We can now see that gender equality will prove sterile unless, as a follow on to the too-long delayed rise in the status of women there is a rise in the status of children.[7]

In other words, the care and interests of children are balanced against women's rights and women must manage the consequences of the way in which the public world in general, and paid employment in particular, is organised. Any conflict between their needs and interests and those of children must be resolved in favour of children. Thus it is women's lives that must be modified, and apart from 'helping' with the housework, men can continue to give priority to their interests both in public and in private, irrespective of their impact on children. To Michael Young, feminism, which challenged these presumptions, was no more than a partisan expression of women's interests.

He was right, however, to recognise that women would be prominent among those critical of a meritocratic society in which 'merit' was defined as 'IQ plus effort' and IQ was a measure of 'the qualities needed to benefit from a higher education'.[8] He was also correct in seeing that women's experience of marriage and motherhood would not fit easily with their professional lives if these were constructed in the same way as those of men. In this chapter I want to show how, in the 1960s, the generation of young women who were the first to take advantage of the opportunities provided by the British welfare state responded to the experience of a more meritocratic education system, looking particularly at those who went on to contribute to the re-emergence of the Women's Movement at the end of the decade. Feminist thinking was far from homogeneous and feminists, then as now, never spoke with one voice about 'the family' and how it might be reformed. Indeed, there were those who, aided by reproductive technology, would discard the family altogether.[9]

First, I want to describe some key demographic features of the 1960s, in particular those concerning marriage, motherhood and employment. Second, I will show how pervasive was the idea that becoming a wife and mother would and *should* take priority over every woman's other activities, however intelligent and highly educated she was. This informed the structure and content of the curriculum for boys and girls both in the grammar and secondary modern schools of the 1950s and 1960s.

46

Demographic background

> Throughout the twentieth century, marriage has never taken place so frequently or occurred at such young ages as during the 1960s: the culmination of a longer term trend toward near universal and youthful marriage.[10]

Marriage followed by motherhood was the destiny of the vast majority of young women. In the 1960s, marriage occurred on average two years after the end of full-time education. Of the cohort of women born in 1941, nearly half were married by the age of 21 and four out of five by the age of 25. The Government Actuary, advising the Committee on Higher Education (the Robbins Committee) in the early 1960s, expected that the average age of marriage would continue to fall and that this 'was likely to restrain the trend of girls to stay at school'.[11]

Children followed soon after marriage. Indeed, in a significant proportion of marriages, they followed within the first year. One in five of all brides and two in five of all teenage brides were pregnant on their wedding day. Legal abortion was not available until 1968 and marriage was the popular alternative to never-married motherhood. Thus lone motherhood was by and large avoided (at least in the short run) by getting married or putting the baby up for adoption. In the early 1960s, only 6 per cent of births occurred outside of marriage. By the end of the decade, this had increased to nearly 9 per cent, a figure slightly below the level in 1945. In the late 1970s the numbers of never-married mothers began to increase again, but it was not until the late 1980s that their numbers increased dramatically *and* the politicians noticed.[12]

Divorce rates had fallen slightly during the 1950s from the high levels following the end of the Second World War and the introduction of legal aid for divorce. They rose during the 1960s from 2 per 1,000 members of the married population to 4.7 by 1970. However, it was not until the 1969 Divorce Law Reform Act took effect that the divorce rate rose more rapidly.[13] Meanwhile, marriage rates continued to increase throughout the 1960s and women were still marrying young. By their late twenties, 85 per cent of women were married. Families were larger in the 1960s. A third of all children had at least three siblings and a quarter at least four. (In 2001, only a third of all children had at least *two* siblings.) However, the birth rate had fallen from the peak in 1964 (when there were over 1 million births), and babies were being born later in marriage. The development of more reliable contraception, improved access to contraception and contraceptive advice (confined to the married until 1969) gave women more control over the timing and size of their families.

Women's employment

Mass secondary education was relatively new when *The Rise of the Meritocracy* was first published in 1958. The 1944 Education Act raised the school-leaving age from 14 to 15 and created a tripartite system of free secondary education. Children were allocated to a grammar, secondary modern or technical school on the basis of their performance in the eleven-plus examination. The private public school system remained intact. There was supposed to be 'parity of esteem' between the three types of state school, but this was never achieved, not least because those deemed to have *failed* the eleven-plus went to the secondary modern school (or more rarely a technical school, for there were fewer of them—altogether, 40 per cent of local authorities had no technical schools). It was the minority of boys and girls who went to grammar school who had the opportunity to go on to higher education, joined by a small number who transferred from the secondary modern to grammar schools, being 'late developers'. In the late 1950s, the majority of boys and girls were leaving school at age 15 and going straight into full-time employment. For the older teenage boys until 1960, there was eighteen months to two years of National Service in the armed forces. This, together with a buoyant economy, meant that unemployment was rare among teenagers. For example, in 1961 only 10,000 of the 330,000 unemployed in Britain were under the age of 19. Over seven out of ten school-leavers left school having achieved neither O- nor A-level passes. Nine out of ten girls had left school before reaching their eighteenth birthday and only one in fifteen of those who stayed on in the sixth form went into higher education. Of these, half entered teacher training colleges, where they outnumbered men by two to one. In universities, men outnumbered women by three to one; very few girls or women entered further education and even fewer studied part-time.

For most girls, education and training took place *before* joining the paid workforce. Nine out of ten university entrants in 1961 were aged under 19. Of the minority of young women who received instruction at their place of employment, a third were training to be nurses (mostly aged 18–22) and a further quarter were training to be hairdressers (mostly aged 15–18).

There was no evidence that girls were less able than boys. We were not told at the time that the pass rate for the eleven-plus examination had been set higher for girls than for boys, in order to avoid girls outnumbering boys in grammar schools. The Robbins Committee found that the proportion of girls who achieved O-levels was much the same as the proportion of boys. Among boys and girls with A-levels, similar proportions went on to higher education. The big difference occurred in the transition from O-levels to A-levels:

It is thus among those with five or more 'O' levels that educational performance differs most sharply between boys and girls. It is also amongst this group that the tendency to early marriage differs most. These two facts may well be connected.[14]

Indeed, they almost certainly were. As Alison Hennegan, reflecting on her schooling in the 1950s, recalled:

I watched the dreary disheartening procession of girls who left school either before 'O' levels or in the middle of 'A' levels. Blinded by the dazzle of their engagement rings, they rushed to submerge themselves in marriages with men they'd outgrown half a decade later.[15]

At my own small grammar school I cannot remember any girl leaving before taking her O-levels, but most left immediately after taking them. The sixth form was tiny and out of a class of thirty taking O-levels, only three continued into higher education (in my case via Cambridgeshire Technical College and School of Art, for the school had become girls only and did not have sufficient teachers to enable me to take mathematics and science A-levels).

Marriage was thus terminating *education*, but it was no longer ending *employment*. (My own local education authority gave me a grant to go to university, but I had to agree to repay it should I get married before completing the course.) Marriage bars in teaching and the Civil Service had been abolished in the mid-1940s. Although women in some occupations did make way for men returning from the armed forces, there was a shortage of labour in the late 1940s and for the next two decades the Ministry of Labour continued to appeal to married women to stay in or return to employment. They also exhorted employers to provide part-time employment compatible with family responsibilities. From the beginning of the 1960s, primary schools were required to create a proportion of part-time teaching posts and later in that decade the Labour Government introduced tax incentives for employers in general to create part-time jobs.[16] In 1951, only 4 per cent of all employees were employed part-time. By 1961, this had increased to 10 per cent, and a decade later to 20 per cent.

Although William Beveridge's social security scheme was based on the model of the male breadwinner supporting a full-time housewife, the *services* provided by the British postwar welfare state were heavily dependent upon women's labour, together with, particularly in the case of health services, immigrants from the New Commonwealth countries.[17] (Immigration matters were the responsibility of the Ministry of Labour until 1961, when they were transferred to the Home Office. Ever since then, immigration policies have been dominated by issues concerning control rather than employment policy.) The expansion of health, education and welfare services created hundreds of thousands of jobs for women. The postwar baby boom, and the second one following fifteen years later in the mid-1960s, guaranteed a continuing demand for these services. In 1951, under a quarter of married women were in paid employment in the formal labour market. A decade later, this had increased to over a third, and by 1971 to over two-fifths. The majority of part-time employees were married women. In 1963, the Robbins Committee concluded that as a result of earlier marriage for women:

A new career pattern had emerged: a short period of work before marriage, and a second period of working starting perhaps fifteen years later . . . The indications are that this pattern will become increasingly common.[18]

The education debates of the late 1950s and early 1960s

One of the dominant themes of education reports published at the end of the 1950s and in the early 1960s was that of 'wasted' talent. The meritocracy that emerged in the 1950s was not very efficient, for the mechanisms for identifying and 'reclassifying' late developers of the kind Michael Young describes in his book were rudimentary. Surveys of national servicemen found that half of those rated in the two higher ability groups had left school at age 15. Moreover, there was a steep class gradient: among those coming from families of manual workers, two-thirds of those rated in the top ability groups had left school at the earliest opportunity.[19]

The impact of the launch of the Russian Sputnik in 1957 was equivalent to the shock of the events of 9/11 in the sense that it required the United States to reassess its position in the world. The US and Britain could no longer take for granted that they were, and would continue to be, technologically superior to the communist world. I was in Cambridge at the time, taking A-level mathematics and physics, and I remember how impressed the lecturers were by the Russians' achievement. It is no accident that the Robbins Committee, which was appointed in 1961 to make recommendations concerning the expansion of higher education, mainly used comparisons with the US and with the Soviet Union.

The committee noted that 'the reserve of untapped ability is greater among women than men'.[20] They did not, however, question the practice of early marriage or consider ways in which it might be possible to reduce the interruptions in education, training and employment associated with having children:

The prospect of early marriage leads girls capable of work in the professions to leave school before they have entered the sixth form and even after sixth form studies, too many girls go straight into employment instead of into higher education. When their family responsibilities have lessened many of them will desire opportunities for higher education. And many if not most married women who have already enjoyed higher education will need refresher courses before they can return effectively to professional employment.[21]

These courses would have to be provided on a flexible and part-time basis. They recommended that financial support be made available to enable married women to take them, including support for older women to take initial courses in higher education. However, they did not develop these ideas, as their terms of reference related to full-time higher education following straight on from school. It was the Open University, inspired by Michael Young and Brian Jackson in particular to take advantage of new developments in distance learning, which, from 1970, created opportunities for men and women of all ages to combine studying with family and/or employment responsibilities.[22]

The committee discussed at length how to fund a much larger population of students. They considered but rejected the idea of replacing student grants with loans, although they believed that as the habit of going to university became more firmly established, the arguments for not doing so would diminish in time. Meanwhile, they were concerned about the impact that a loans system would have on women:

The effect might well be either that British parents would be strengthened in their age-long disinclination to consider their daughters to be as deserving of higher education as their sons, or that the eligibility for marriage of the more highly educated would be diminished by the addition to their charms of what would be in effect a negative dowry.[23]

Another theme concerned the view that although educating girls was less likely to be considered a 'waste' than in previous decades, they nevertheless needed a rather different education from boys. Differences in the curriculum offered to boys and girls were structured into both grammar and secondary modern schools. The grammar school to which I went in the early 1950s had two streams—a Latin stream and a science stream. In other words, C. P. Snow's two cultures were built into the way the school was organised. So too were gender differences. Girls who chose to go into the science stream were unlikely to be taught physics and chemistry. These were subjects for the boys. Domestic science was timetabled against these subjects and girls were expected to take this along with biology. (Somehow, my mother negotiated with the school for me to stay in the Latin stream but to take physics and chemistry as well. I had to give up geography, history and biology. Nevertheless, I learnt to sew and cook at home and my twenty-first birthday present—at my request—was a sewing machine. I was not unusual among my women friends at university in being able to sew and cook and enjoying both.) The Robbins Committee noted that girls on the whole chose to study the humanities and boys the sciences. They recognised that in part this reflected a shortage of mathematics and science teachers in girls' schools (as I had experienced). In addition, in the state sector these teachers were more likely to be male and so in coeducational schools girls were not provided with female role models in these subjects. The committee noted that 'at present very few girls in this country seem to be attracted to a career in applied sciences, and the contrast with some other countries, notably the Soviet Union, is very strong'.[24]

The committee listed the kind of refresher courses married women graduates would need on their return to the labour market. They were courses for doctors, teachers and social workers, as well as for the professions in commerce and languages.[25] Nowhere in the report did the committee seriously challenge the highly gender-segregated labour market in Britain.

The education offered to children of average and less than average ability was also highly gendered. In 1959, the Crowther Committee reported on the case for raising the school-leaving age to 16. They discussed the curriculum that older children would follow. They recommended that 'girls should be encouraged to qualify before marriage in a greater number of professions or occupations which will provide opportunities for them in later years'.[26] The committee did not feel there was much scope for giving the 'intellectually able' girls education specifically related to their special interests as women, but for less able girls:

. . . the prospect of courtship and marriage should rightly influence the education of the adolescent girls. Though the general objectives of secondary education remain unchanged, her direct interest in dress, personal appearance and in problems of human relations should be given a central place in her education.[27]

They did give thoughtful and perceptive consideration, however, to the need for *both* boys and girls to be taught what they called 'sexual ethics', not only in the context of marriage but also in the light of changing family structures and relationships, and what they called:

. . . the emancipation, or isolation, of the individual (it can be looked at both ways) and the rejection of traditional authority [and] the conquest of the field of communications by the mass production techniques which were first applied to the manufacture of goods.[28]

The committee that considered the education of teenage girls and boys of average and less than average ability was chaired by Sir John Newsom and reported in 1963. One of their aims was to develop a curriculum that would 'make fuller use of the *natural merits* of older boys and girls in the work they will eventually undertake'.[29] Boys *and* girls needed lessons on personal relations in courtship, marriage and family. The report's recommendations were, in addition, very explicitly based on the importance of preparing *girls* for marriage and motherhood. After all, girls had 'a key role in establishing the standards of the home and in educating their children'.[30] This meant that:

The domestic crafts start with a built-in advantage—they are recognisably part of adult living. Girls know whether they marry early or not, they are likely to find themselves eventually making and running a home.[31]

They proposed that secondary schools should have a separate 'housecraft flat' to practise in. To make the experience as realistic as possible, infants should be brought into the flat, so that the girls could play with them. In addition, they should visit infant classes, children's homes and old people's homes. Their proposals for 'realism' did not end there:

A second element of realism needs to be introduced in claims on the pupils' time. Real housewives have to take children to and from school, keep appointments, and fit in their cooking, sewing and cleaning and their own recreation with demands which are outside their control.[32]

Girls therefore needed 'time management' exercises to teach them that their time would be at the disposal of others, whether professionals or their husbands or their children. It is interesting to note that these attitudes were not confined to the poorly educated woman. A correspondent to *The Times* in

1958, when the first woman life peer was admitted to the House of Lords, facetiously wrote:

If the new lady peer should arrive a little late for the debates it is to be hoped that the noble lords will not fuss. They were probably kept in waiting for the window cleaner to be finished or the man to mend the vacuum cleaner or perhaps there were Brussels sprouts to prepare for the evening meal.[33]

A national government survey of women's employment conducted in 1965 found that nearly half of full-time housewives reported that their husbands disapproved of them working outside the home, compared to only one in six of the husbands whose wives were employed.[34] Family law at this time still gave husbands considerable control over many aspects of the lives of their wives, including how they spent the housekeeping money and their access to credit. Against this background, it is therefore not surprising that Sir John Newsom could hold the view that 'in the main girls lack the ambition to acquire skills'.[35] This was the context in which the minority of my generation, as Carolyn Steadman wrote, 'were allowed to travel through the narrow gate at eleven towards the golden city'.[36]

Untidy contradictions and conflicting demands in the golden city

Education policies had a basis inspired by a deep-rooted philanthropy. It was education for the working class, not conceived of as a continuity with the traditions of self-organisation and self-education for socialism, but as an avenue to individual self-improvement, a share in what had hitherto belonged only to the few. It was up to those of us who were privileged to enjoy its greatest benefits to make the most of them. To take what was offered and run. In the end, with the expansion of higher education, a significant proportion of us weren't content with that.[37]

Young women of my generation who had succeeded within the terms of a meritocratic education system were confronted very quickly on graduation with the realities of the structural inequalities in the labour market, which were based on class and gender. This was nothing new. Eleanor Rathbone, in her trenchant feminist analysis of the inadequacies of the wages system from the perspective of women and children, had observed forty years earlier:

Everyone knows that broadly speaking, there is a double standard of pay for the two sexes. With the exception of a few occupations of which the medical profession and textile industry are the most conspicuous, women receive a lower rate of pay than men, even when they are engaged in the same occupation and do work which is equal in quantity and quality.[38]

In forty years, too little had changed. In the mid-1960s, the annual median full-time earnings of women were half those of men. Equal pay in principle had been introduced in the Civil Service and in the teaching profession in the

1950s. However, the principle of equal pay for equal work, let alone for 'work of equal value', was far from widely accepted, let alone practised. After all, the majority of the Royal Commission on Equal Pay, which reported in 1946, had *not* recommended its *general* acceptance for reasons little different from those expressed by the distinguished economist Alfred Marshall nearly fifty years earlier. He, while welcoming an increase in women's wages because 'it tends to develop their faculties', was concerned that 'it tempts them to neglect their duty of building up a true home and investing their effort in the Personal Capital of their children's character and abilities'.[39] Even those of us whose careers were not immediately and directly affected by marriage and mother-hood and who entered non-traditional female occupations discovered that despite having identical qualifications and class of degree, we attracted a lower salary than our male counterparts. For example, one of my fellow mathematics graduates was taken on as a trainee in a large industrial chemical company and another joined an aeronautical engineering company. Both were paid about three-quarters of the salary of their fellow male trainees.

The most significant direct challenge to the value placed on women's skills in the workplace in the 1960s came not from fresh young graduates but from women in the Ford car factory at Dagenham in Essex. In 1968, 400 women sewing machinists demanded the regrading of women's jobs and equal pay. They had noted that whereas a quarter of men were doing jobs in grade C, only 2 out of 900 women were on grade C. Audrey Wise, who in 1974 became a Labour MP, was an active trade unionist at the time and was a speaker at the first women's liberation conference held at Ruskin College in 1970. She was in touch with the Ford women strikers. She found that there were five grades in engineering, the bottom one being a labourer. The women's grade was *below* that, despite the fact that they had to pass the same tests as the men in order to get a job at all. It was not enough to claim that all women should get the male labourer grade (the official union line at the time). As she later wrote:

It was a profound insult, because it assumed that all women were unskilled and that the most you could aspire to was the wage of an unskilled man. It gave no recognition to the skills of women. I think there's a lot of rubbish talked about some work being unskilled. But that wasn't the point. The point was that men were graded. The grade might be imperfect, but the skills were recognised, and women, it was implied, had no skills worth recognising.[40]

After three weeks, this 'petticoat strike', as the newspapers called it, ended. They had gained 92 per cent of male skilled rates.[41] Subsequently, a National Joint Action Campaign Committee for Women's Equal Rights was formed, and they organised a big equal pay demonstration in Trafalgar Square in May 1969. Audrey Wise explained that this Joint Action Committee did not include equal pay in their name 'because they realised it affected more than wages. It affected recognition, it was something in the head as well as in the pocket'.[42] It was not only middle-class women who were interested in feminism at this time, although the relationship between the politics of class and the politics of

54

gender was, and remained, contentious both in theory and in practice.[43] The politics of 'race' were less visible in the debates in Britain at this time.

By the end of the 1960s, equal pay had to be taken seriously by trade unionists and politicians, not least because under the EEC's Treaty of Rome, equal pay was a condition for membership and there was growing support on all sides of industry for Britain's entry. In 1970 the Equal Pay Act was passed, albeit with many loopholes. The crucial back-up of anti-discrimination legislation took another five years to reach the statute-book.

Michael Young does not discuss the differences in rewards for men and women outside of the context of marriage and family. In the chapter entitled 'Rich and Poor', he describes how inequalities in *income* were considerably reduced in the meritocratic society by paying everyone the same. However, differences in *standards of living* were perpetuated by means of tax-free 'expenses', most of which were enjoyed by men outside the home and thus, he suggests, were not shared by women. These expenses were justified in the name of 'efficiency' and to ensure that the intelligent elite—the meritocracy— enjoyed the highest rewards. In the following chapter he reported that:

Through the women's circles the activists have been able to assert their influence and show their men-folk . . . that they are a force to be reckoned with. In so doing they are making a protest against the standards, those of achievement by which men assess each other. Women have always been judged more by what they *are* than by what they *do*, more for other personal qualities than for their intelligence, more for their warmth of heart, their vivacity, and their charm than for their worldly success. It is therefore understandable that they should wish to stress their own virtues.[44]

However, men are *also* judged by and rewarded for what they are. After all, in Britain since the nineteenth century it has been because they are, or will be, husbands and fathers that many men have successfully claimed a higher wage—a family wage—than women.[45] White men were, and are, paid more than black men in Britain. Michael Young's critique of the meritocracy described in his book did not fully address the extent to which merit and skill are gendered concepts. In the 1970s and subsequently,[46] feminist scholars investigated why and how 'skill is increasingly an ideological category, developed out of the struggle of men to retain their dominance in the sexual hierarchy at work, rather than a real distinction based on the nature of the jobs that men and women do'.[47]

In jobs we do full work for half pay, in the home we do unpaid work full time

Many women married quickly after graduation, as it was expected that they would—and should. Once babies arrived, the presumption that 'a woman's place is in the home' became very real.[48] As Sheila Rowbotham, who was very active in contributing to the re-emergence of the Women's Movement and spoke at the first conference at Ruskin College in 1970, later wrote:

We, the newly educated, had been told we were equal. But a prosperous welfare capitalism did not seem to think that meant more nurseries. The contradictions of childcare and housework were then an extremely important influence in bringing women into the women's liberation movement.[49]

One of the key differences between my generation and that of our mothers was that our experience of the welfare state meant that we felt *entitled* to challenge the situations in which we found ourselves. As Carolyn Steadman reflected:

The 1950s was a period when state intervention in childhood was highly visible . . . [and it] imparted a sense of self. I think I would be a very different person now if orange juice and milk and dinners at school hadn't told me, in a covert way, that I had a right to exist, was worth something. My inheritance from those years is the belief, maintained with some difficulty, that I do have a right to the earth. I think that had I grown up with my parents only twenty years before, I would not now believe this.[50]

The 'traditional' ideas about women's place in the home provoked various reactions. There was agreement that there was a problem about the invisibility of and lack of value placed on women's work both within the family and outside, but not about either the roots of that problem or the appropriate strategies to tackle it. Some required more radical changes than others, but all recognised that 'public' and 'private' inequalities were inextricably linked.

Loneliness was one feature of being a full-time housewife for those who had moved away from family and friends—usually because their husband's job determined where they lived. Working-class girls who had gone to university may have come from tightly knit communities, but they were likely to have married into the professional classes. Their upward social mobility required geographical mobility. However, it would be a mistake to be too sentimental about working-class communities at that time. Hannah Gavron's small study of housewives in the mid-1960s, for example, found that in her London-based sample:

The young working class mother in this sample was confined to her home in a way that previous generations may not have been. The extension of employment among older married women, combined with changed urban conditions, has meant a fair degree of isolation for the mother with young children who has to be at home.[51]

In 1960, Maureen Nicol was a mother in that position. She wrote a letter to *The Guardian* responding to an article written by Betty Jarman, a journalist with young children living in the suburbs and feeling very isolated. As a result of the responses to her published letter, she set up the National Housewives Register (initially called the Liberal-Minded Housebound Wives Register!) and within a year had 2,500 members: 'We were sneered at by the tabloids who implied we were these silly bored middle class housewives, and why didn't we buckle down.'[52] However, the Register put women in touch with each other and some subsequently became very involved in the Women's Movement. Ellen Malos, one of the founding members of Bristol's Women's Centre and of Bristol Women's Aid, as well as of the National Women's Aid

Federation, recalls that in the early 1970s the Register 'invited the Women's Liberation Group to speak to them and several of the women at that meeting became very active Women's Liberation Movement members'.[53]

In 1961, the pre-school playgroup movement started. This was also triggered by a letter to *The Guardian*. The letter was from a young mother who had started a group of her own because there was no state nursery place for her daughter, and who was finding it difficult to meet other mothers with small children because she was new to the area. Jill Faux, who in 1973 became the association's first Development Officer, recalled that 'the response to *The Guardian* letter was overwhelming'.[54] She had a middle-class background, had passed the eleven-plus and had achieved ten O-levels, but had not gone to university because her parents and grandparents could only afford to support her brothers through university. She wanted to be at home while her children were very young:

But having said that I was going to stay at home with the children, at least until they went to school, it was imperative for me to get some sort of satisfaction. I couldn't just do it with understanding because I would probably bawl them out or hit them . . . that's why as far as I was concerned the playgroup movement's most important aspect was the adult education rather than the child education.[55]

She is convinced that the playgroup experience was a stepping-stone to involvement in other community activities: 'If I look round now at people who I knew at the time, many parents whose children had outgrown the playgroup would go off and do almost anything having gained an enormous amount in self-confidence.'[56]

The editors of a recent collection of personal accounts of those involved in various groups, organisations and movements that arose in the 1960s, from which the experiences described above are drawn, note the wide range of what they call 'do-it-yourself' politics:

The in-your-face confrontation was just part of a spectrum. Many of the innovations described in this book arose on quiet observations of needs which were being unmet by the welfare state. The range covered is extensive: child poverty, the problems of old people, women living with violent partners, prisoners' wives and those arrested on drug offences, mothers' lack of child care—the list could go on. The innovators were coming at the gaps in welfare provision from many angles, but this collection shows that they shared one characteristic in common—a dogged determination.

Behind this resolve was the tacit assumption that people deserved dignity—a presupposition which would have been impossible without the welfare gains made by an earlier generation . . . Rights were not abstract or about politics alone, they were active and about sex as well as economics.[57]

The young women who became involved in various left-wing organisations and activities and more formal politics also found themselves facing conflicting and confusing expectations:

Straddled across the gap between hope and experience, some young radical women began to wonder. Why did men split us into comrades and 'chicks', for example? The first were tolerated in the publicly important sphere of politics. The second were to be bedded, in the trivial realm of lust and passion. Why, I can remember wondering, couldn't you be a woman and a person doing both?[58]

Sheila Rowbotham included in her collection of essays, *Threads through Time: Writings on History and Autobiography*, her contemporary reflections on the 1960s. She describes how re-emerging feminist ideas were being reinforced, fed and reworked in various ways as a result of wider political movements and events taking place in the US and in Europe at the time:

In Britain we had also seen civil rights demonstrations on television, we had read about black power and then learned about the struggle which was not simply about formal rights but also raised issues of cultural identity, access to symbolic space, the power to define one's self, a challenge to how one was regarded and represented. Some of us at the Dialectics of Liberation conference in 1967 had puzzled over Stokeley Carmichael's hostile response to a young white woman's question. It seemed the dialectic could run into disturbing blockages.

Equally influential was the anti-imperialist movement against the US role in Vietnam. Vietnamese women's sufferings and bravery as fighters made a deep impression on young women supporters in the West. Despite the differences in our circumstances, they gave us inspiration and a political language of colonialism which we could adapt.[59]

Movements and events in Germany and France, notably in 1968, influenced young women too. Rowbotham observes that those who joined the Women's Movement in response to the media's mocking reports of 'women's lib' were not necessarily involved in Marxist left-wing groups. They were the young women who, having succeeded in the meritocratic education system, had joined the expanding administrative and professional jobs in the welfare state. In this way they were doing what the Robbins Committee had hoped they would do, at least until they married and had children.

For working-class young women, this was a more complicated journey, which is vividly illustrated by the contributors to Liz Heron's collection of essays by women brought up in the 1950s,[60] by Jean McCrindle and Sheila Rowbotham's 1977 collection,[61] and by Mary Ingham's 1981 interviews with women who had entered grammar schools in 1958.[62] To quote Valerie Walkerdine:

They held out a dream. Come they told me. It is yours. You are chosen. They didn't tell me, however, that for years I would no longer feel any sense of belonging, nor any sense of safety, that I didn't belong in the new place any more than I now belonged in the old.[63]

Young working-class men who went into higher education also felt both out of place and disconnected from their origins.[64] Nevertheless, as Bernice Martin has argued, it is important to note when comparing the experiences of the prewar generation, the generation described in this paper and subsequent generations, that:

58

The generation of post-war 'baby boomers' is the first to display generally sceptical feelings about authority and to operate a situational and personalised morality. What is particularly significant about this regularly replicated set of findings [from the European Values Survey] is that generational differences are far more significant than class differences in relation to these cultural values, with each younger age cohort displaying a stronger version of the newer values.[65]

For some young women in the late 1960s and 1970s, their involvement in the Women's Movement helped them to make sense of their situation, because 'shared individual experience is an important part of the social discovery of a common condition'.[66] This was one very important way in which the 'personal' became 'political'.

Conclusion

> You should never have educated us, the ordinary girls of the fifties, for we are dangerous. We are set on becoming, and you will not stop us now.[67]

Michael Young correctly anticipated that women would be prominent among the critics of the values of the meritocracy he satirises. He suggested that women might want to define 'merit' differently from men, but he accepted a split between economic and personal life and between work and home. The meritocracy he described is based on rewarding intellectual work, particularly in the sciences, and although he was clearly sympathetic to the Technicians who had an average or lower IQ, he barely recognised or valued women's emotional work within the home. He did not consider how society might be organised differently from the tradition of leaving domestic work and childcare to wives and servants. In this he was a product of his time for, until the second-wave Women's Movement developed at the end of the 1960s, few in postwar Britain questioned that marriage and children were young women's destiny and that these would take priority over everything else. Paradoxically, it was the experience of being a young citizen in the early years of a postwar welfare state, based more closely than ever before on the principle of universality, combined with success in its meritocratic education system (imperfect though it was), that gave some of the generation of young women educated in the 1950s the confidence and determination to question, and to try to reform, both the 'private' world of the 'family' and the 'public' world of politics and economics. This was attempted both individually *and* collectively.

Thirty years on, many of the reforms of family lives, workplaces and civil society of which we dreamed and about which we argued so fiercely are far from realisation. It is true that marriage and children are not now accepted as their immediate 'destiny' by a much higher proportion of young women, and there are far more opportunities for girls and women in education and employment. However, the labour market is still segregated by gender and there is still a gender pay gap, albeit a narrower one for those able to work full-time. Those women who succeed within it are often those who have accepted men's values and priorities, and there is evidence that young women are still deciding that being a mother is not easily combined with a successful career.

Nearly a quarter of the women born in the late 1950s who became graduates remained childless, compared with one in six of those with no qualifications.[68] Since the early 1990s, the high cost of housing and a more consumerist society means that many more families, including middle-class families, must depend on two earners. The 'long hours culture' in the workplace, which has developed in Britain in the past twenty years, has coincided with a dramatic reduction in the 'career-break' that mothers with young children take. Today, most do not even stay out of the labour market for fifteen months, let alone the fifteen years envisaged by the Robbins Committee. Carers who work part-time (still mainly women) continue to be disadvantaged in terms of pay and opportunities. Today, children seem to be more valued as young consumers than as young citizens. Childcare services in Britain are still under-developed compared with many of our European partners, and few of us envisaged that nurseries would be so heavily dependent on the private for-profit sector. While 'wages for housework' were the subject of fierce debates,[69] the marketisation of childcare and of social care were certainly not part of the futures we discussed. The 'complicated-and-slippery notions of *public* and *private*'[70] have taken on different meanings in a society that is now more heavily dependent upon the market.

Debates about how we value and organise men's and women's work in the home *as well as* in the wider society, which Michael Young only partially addressed and with which the Women's Movement began to re-engage at the end of the 1960s, have remained contentious and very important.

The Chequered Career of a Cryptic Concept

CLAIRE DONOVAN

Introduction

MICHAEL Young's *The Rise of the Meritocracy* has attracted a mixed reception over the years and has variously been taken to be for, against or ambivalent towards a society being ordered along the meritocratic principles it spells out.[1] The text can and has been read as supporting all of these positions. Young was advocating the desirability of removing hereditary privilege as the basis for social order and (with echoes of Plato's *Republic*) promoting the efficiency and justice of a division of labour based upon mobility of individual talent and effort, or 'merit'. He was also alerting us to the danger that if taken too far, a fully evolved meritocracy would be based on a brand of positivism that smothered human values and decency, and (with echoes of Orwell's *Animal Farm*) would crystallise into a smug and self-replicating elite class or oligarchy that would pull the ladder of opportunity up behind it, and hence no longer be a true meritocracy of talent.

Life can sometimes be stranger than social science fiction, and in later years Young looked on while within the political realm his 'meritocracy' was shaping up to become its own antithesis, located at the heart of modern democratic thought. In his BBC obituary, Young's invention is placed 'at the centre of Blairite thinking',[2] although six months earlier he had publicly reclaimed his concept, stating 'It would help if Mr Blair would drop the word from his public vocabulary' and 'he [Blair] has caught on to the word without realising the dangers of what he is advocating'.[3] Young had, however, long recognised that *Meritocracy* was largely misunderstood and that the idea of 'meritocracy' had taken on a life of its own independent from his original, albeit mixed, intention.

But why was this so? Referring to both political and academic spheres, Young speculates that *Meritocracy* is an influential book, that 'the most influential books are those that are not read', that people have commented upon or referred to his text without ever having read it, and that most of these people have not recognised the text as satirical.[4] This chapter takes up his challenge and reviews the political science serial literature from 1958 onwards that cites *Meritocracy*, to investigate whether there is 'citation without knowledge' and if the text has been properly recognised as satire. The chapter then goes on to study the career of the 'meritocracy' concept and the various pathways it has taken in political science papers that do and do not refer to his original work.[5]

Published by Blackwell Publishing Ltd, 9600 Garsington Road, Oxford OX4 2DQ, UK and 350 Main Street, Malden, MA 02148, USA

How the text is presented

The full title of Young's work[6] is *The Rise of the Meritocracy, 1870–2033: an Essay on Education and Equality,*[7] and it is presented as a PhD thesis in British historical sociology, written by a fictional Michael Young in either the year 2033 or 2034. The mock futuristic PhD was, to say the least, an unorthodox choice of format, which proved to be so problematic that Young (whose *alter ego* was in this instance literally ahead of his time) feared his manuscript would never be published. Chatto and Windus, who Young describes as 'an old, respected, and literary English publisher', were prepared to publish the work if it was rewritten as a novel in the style of Aldous Huxley's *Brave New World*. This Young dutifully did, 'with the young and ravishing Lady Avocet as the heroine having a love affair with an elderly plumber'. Needless to say (and probably mercifully on the grounds of crimes against literature), this version did not appear in print. Another publisher, Longman, somewhat missed the point and rejected Young's original text on the grounds that they did not publish PhD theses, an event Young describes as 'fair warning that the book, if it ever did see the light of day, was going to be misunderstood'.[8]

The manuscript was rejected by eleven publishers, but eventually went to print due to a chance meeting on a beach in North Wales and the kindness of an old friend of Young's, Walter Neurath, who, with his wife Eva, had founded the publishing house Thames & Hudson. The book first appeared in 1958, and shortly afterwards was reproduced by Penguin and became a bestseller, appearing in seven languages.

Although later editions lost the full original title, when handling the book it is very clear that this is a satire, or what we might call a '*social* science fiction'. On the first page of the text proper, we are told that the Populist Movement has called for a general strike in the coming May of 2034, and that there has been wide-scale civil revolt, including spates of unofficial strike action, the 'gutting' of the Ministry of Education and even the destruction of an atomic power station.[9] On the last page of the book, a footnote tells us that Michael Young was killed in the Peterloo riots of May 2034, and that the publishers have left his thesis unaltered, although 'The failings of sociology are as illuminating as its successes'[10]—a hint that the fictional Michael Young's account of the meritocracy should be taken with a pinch of salt. Given that his misreading of the social and political situation cost him his life, it is doubtful that on the strength of his analysis the pretend Michael Young would have been awarded his doctorate posthumously.

The book is divided into two parts. The first, 'Rise of the Elite', gives a largely historical materialist account of the conditions that led to the shift in British society from agrarian feudalism to industrialism to a meritocracy, a change driven by the increasing demands of international competition to maximise the efficiency of the whole workforce. It also describes the decisive role that the Labour Movement played in securing the transition to a meritocracy through its pursuit of policies aimed at promoting equality of opportunity and eradicating hereditary privilege. We are introduced to the formula I + E = M (intelligence, or IQ, plus effort equals merit), which decides every person's station in life as educational selection becomes the rational and moral imperative upon which the meritocracy is built and sustained.[11] The membership of the meritocracy is limited to the 5 per cent of the population who have the most powerful jobs, the highest status and the greatest material rewards. It is made up of those selected to receive the best education. Their elite status is earned through their own intelligence and effort, and hence merit. Those who are excluded from the elite have simply failed to make the grade although, the argument goes, their interests are best served by the meritocracy, as this is the most efficient use of the country's talent in the arena of international competition and the benefits from this flow to all.

The tone in this first section is largely positive, praising the creation of the meritocracy as the basis of the social order rather than heredity, but the mood becomes increasingly menacing in the author's mounting contempt for those who fall outside of the elite, eroding our faith in his academic neutrality. As we would expect of a thesis, there are many footnotes, and these largely refer to genuine government reports and academic texts.

The second half of the text, 'Decline of the Lower Classes', is the larger projection into the future, where we encounter the undesirable aspects of a fully fledged meritocracy, and the author is unmasked as an intolerant voice, who holds the grievances of the masses in increasing contempt as he defends the interests of the elite of which he is a part. In this dystopic vision, the working class is stripped of its articulate potential leaders, the trade unions come to represent elite interests, domestic service is reintroduced, the meritocracy becomes anti-democratic as Parliament is weakened by the rule of the Civil Service, and ultimately the meritocracy itself becomes a closed self-replicating elite, which has pulled up the ladder of opportunity behind it. Some of the references in this section are genuine and largely Fabian in orientation, but most are inventions (for some unknown reason, there is a preponderance of bird names in phoney citations; for example, Dr Nightingale, Dr Puffin, Professor Eagle, Rook, Stork and Shag), and Young even invents an 'interesting' reference to himself in a 1967 *British Journal of Sociology* paper, 'The role of the extended family in channeling aspirations'[12]—'Note the earliness of the date,' he says.[13]

The book is also peppered with various flights of fancy, and we are witness to numerous futuristic inventions, some more prophetic than others, such as the invention in Britain of a Social Science Research Council—which was actually created in 1965, with Young as its first chair. However, he was less successful in predicting that milk would be on tap in every home, that in the 1990s Chinese would become the second language in schools and, most outlandish of all, that sociology is a highly respected enterprise. Of course, the most enduring of Young's inventions is that of the 'meritocracy' itself, which makes its first outing in this book. If the interested reader was eager to trace the original source of this concept, he or she would find the following in an early footnote:

The origin of this unpleasant term, like that of 'equality of opportunity', is still obscure. It seems to have been first generally used in the sixties of the last century in small-circulation journals attached to the Labour Party, and gained wider currency later on.[14]

Here Young is teasing himself, and the reader. Until 2034, the jury is of course out on whether Young's vision of a meritocracy as a calcified regime will come to pass, although in his later opinion he felt that it was already taking shape in Britain at least.[15]

In any case, it is very difficult to see how *Meritocracy* can be mistaken for a standard academic text.

The satire

In a new introduction to the Transaction edition, the real Michael Young mulls over how his book was received and how his invention 'meritocracy' has been used. He cites Daniel Bell's view that the logical form of a post-industrial society is that of a meritocracy, where differential status and income are tied to technical expertise and higher education, which generally excludes people without the relevant educational qualifications.[16] Young holds that *Meritocracy* was 'always meant to make that kind of case' and that, for whatever reason, most people have 'accepted that must have been the case I was trying to make'.[17] What we may call the utopian version of meritocracy, presented in the first half of his book, is founded upon the principle of equality of opportunity, and embodies the I + E = M formula, where following educational selection (or I) people are allotted different roles in society, and those who enter the higher echelons must continue to be high achievers (or E) to deserve (or M) the benefits and material trappings that belong to the elite. Another premise is that of absolute mobility, to ensure that each generation will continue to be educated, employed and rewarded according to achievement or talent and not birth. However, while this was part of Young's intention, those who believe that he was presenting a utopian meritocracy have not, in his view, correctly interpreted his text:

They have neglected, or not noticed, the fact that the book is satirical, and although sociology, and therefore properly earnest, it is also in an older tradition of English satire. I know that in those island clothes the book may not travel so well. But if the book is not seen to be counterargument as well as argument, the point of it (or at least a good half point) will be lost.[18]

In Young's words, 'Another line of argument is also made much of in the book. It is that a meritocracy could only exist in any full form if there were such a narrowing down of values that people could be put into rank order of worth.'[19] He evokes the work of John Rawls to describe the counterargument in the second part of his book, which we may call the dystopian version of meritocracy. Rawls recognised that equality of opportunity could eventually lead to a 'callous meritocratic society'.[20]

Young explains that as a satire, his book was meant to argue both sides of the case for and against a meritocracy: 'The two points of view are contrasted without. The imaginary author has a shadow.'[21] He continues:

The imaginary Michael Young of 2034 is meant to seem more dour and portentous than I am. I am, by apparently taking his views so seriously, trying to make fun of him. . . . I tried to make him out rather ridiculous because I also wanted to show the strength of the opposite case. I wanted to show how overweening a meritocracy could be, and, indeed, people generally who thought they belonged to it, including the author to whom the book was attributed.[22]

Young's *alter ego* was unwittingly 'the mouthpiece for another story, showing how sad, and fragile, a meritocratic society could be'.[23] We must, however, be aware of a further twist—that when academics cite the Michael Young of *The Rise of the Meritocracy* they are in fact using the words of his often misanthropic doppelganger.

The tests

Young's citation challenge

Past research has demonstrated that texts may be referred to without apparent knowledge of their content, and has even shown that some social scientists have referred to 'classic' or foundational works incorrectly.[24] Young himself takes this argument one step further. Observing that *Meritocracy* is an influential book, he makes the bold assertion that 'the most influential books are those that are not read', that people have commented upon or referred to *Meritocracy* without ever having read it, and that most of these people have not recognised the text as satirical,[25] but only as the utopian version of the meritocracy presented in the first part of the book. This chapter tests Young's retrospective hypotheses in the form of a citation and content analysis to examine (a) whether people who comment upon the text have read it, and (b) if they recognise or make reference to the fact that the text is satirical.

Obliteration

The idea of 'obliteration' refers to work presented in original sources or foundational texts that ceases to be cited because the concepts or methods eventually become absorbed into the assumed knowledge of a field. This chapter goes beyond Young's hypotheses to examine whether the intended spirit of *Meritocracy* has survived over time. It examines papers that discuss meritocracy, but do not cite the original work, to test the prevalence of utopian, dystopian or other versions.

The fictitious formula

Young realised that 'there was nothing new in the proposition that IQ + effort = merit; only the way it was formulated',[26] although he was lampooning the idea that these combined factors, whether brought about by nurture, nature or a combination of both, could produce a moral imperative:

Even if it could be demonstrated that ordinary people had less native ability than those selected for high position, that would not mean they deserved to get less. Being a member of the 'lucky sperm club' confers no moral right to advantage. What one is born with, or without, is not of one's own doing.[27]

This chapter investigates whether this fictitious formula (in the form of I + E = M, or IQ + E = M) has been taken seriously as a measure and has gained any currency. The content analysis scans all papers for the inclusion and use of this equation, as a further test of whether the text has been read and understood as satirical.

The methods

A sample of political science papers[28] is taken from the Institute of Scientific Information's (ISI's) Web of Knowledge v.3.0.[29] This online resource provides detailed information on indexed serial literature in the form of journal papers, reviews and other contributions. For the social sciences, the Social Science Citation Index covers 1,725 journals from 1945 onwards. While the sample is limited to journals rather than books, references to books can be traced through the bibliographies of ISI-indexed papers.

Citations to The Rise of the Meritocracy (testing Young's citation challenge)

The bibliographies of texts therefore allow us to identify which papers cite Young's work. Combinations of Cited Work searches were conducted, combining the Science Citation Index (SCI), the Social Science Citation Index (SSCI) and the Arts and Humanities Citation Index (A&HCI) for all available years, and 283 citing texts were found:

RISE OF MERIT*	1
RISE MERIT*	275
MERIT*	7

Non-English-language papers were filtered out, leaving a total of 261 texts. Of these, 14 (5.4 per cent) were political science publications, following sociology (24.1 per cent), education and educational research (20.3 per cent), social sciences, interdisciplinary topics (7.7 per cent) and law (6.9 per cent).[30] Ten of the political science texts were classified as articles, and four as reviews. The distribution of years of publication is as follows:

Publication year	Record count	Per cent
1959	1	7.1
1960	1	7.1
1973	4	28.6
1975	4	7.1
1976	2	14.3
1977	1	7.1
1980	1	7.1
1982	1	7.1
1993	1	7.1
1998	1	7.1

Content analysis was then applied to these texts to give yes-or-no answers to the following questions:

1. Are sections of *The Rise of the Meritocracy* quoted, or does the text demonstrate enough knowledge of the work for us to assume that it has been read?
2. Is *The Rise of the Meritocracy* understood as dystopic/satirical?
3. Is the sampled text for or against the idea of a meritocracy?

Use of the concept of 'meritocracy' (testing for obliteration)

It is possible to search the titles, keywords and abstracts of ISI-indexed journals for particular words. It is important to note that ISI only holds data on keywords from 1992 onwards, and abstracts from 1993 onwards. This will affect the distribution of papers in the sample. Again, all three ISI indexes were used for all available years, using General Search: Topic: MERITOC*, and 268 texts were identified. Works that cite *Meritocracy* were excluded from this sample, leaving 229 papers, and non-English-language papers were removed, giving a total of 207. Of these, 15 (7.2 per cent) were political science publications, with sociology (22.2 per cent) and education and educational research (17.4 per cent) being dominant. Eight of the political science papers are classed as articles, six as reviews and one as editorial material. The years of publication are as follows:

Publication year	Record count	Per cent
1987	2	13.3
1993	1	6.7
1995	1	6.7
1999	6	40.0
2000	2	13.3
2001	1	6.7
2003	2	13.3

Content analysis was used to answer the following questions:

1. Is the concept of 'meritocracy' defined, and if so, is it utopian or dystopic?
2. If the concept of 'meritocracy' is not defined, can we infer that it is viewed as utopian or dystopic?
3. Is the sampled text for or against the idea of a meritocracy?

$I + E = M$ (using the fictitious formula)

All papers were scanned to see if this formula had been used or discussed as a substantive measure, and if so, within what kind of context.

Results

Testing Young's citation challenge

Even using primitive analysis, we find various points of discussion about the political science texts that cite *Meritocracy*. Most use was made of the book in the mid-1970s, reflecting an interest in debates about distributive justice, its first standard use being fifteen years after its original publication. There are two reviews of Young's book, and I am happy to report that both reviewers have clearly read the text and have understood it as satire. There are two reviews of other books and these cite *Meritocracy*: a 1973 review of Rawls' *A Theory of Justice*, and a 1998 critique of Noberto Bobbio's *Left and Right*. The remaining ten works are standard journal papers. It is somewhat surprising to find that, with one exception, all the political science papers originate from the United States, the one exception being the Briton Perry Anderson, who was then resident in Italy:

Paper	Year	Type	Quoted/ read?	Dystopic/ satirical?	For or against 'meritocracy'?	Country
1	1959	Book review	Y	Y	Against	US
2	1960	Book review	Y	Y	–	US
3	1973	Article		Y	Against	US
4	1973	Article		Y	–	US
5	1973	Article	Y		For	US
6	1973	Article		Y	Against	US
7	1975	Book review	N	N	–	US
8	1976	Article	Y	N	–	US
9	1976	Article		Y	–	US
10	1977	Article		N	Against	US
11	1980	Article		Y	Against	US
12	1982	Article	N	N	Against	US
13	1993	Article	Y	Y	Against	US
14	1998	Book review	N	Y	Against	Italy

Quoted/read		Dystopic/satirical		For or against 'meritocracy'	
Yes	No	Yes	No	For	Against
5	3	9	4	1	8

We find that three texts that cite *Meritocracy* display no evidence of the writer having read it. One is the review of Rawls, which just mentions Young's book in a footnote; another review refers to *Meritocracy* in passing; and one article merely speaks of Young's book in the same breath as a serious 1967 book chapter by another author, as 'two particularly valuable contemporary criticisms of the ideal of meritocracy'. The writers of five texts have either cited from or have clearly read the book, two being reviews of it. The article that displays the most comprehensive understanding of Young's book is a critique of liberal notions of distributive justice, and invents the ironic term 'Neo-Youngian' for the argument that those people who are socially excluded in terms of having no access to goods through distributive processes are in that situation due to their own apathy or incapacity. However, two papers that cite Young appear to have missed the point, one using Young to talk of the Civil Service as a 'true meritocracy of talent', while the other cites the Populist Movement's Chelsea Manifesto, which sets out a more humanistic way in which to value people, but does not indicate that this was held in sharp relief to the values of the meritocracy. Of the five authors who cite the book, only three appear to have really understood it in Young's terms.

Four texts demonstrate no understanding that Young's book is satirical. One displays no evidence of the writer having read the book, yet goes on to argue that Young extrapolates from documented trends in British education to argue 'that this theory of equal opportunity justifies a continuation of the British class system or a version of it'. The writer of one paper, who displays no evidence of having read Young's book, nonetheless has sufficient knowledge to make a jibe at two highly statistical advocates of meritocracy, noting that 'one of the most charming things . . . is that they don't know Young's book is a satire'.

In terms of testing Young's hypothesis, we find that just three out of the fourteen papers demonstrate the authors have both read his book and understood his intent. However, five that seem not to have read the book nonetheless understand its import. Overall, nine texts recognise Young's book as dystopic or satirical, and eight are clearly against the idea of a meritocracy. There is a decay effect as citations to Young's book—or evidence that an author has sufficient familiarity with the book—ebb, along with the understanding that the work is satirical. However, this contrasts with a trend towards being more critical of a meritocracy. In short, Young's hypothesis stands, and his intent seems to have been successfully transmitted.

CLAIRE DONOVAN

Pathways of 'meritocracy'

The journal texts that use meritocracy in their title, abstract or as a keyword, but do not cite *The Rise of the Meritocracy*, are published between 1987 and 2003. It was noted above that ISI only lists keywords from 1992 onwards, and searches abstracts from the year 1993, and this impacts upon the distribution of papers, as any earlier papers that discuss meritocracy may be missed. There is increased interest in this area post-1999, and although this is largely due to five reviews of one particular book, Nicholas Lemann's *The Big Test: the Secret History of the American Meritocracy*, there are also six full journal papers. There was one further review in 1987, and one editorial piece that also includes an interview. There are eight full papers in total:

Paper	Year	Type	Defined/ inferred	Utopian/ dystopian	For or against 'meritocracy'?	Country
15	1987	Book review	D	Dystopian		US
16	1987	Editorial/ interview	I	Dystopian		US
17	1993	Article	D	Utopian		US
18	1995	Article	I	Utopian		US
19	1999	Article	I	Utopian	For	US
20	1999	Book review	D	Both	For	US
21	1999	Book review	D	Dystopian	Against	US
22	1999	Article				US
23	1999	Book review	D	Dystopian		US
24	1999	Article				US
25	2000	Book review	D	Utopian	Against	US
26	2000	Book review	D	Utopian	Against	US
27	2001	Article	D	Utopian		US
28	2003	Article	D	Both	For	US
29	2003	Article			Against	Canada

Defined/inferred		Type			For or against 'meritocracy'	
Yes	No	Utopian	Dystopic	Both	For	Against
12	3	6	4	2	3	4

Again, we find that the texts are almost exclusively American, the exception being one Canadian article. It is remarkable to note that two articles have 'meritocracy' in their title (they are coupled together as a 'for and against' piece) but neither of them mentions meritocracy.

Nine of the offerings do set down what they take meritocracy to mean: five subscribe to the utopian version, three to the dystopic reading and two employ both. We are able to infer the type of 'meritocracy' used in a further three further papers, one of which is dystopic and two utopian. So in total six papers subscribe to the utopian reading and four share Young's cynicism, while two discuss both views but identify with neither. The utopian reading coincides with liberal notions of distributive justice, and we find that two of these papers use this definition, but are opposed to this kind of meritocracy. In short, we find that there is almost equally divided opinion about the meaning of the term and those who are for and against the idea of a meritocracy. In this sense, although not cited, the two parts of Young's book are alive and well, and still shadowing each other.

For example, versions of the utopian meritocracy include defining the 'level of meritocracy' as 'the degree to which individual merit is a factor in determining economic outcomes'; arguing that 'educational expansion is critical for signalling modern ideas of mass opportunity and meritocracy'; and the assessment that 'America is likely to retain strong meritocratic tendencies' and to continue heavily using intelligence testing because 'People believe in it. Institutions are used to it. And most importantly, even as we recognize that testing has its drawbacks and limitations, the alternatives are either impractical, undesirable, or worse.' The utopian vision sees meritocracy as going hand in hand with democracy. On the other hand, the dystopic readings include seeing meritocracy as 'the classic dilemma facing all democratically-inclined societies' in the form of 'how to select, on the basis of merit, a sufficient cadre of leaders of all types required to move society forward, without ending up with a self-servicing and self-perpetuating elite that dominates the rest of society'; and arguing that governments use a 'meritocratic veneer' to say that institutions promote equal opportunities, while they instead promote systemic structured economic inequalities; and although not cited in the bibliography, Young is correctly remembered when one author notes that 'The phrase "meritocracy" came from Michael Young . . . who worried that the new educated ruling elite would have so powerful a basis of legitimacy as to make inequality even harder to reduce.' The dystopic version of meritocracy is concerned that it is ultimately unjust and can be anti-democratic.

It is interesting to observe that new forms of 'meritocracy' are being invented. For example, Lemann's book talks of 'real meritocracy', echoing the Chelsea Manifesto by arguing for the concept of merit to be expanded to include qualities such as 'wisdom, originality, humor, toughness, common sense, independence, determination'. In sharp contrast, one mathematically inclined paper talks of 'no-meritocracy' (where merit determines no out-comes), 'low-meritocracy' (where merit determines outcomes 10 per cent of the time), moderate or ambiguous meritocracy (50 per cent), and the 'perfect meritocracy condition', where 'those who choose to work hard always prosper'. But however meritocracy is formulated, we find that Young's original argument and counterargument remain dominant and are still in conflict.

$I + E = M$ (using the fictitious formula)

None of the political science papers use this equation, although some do talk about it in longhand. In the political science case study, there is therefore no evidence that this equation has gained any currency as a serious measure.

Conclusion

This review of the political science serial literature has been very successful in testing Young's retrospective hypothesis, which is found to be positive. The content analysis has also been a valuable device for tracing how the use of the term 'meritocracy' has evolved and taken on a life and a meaning that is divorced from Young's original contradictory intent, although the spirit of ambiguity embedded in *The Rise of the Meritocracy* still thrives. Young created a dual tension between the utopian and dystopian visions of meritocracy, which act to counterbalance each other within the original text, but inside the political science literature there has been a tendency for this tie to snap and the utopian and dystopian versions have taken separate journeys.[31] Various 'narratives' for and against meritocracy emerge and, noting the influence of other books, perhaps counter-intuitively, those who cite Rawls are more likely to be against the idea of a meritocracy than those who cite Bell.

To sum up, Young's challenge has been vindicated. We can also see that there has been a dualism in the subsequent intellectual development of his concept of meritocracy, although the satirist in him, rather then the social democrat, would perhaps have approved of this. To use his own words, the decision for or against the meritocracy is one that he 'left to the reader, the hope being that, on the way to making up his or her mind on one of the great issues of modern society, he or she will also have a little fun'.[32]

Looking Back on *Meritocracy*

MICHAEL YOUNG
(interviewed by Geoff Dench on 22 March 1994[1])

Michael, I want to talk about the Meritocracy *book a bit, because this is your one written work of fiction, and I think that's a very interesting medium because you can explore things that you feel ambivalent about in fiction in a way that you can't in other contexts. And I think I can see lots of contradictions being worked out perhaps in there. How did you actually come to write* Meritocracy *in the first place? Was it because of a need to work things out in some way?*

I've always found *equality* as a notion extremely difficult. I know I'm for it, but I'm not absolutely sure what I'm for. I think it's more true to say that socialism is about fraternity than what Tony Crosland said, that socialism is about equality, but I think of them as bound up together. And I could see one thing, in talking about equality—especially to a philosopher friend of mine called Prudence Smith, who has a very searching analytical mind—which showed me how shoddy my thinking was (this was after the war) on these subjects. [This is] that I didn't understand what I meant by the 'equality' that I was so much in favour of. But I could also see that equality of opportunity, which had so much more of a following than equality, was itself going to produce greater inequality and was one of the basic contradictions I guess of the whole society—all modern societies—because they all believe in equality to some extent. I mean, all advanced ones, they all have some adherence to democracy; one man, one woman, one vote, et cetera, and they all believe in equality of opportunity, which legitimises inequality in a way that wasn't possible before the idea of equality of opportunity as having a great practical relevance to education was very thought out. So I do think of it as a very deep-lying contradiction in society.

I tried to put it down in a Fabian essay, in a book of Fabian essays, modern Fabian essays, and some of it, and luckily (it was one of those lucky things like the Consumer Advisory Service), Dick Crossman, who was the editor of this, thought that it was a hopeless essay and I was calling in question equality of opportunity and all sorts of things that good Labour Party members ought to have been for, to have been in favour of, and wouldn't put it in the book of essays. So I thought: well, I'm not going to get it published as an essay; I'd better try and make it into a book. And I made it into a book. But I thought it was much . . . I hoped there wasn't any ambiguity about my own position, but of course there was, as people saw it, read it. And what I was trying to state was the contradiction and the ambiguity in modern society and put both points of view as clearly as I could—but in making fun of both of them too, and specially making fun of the people who believed in equality of opportunity, because I wasn't siding

By kind permission of Jane Gabriel, Gabriel Productions Ltd. © 1994 Gabriel Productions Ltd
Published by Blackwell Publishing Ltd, 9600 Garsington Road, Oxford OX4 2DQ, UK and 350 Main Street, Malden, MA 02148, USA

with them. But I hoped that my own tiny voice was also apparent there, and what I thought.

In what ways were you misunderstood, do you think, by some readers?

Oh, I mean all the time, I have been understood in I think roughly the same way. I wrote it as an attack on the 'meritocracy': it would be a more wounding, stratified system perhaps than had been known since the days of slavery. But people have taken it that I was lauding this society and wanting it to push ahead and arrive as quickly as possible.

Was there an impetus within the Labour Party towards meritocracy?

Yes, certainly, and even more in the Conservative Party; it's something they've agreed on.

How far do you think that the book itself helped to resist this by promoting the comprehensive idea?

No, it didn't.

You feel that things have developed in this direction?

Yes.

So the book would be as relevant today as it was then?

Well, it's obviously out of date, but there has just been a new American edition. I've written a new introduction, I've tried to bring it up to date but not very satisfactorily.

Did the book draw at all on the work that you had started doing in Bethnal Green?

No.

Because one of the things that I found interesting in it was that it developed the idea of fraternity, but it takes women as central in actually promoting it. Now, does this arise at all out of the discovery of the strength of the mother/daughter relationship within the community?

Yes, perhaps it does; I hadn't thought of that before. But it's my own point of view in the book—that what I had thought of as women's values, as against men's values, that women's values are the ones that I was trying to side with and espouse. And I think, I mean I still do, that there's something in it; I think there is a sort of fundamental divide, I suppose, between valuing people according to what they are and valuing people according to what they do. I think generally men care more for the second and women more for the first, and I was trying to argue for the first. And if you think that way, then of course there's no doubt that if you really value people for what they are, I mean what they are deeply, as human beings, then of course you can't have a class or caste system that's going to be very strong, however much the men do. But I was imagining that women might win the day and—or women as of that time anyway—and that would be wonderful if they did.

Because in the female community there are no classes?

No, there are classes, but I thought, I mean I thought the women then weren't so much harnessed as they have since become to the productive, the economic system. I mean the women's values that I was trying to bring out were the values of women who were in homes, and with children, and good mothers and good grandmothers and so on, I suppose. But women who go into the productive system, I mean they have the same sort of values—but not to the same extent—as men.

But were you in a sense looking for this when you left the Labour Party research to go to Bethnal Green, because the Labour Party in government was all about production and the state, and you were moving over to look at the moral economy really. Or wasn't this conscious?

Yes, the Labour Party had a fair amount about the moral economy. The speech I didn't write for Attlee in the 1945 election said that socialism is no more than the family writ large on the canvas of society. I mean, the moral base of the Labour Party, at that time anyway, was fairly strong because it came straight out of places like Bethnal Green. Class loyalty, solidarity, mutual support and so on; and there were non-conformist churches above all, I suppose. It was still a very strong strand, all the stronger because it was mostly taken for granted and not very much out in the open. It was a moral party; it no longer is.

But there is another contradiction here, which again comes out in the meritocracy, between the family as a selfish institution because it's smaller than the state but also the family as a source of moral value for an individual. How do you feel about that? I mean, do you see the family as more of a selfish than a moral institution?

No. Must be both.

Depending on the level.

It's our only moral institution of any fundamental importance. Nothing else.

How did the Labour Party in the fifties feel about the family, because the Labour Party at the moment is very confused. Was it then?

Yes, it was, that was I suppose a strand in the family studies, and what I did in that last Labour Party document. It was still the case that families were thought, at any rate by advanced thinkers in the Labour Party, as being *passé*, finished, and there had been quite an influence, world-wide, on socialism, from Russia, where the family wasn't exactly held in the highest possible esteem. And that kind of feminism that flourished then was on a great deal about the fetters; the way in which the family had fettered women, prevented them from realising their individuality, and so on. [It was] regarded as rather a conservative, and worse, institution by some people; but it was already changing.

In the early thirties it was really quite strong, and my mother, I know, would not use the word 'family' really; she was an advanced thinker of her time! I mean it was just something you just didn't talk about, was obviously no good. You were leading new liberated lives (God!) as cohabitants—even if they weren't called that then.

But the main argument in Meritocracy *is between individual and group, individual and state, and one of the things that it is addressing is the issue of whether you need to reward people. In your own life, you feel very strongly pulled to do things; you don't feel that you need a reward. And one of the things perhaps that the Labour Party is itself still mixed about is the need to reward people for labour—and this comes back to the citizen's wage, things like that. How did you actually feel when you were writing* Meritocracy; *did you feel then that the Labour Party had got it wrong and that you were moving away from that position, or not?*

No, I don't remember that sort of thinking being in my mind. I suppose part of the sort of female position, the Lady Avocet position [character in the book], was that public service, doing things out of loyalty and love, could turn out to be some of the best things that were done. I suppose this comes back to the family too. And some of the best institutions in the country were those in which there were people who did [*reply lost here*].

In the fifties there was still very much an idea of serving the state; of public service, and being rewarded by the state for things that you contributed to it. That seems much, much weaker now. In many circles in this country there is a feeling that the state, society, owes you a living. Do you think that this is a long-term shift, or do you think this is just something which is superficial and will disappear again quickly?

No, a long-term shift towards a more individualistic society. Most people, if they are to be rewarded in other ways than by money, need to be rewarded by respect given by others. And if there aren't many important 'others' in your life—for instance, in some sort of community setting, or extended family or something—then there aren't the people to give you the respect that can be a very powerful motivating force and incentive. And if you are to a greater extent on your own, with your own nuclear family or whatever, and you haven't so many people in your life that matter to you, or matter not in the same kind of way, and objects and things have to quite a large extent taken the place of people, what you do with your daily life, then money becomes ever more important as a way (I mean quite apart from what it will buy, the comfort it will give and the security it will give), but it becomes also a sort of symbolic token of respect.

If you earn money then you are worth something to other people; to the much wider community, whose members you may not know at all individually, but it has given you something. And I mean that's why we need work, because it is a way of getting that kind of respect from others.

76

Still, we are social animals, but the society in which we are animals in common has become one in which we don't see the other animals, even hear them in the night! With their strange noises. They are there, but they are kind of invisible and they [affect us] greatly. And we like to have the feeling that they have some concern for us, even though it's only shown through giving us a certain salary or bit of money.

But do you think the way things have changed is consistent with the predictions or fears in the Meritocracy *book?*

Yes. Yes, I think the circle has been squared really, fairly satisfactorily, as I feared it would be, and there is in some ways greater equality. Not just voting, we had that before, but I think that there's . . . people can meet each other more freely from different classes than they did. There's still all kinds of barriers, [but] I mean you can't see, you can't immediately mark out people by their dress and their demeanour as you could. Poor people aren't stunted as they used to be; it was quite unusual in South Shields in 1910 for any man to be higher than five foot. They are more equal in height and more equal in other ways, nutrition has become much better, et cetera.

But at the same time, alongside that, while equality might have extended itself much more widely, it has only extended itself because the demands of the kinds of technology-driven society we have are for more and more highly competent people to pull levers and to design the levers. And that means an education system which is harnessed to the productive system even more closely than it was before. And it has taken the heart out of millions of children as a consequence and has led to the . . . some of the awful things that are happening to families and communities. But still the momentum of it is tremendous, world-wide. And how to take a grip on that, in the interests of a sort of equality that would be wider but not stultifying, is the great intellectual task.

So the book hasn't been self-defeating in the sense of preventing what you feared happening?

No, no. Not only has it come out as I feared it would, but it hasn't been taken as a warning but been taken as a sort of blessing. Very bad luck.

Thanks.

Relevance to Modern Britain

A Brief Profile of the New British Establishment

JIM OGG

An under-researched model

THE two goals of economic prosperity and social justice have been at the forefront of New Labour policy throughout its time in office. Its line of argument is that social inequalities can only be reduced under conditions of economic growth, a point that has been constantly reiterated and re-marketed by central government offices. This growth requires a well-educated work-force, and education therefore is the key to achieving a wealthy and just society. Underpinning this tripartite schema is the concept of meritocracy—establishing a social system in which jobs and social recognition are allocated according to individual merit. A meritocracy grounded in education offers the means whereby the circle of prosperity and justice is squared. Education and the possession of qualifications create wealth, and wealth creates the conditions for social justice.

But does this formula work? *The Rise of the Meritocracy* is obviously highly relevant here. For although Michael Young was supportive of ending old social class-based inequalities, he was of course also wary of the danger that a rigid application of the ideals of meritocracy might lead to a *new* class system. But since he wrote *Meritocracy*, while many Western societies have moved in that direction, the nature and extent of the shift has not been adequately theorised or explored. This is unfortunate, because it is looking increasingly likely that current educational systems may not actually provide the driving force of economic growth that has been claimed. If anything, it may be the growing economic prosperity that is causing the exponential growth in higher education.[1]

Today, there are worrying signs that instead of a well-educated population forming the vanguard of the nation's producers, a new elite is forming, based on the transfer and acquisition of cultural capital gained by 'playing the educational system'. Colleges and universities may be less likely to provide the conditions under which individuals can flourish intellectually. Instead, they may be becoming a new source of social inequalities, as qualifications replace earlier social-class distinctions between the haves and the have-nots.

The phenomenon has, of course, been subject to some passing analysis, starting with Daniel Bell's discussion of the new 'cognitive elite' in 1977, influencing ideas about a new 'service class' in Britain and leading to revisions to standard social stratification made by John Goldthorpe. But the possibility of a major shift to a new type of elite, and a new form of social

Published by Blackwell Publishing Ltd, 9600 Garsington Road, Oxford OX4 2DQ, UK and 350 Main Street, Malden, MA 02148, USA

structure, still awaits thorough and systematic investigation—possibly because there are some conflicts of interest here for senior academics, who may be reluctant to acknowledge their own powerful position in the new social order.

A short essay in a collection like this is not the place to launch such a major enterprise. It does, however, provide a good opportunity to start outlining some features of how meritocracy is currently manifest in Britain, which any serious subsequent analysis will need to encompass and explain. Much of what was foreseen by Michael has already materialised, and although his own concept of meritocracy may not prove to offer the best characterisation of emerging British society, the general idea is bound to prove central when full analysis does get under way.

The merits of education

What I have attempted to do here is to provide a snapshot of graduates—the group that may compose or contain our new elite—by briefly comparing their lifestyles and attitudes with those of other educational 'classes'. The data are from the *British Social Attitudes* (BSA) surveys, and I divide their sample into three groups—graduates, people with qualifications lower than a degree but higher than GCSE, and people with GCSEs or no qualifications at all. Only adults below the age of 65 are included, as the cohorts of people above this age were not exposed in full measure to the educational boom that started in the 1970s. The BSA surveys have taken place annually since 1983 and, looking at the separate surveys since the 1990s, we can see that in this population (aged 18–64) about one in five are graduates, one in four have only GCSE qualifications or lower, and about half fall in between. Over the years, the disparity between these three categories is reducing, with more graduates and fewer unqualified. Nevertheless, and pertinent to the argument by Jon Cruddas elsewhere in this volume, there remains a strong core of the population who are poorly qualified.

In the tables that follow, these three groups are divided themselves into three subgroups based on age—under 35, 35–49 and 50–64. This age division is important for a number of reasons. As noted above, the main growth in education has occurred since the 1970s and there are relatively few graduates in the population aged 50 and above.[2] The worth and social recognition of education has been very different for this generation compared to younger graduates, and these differences may be reflected in their respective values. But perhaps more important is the fact that, over the past thirty years, more children from professional and middle-class backgrounds have been entering higher education than from working-class backgrounds.[3] This trend, which runs counter to the principle of meritocracy, is important to bear in mind when comparing the values of differently educated age groups. Attitudes and values are also generally formed early in life and tend to be stable in middle age and beyond. The final reason for looking at age is that the concentration of

82

a new elite—if it exists—may well be associated with a particular stage in the life course, when investment in education pays off, notably at the peak of an active career.

Work and income

The fundamental influence of education in modern Britain is reflected in the way that it is linked with access to well-paid, socially valued work. We can see from Table 1 that the distribution of household income is strongly associated with education for each of the three age groups. Households containing graduates are far more likely to have incomes of £38,000 or above; and where the graduate is aged between 35 and 49, almost two in three households are above this threshold. Reflecting, perhaps, the greater rewards available to them, a higher proportion of graduates are also actually in work; while one in two young or older persons with low-level qualifications, or none at all, do not do any paid work. This is also related (though not detailed here) to the higher incidence of working women, and of two-income households, among graduates.

The low rate of employment among the young unqualified reflects not only their greater difficulty in finding and keeping a job, but also the fact that less qualified women are more likely to define themselves as not actively seeking work. Among the senior group, low rates of employment also reflect the more general fact that leaving the job market permanently (through early retirement, unemployment or ill health) is more common among the unqualified

Table 1: Work and income (column percentages)

	Under 35			35–49			50–64		
	Graduate	Middle	Low	Graduate	Middle	Low	Graduate	Middle	Low
In paid work	77	68	53	85	86	67	73	70	53
Household income more than £38,000	40	21	11	59	35	12	51	29	11
Has a say in job	66	47	47	68	59	47	68	63	58
In higher occupation[a]	28	31	2	29	8	0	24	8	2
In lower occupation[a]	14	50	69	7	36	72	12	33	65
In public- or voluntary-sector employment	37	14	10	43	27	16	44	33	24
N (BSA 2004)	186	431	131	196	494	225	121	331	303

[a] Based on NS-SEC occupational classification; 'higher' = higher managerial and professional occupations; 'lower' = lower supervisory, lower technical, semi-routine and routine occupations.

above the age of 50. So whereas three in four graduates and one in three 'middle'-level qualification individuals have jobs at all ages, about half of the young and the senior among poorly qualified individuals are absent from the labour market.

Table 1 is also instructive in showing how graduates tend to gravitate to higher-status jobs, where qualifications are particularly important in securing work and working conditions are better. Around one in four graduates are in higher occupations, a proportion that does not vary across the three age groups. Graduates are more likely to have a say in their jobs, reflecting more job satisfaction. They are also attracted to the public sector, which has been expanding under New Labour, although the number of jobs is still lower than in the early 1990s. Of particular interest is the widening gap in the younger age group between graduates and the less qualified. Many graduates are today attracted by the better working conditions that the public sector represents, compared to less stable careers in the private sector.[4]

These figures show that there are clear gains to be had from possessing a degree, such as getting a job, having a higher salary and having some influence over the work being done. These provide key incentives for professional and middle-class parents to invest in the education of their children.

Political involvement

Not surprisingly, the pattern of graduate employment is linked to much greater participation in the political process (Table 2). Graduates in all age groups are much more likely to take an interest in politics and to hold the view that their participation is worthwhile, and does have an effect. Similarly, they show more trust in public servants to carry out their jobs impartially, including police to not bend the rules. On top of this, and at first sight perhaps a little contrarily, they express belief in active politics and personal action. What this ultimately shows, perhaps, is that this group feels that it is able to influence political decisions. This is why it records greater trust in the system. Also, though not shown here, members of this group have greater confidence that people like themselves do have a say in how things are done, and that voting does make a difference.

For political dissidents, on the other hand, especially among the poorly qualified group, all this would probably confirm their scepticism about the political process. There is actually not much difference between the educational 'classes' in support for the main parties. And these findings could prompt the conclusion that *party* politics may indeed no longer have a great relevance to many people, and that graduates may be operating as a confident 'insider' cross-party elite, united by their views and their ability to influence society in their daily lives regardless of which party is in power.

Table 2: Political involvement

	Under 35			35–49			50–64		
	Graduate	Middle	Low	Graduate	Middle	Low	Graduate	Middle	Low
Has a great deal or quite a lot of interest in politics	37	17	7	51	29	14	66	41	20
N (BSA 2004)	186	431	131	196	494	225	121	331	303
Would never:									
• Boycott a product	21	28	–	2	19	41	10	18	35
• Go on a demonstration	29	36	–	19	34	49	25	40	50
• Express views via media	26	39	–	27	39	58	16	44	56
N (BSA 2004)	53	106	24	50	142	53	32	108	83
Agree doesn't really matter which party is in power; in the end things go on much the same	60	74	78	56	71	85	51	65	84
N (BSA 2003)	347	514	217	459	448	327	286	272	468
Sometimes politics and government seem so complicated that a person like me cannot really understand	42	66	78	38	60	74	39	56	75
N (BSA 2003)	271	365	157	343	339	236	230	206	349
Most people can be trusted	51	37	29	64	45	29	66	57	35
N (BSA 2000)	192	268	118	212	208	197	145	111	270

The welfare state

Confidence in the current political system is reflected further in people's views on the efficacy of the welfare state (Table 3). Again, these are not quite what might be anticipated. Thus it is non-graduates, the group that contains most of the people who are actually dependent on benefits, who demonstrate the most critical assessments of it, especially among the older age cohorts. They record the highest rates of agreement with a number of statements asserting that people are cheating the system—including that people who are on the dole are often on a fiddle, that unemployed people could find work if they wanted to, and that people on social security often don't deserve it. Graduates, on the other hand—who as the highest paid workers might be expected to be suspicious about how their taxes are spent—emerge here as more sure that money is being well spent, and is going to people who genuinely need it, although here again the gap seems to be narrowing among younger people.

A possible explanation of this distribution is that the welfare state is what makes 'meritocrats' feel morally entitled to be doing well. Knowing that they are supporting 'losers' in the competitive system reduces the guilt that some may feel for their personal success, and also perhaps in some cases for the detachment from family responsibilities that they needed in order to achieve success in the first place. Unqualified respondents, though, who are either dependent on benefits themselves, or living among people who are, may be in a better position to see how things actually work (or don't) in practice. This may be why it is older people who are most critical in their assessments. But, once again, there are some signs that even younger graduates may be losing confidence in the welfare state.

These different interpretations of welfare throw further light on how political parties may have become relatively detached from class position. There is something of a consensus now among the main parties on what the welfare state should be doing—as indeed on many things. What varies is the degree of *trust* that people have in how it is operating—and this occurs on the basis of class rather than political affiliation.

Table 3: Attitudes to welfare

	Under 35			35–49			50–64		
	Graduate	Middle	Low	Graduate	Middle	Low	Graduate	Middle	Low
Agree strongly:									
• Many people falsely claim benefits	44	61	55	29	63	63	27	59	65
• Should be proud of welfare state	13	5	7	23	11	9	32	21	22
• Think levels of benefits are too high	49	62	42	38	58	54	34	55	56
• Think gap between high and low incomes is too large	69	74	74	67	71	72	72	76	76
N (BSA 2004)	186	431	131	196	494	225	121	331	303

Attitudes to immigration

Finally, Table 4 shows a series of attitudes on immigration as recorded in a self-completed questionnaire that formed part of the 2003 BSA survey. New Labour's stance on immigration policy is entirely in keeping with its overall meritocratic principles. A prosperous economy in a globalised world requires an immigrant workforce, and it is best if such a workforce is composed of meritocrats who have proved their social worth in their country of origin. As spelt out in policy documents and current plans to introduce a points system of eligibility, well-educated and skilled immigrants would be encouraged to

Table 4: Attitudes to immigration

	Under 35			35–49			50–64		
	Graduate	Middle	Low	Graduate	Middle	Low	Graduate	Middle	Low
Agree it is impossible for people who do not share Britain's customs and traditions to become fully British	34	38	51	36	54	62	43	58	63
Immigrants improve British society by bringing in new ideas and cultures	44	23	22	46	27	25	66	42	22
Immigrants are generally good for Britain's economy	22	7	8	37	17	12	39	23	21
Immigrants take jobs away from people who were born in Britain	28	50	62	21	41	52	28	42	56
Government spends too much money assisting immigrants	57	62	73	46	64	76	43	66	75
Immigrants increase crime rates	26	38	39	15	36	51	17	44	45
N (BSA 2003)	62	113	37	96	83	71	45	60	101

apply for British citizenship. Because they are highly educated, it is assumed that this new group of elite immigrants would be able to integrate into Britain's culture and way of life whilst retaining their own ethnic identity. They would thus avoid the social exclusion that has befallen previous waves of immigration, and thereby escape the racism common among many sections of the working class and less educated population.

The BSA data show clearly that much of the British population does not appear to share these views—or, at least, that there is a misconception about the objectives of such a policy. Multiculturalism, a driving factor behind New Labour policy, is favoured by the highly educated, and especially the highly educated young, whereas assimilation or integration is given preference by the less educated. Graduates of all ages are more favourable to the idea that immigrants improve British society by bringing in new ideas and cultures, also one of the key issues in New Labour's policy. The view that Britain's economy needs immigrants is a minority one among all respondents, but it is particularly low among young non-graduates. This is no doubt because the majority of poorly educated respondents believe that immigrants take jobs away from people who were born in Britain. Although not measured here, they also seem likely to believe the same for other resources such as housing and schools. Hostility towards immigrants is stronger among the poorly educated within all age groups. But unlike graduates, poorly qualified respondents hold more or less the same anti-immigration sentiments whether they are young or old, and there is even some evidence of a hardening of attitudes among younger age groups. On the evidence of these figures, there is no reason to suppose that an immigration policy steeped in meritocratic ideals will enhance social cohesion.

Conclusion

Since Michael's book, many writers around the world have demonstrated the important role the idea of meritocracy has in legitimising the power and social status of a select few.[5] In the past, elite forms of education were the main vehicle to propel people to the top, and many modern governments have introduced positive discrimination policies in one form or another to increase the number of individuals from lower social class backgrounds entering universities. Although this remains true today, the explosion in higher education is adding a new dimension to the meritocracy landscape. As Britain and the rest of Europe grapple with the complexities of how to maximise life chances and to protect vulnerable groups, the expansion of the state in areas such as education, health and housing has reached a new zenith. The managerial infrastructure to support this growth relies increasingly on highly qualified administrators, but as our brief excursion into some key values suggest, these individuals share a world-view that is very different from that of poorly qualified people. The latter group are either excluded altogether from employment in these sectors, or absent from the middle and higher echelons within them.

Such divisions can only lead to frustration, discontentment and alienation among people who see themselves excluded from society because they lack qualifications. If this in itself is not cause for concern, demographic shifts in Britain introduce a further twist to an already complex situation. Although predictions of a generational conflict may be alarmist, it is not difficult to envisage the resentment a young, unqualified (and probably unemployed) person can feel towards older qualified workers in positions of authority. The different values held by graduates and non-graduates point to the need to monitor for such signs of social fracture. Meanwhile, it is certainly not too soon, and hopefully not too late, to start trying to restore social worth and job stability outside of the meritocratic core, as a matter of some urgency.

Face, Race and Place: Merit and Ethnic Minorities

MICHELYNN LAFLÈCHE

Meritocracy—an emerging principle?

As a concept or a principle, meritocracy does figure in the context of a number of the issues we examine at Runnymede. This is not because we seek to find it there, but because it seems to emerge any time we talk about equality, particularly if it's an employment-related issue, about promotion through organisations.

When preparing this chapter, my brief was principally to look at what different members of minority groups, broadly speaking, understand by the term 'meritocracy'. For example, does it mean anything when Tony Blair promises them that 'merit' is what will take them where they want to go? Do any specific problems arise *for* minority groups, again, broadly speaking, because of concepts of meritocracy or the way in which other people or they themselves understand, interpret and implement those concepts?

Two interesting pieces of work already in hand at Runnymede have some relevance to these questions—though this was not what they had been principally aimed at producing. In using examples from them below, I am highlighting aspects of these projects that I think are interesting and relevant for future work.

What does meritocracy mean within organisations?

The first of these Runnymede projects centred on employment-related concerns, looking at the progression of senior managers through organisations and at related race equality issues. Two briefing papers have been published on the subject so far.[1] In that particular project we interviewed extensively, with the interviewees being accessed via three different participating organisations. We interviewed black and other minority ethnic managers from visible minorities, and white managers, who were all at fairly senior levels. We also interviewed what we came to call 'strategic policy-makers'—those who determine what policy is needed and are responsible for drafting it, often located in human resources (HR), but sometimes in other parts of the business. We interviewed them about what race equality looked like in their organisation.

The obvious, but crucial, opening question was 'Does race equality exist?' Was race equality a meaningful concept for them to be thinking about? Was race equality something they wanted to aspire to—as an organisation, as

Published by Blackwell Publishing Ltd, 9600 Garsington Road, Oxford OX4 2DQ, UK and 350 Main Street, Malden, MA 02148, USA

individuals within that organisation? The responses gave us outcomes that we certainly didn't expect, sometimes in contradiction of things we'd said in earlier pieces of work conducted as part of this research programme.

Our research in 2000 had led us to conclude that organisations, and white managers within those organisations, thought they were doing really well in their policies and practices on race equality issues.[2] Black managers, however, thought that what the organisations and the white managers were doing was really poor, in terms of implementing these policies and practices, so that the outcomes were not equal, and certainly not experienced positively by these managers within the organisations.

What we found from the final phase of this work was that in fact white managers felt much the same as black managers did.[3] However, they had been, and still were, more comfortable with verbalising their thoughts than with providing written responses to the survey questionnaire—despite knowing that what they were saying in the verbal exchanges was being written down by us.

Principally because of such findings, it's preferable to start with the end of the story, with this final response-gathering phase, because in five years from now these kinds of responses should be the last thing we would want to find ourselves hearing.

The combined response phase

We brought all the white managers and all the black managers together in one room with two facilitators—a white facilitator and a black facilitator who had been working individually with the groups. We wanted them to respond to the following question:

If yours was an organisation that you thought practised race equality, what would that mean in 5 years' time for you? How would you envisage your organisation at that stage? And what would be your expectations arising from that look ahead?

And the answers, presented here almost at random, were as follows:

- There would be more diversity at all levels, with a much higher proportion of minority ethnic managers.
- We would hear the benefits of the business case clearly articulated.
- There would be a higher retention of minority-ethnic managers at all levels.
- We would hear more openness on promotions, and there would be better communication in the organisation. And this means we would see more articles about how our company is a diverse and fair employer.
- We would feel proud to work for a company at the forefront of promoting and implementing diversity.
- We would feel more culturally aware as a result of having a truly diverse workplace at all levels.

- We would feel part of a real meritocracy, and be promoted purely on ability.

This is a particular group of individuals—highly educated, highly qualified, well advanced into good careers that are on track for long-term success and continuity—for whom there is a concept of meritocracy that they want to see applied throughout the organisation for which they work. Possibly the biggest thing to remember about their responses is how they understood that merit was something you should aspire to, but that you couldn't aspire to it when merit itself was mediated by racism. That was the daily experience of racism for these individuals at these senior levels—but it was an experience their colleagues failed to recognise them having.

Defining the 'good manager'

One of the questions that we explored with these group members was what it took to *be* a good manager and a successful manager by first allowing them to define what that meant.

We worked with them on an individual basis at this point and, interestingly enough, both sets of managers came up with the same answers, but with precisely opposite interpretations of what they meant.

- The answers were that in order to be a good manager in these organisations you had to have merit—which meant you had to have the right qualifications and demonstrate the ability to use your qualifications in the job you had.
- When asked to elaborate, they then began to unpack what that meant for them. In fact, it had little to do with their qualifications; it had very much more to do with three things, in the following order:

  (1) it was about face,
  (2) it was about race and
  (3) it was about place.

Issue (1) was that your face had to fit, and that was very much a gendered issue. In these organisations, men who were white were thought to be far more likely to be able to progress and demonstrate their own merits, because of those particular aspects or perceived attributes about themselves over which they had no control.

Race—issue (2)—was equally important in that sense, or almost equally important, in that if you were black—male or female—you were unlikely to be able to fit in, because your culture (as it was described, as opposed to your colour) wasn't going to fit with the culture of the organisation, or with the cultures of the organisations with which your organisation had to interact.

Place—issue (3)—was about where you were. You had to be in the right place at the right time. It had little to do with qualifications; it had to do with being in the right room at the right time to be recognised by the right individuals, who had the power to bring you through the organisation.

Complementing all three issues was the idea that you had to have a whole set of social structures around you that enabled you to be in the right place at the right time, have the right face to fit that particular place, and look as though you belonged there.

Merit, perceived value and racism

From the point of view of the white managers responding to this particular set of questions, this *was* merit: merit was about all of these aspects, all of these soft aspects that have nothing to do with ability or qualifications or demonstrated capacities. Merit had everything to do with your right to have all these other things to support you. Your right to be supported in this way was predicated on your being valuable in yourself, which meant in turn that you had, say, a cleaner taking care of your home, somebody to wash clothes, systems to ensure that you could attend every evening reception and drinks-after-work activity that would ensure access to the right people, to guarantee the next step in your career progression. That was merit.

For black managers, merit was in fact focused on the ability issue. They recognised all of the above-mentioned aspects as part of the organisation's need for and way of recognising merit when it presented itself. But it wasn't *their* interpretation of what merit meant, and of what a meritocracy should be based on.

For our part, we hadn't expected to see such a convergence and then such an opposition between views of what merit meant. What was particularly interesting was the idea of merit being seen potentially, in five years' time, as the criterion for judging the level of racism, and in their view hopefully the lack of racism, within an organisation, while at the same time their being absolutely clear that the concept of merit as currently applied within the organisation was in fact based on some form of largely indirect racism—be it individual or organisational racism.

There was then a real contradiction in terms between what people understood as the possibilities for applying merit judgements and how meritocracy was actually working within their organisations.

How do ideas of merit affect identity?

Runnymede's other piece of research that indirectly addresses notions of merit is called 'This is Where I Live', a project focused on young people.[4]

In this project, we ran fourteen focus groups across the United Kingdom (including Northern Ireland) with young people from different ethnic backgrounds, including white communities. The groups were mainly from disadvantaged backgrounds. Only a couple of groups could be described as relatively privileged and they were a thought-provoking contrast with the other groups. Thinking specifically about young people from disadvantaged backgrounds, the concept of merit wasn't something that had great resonance with them. Again, it wasn't an issue that we had particularly wanted to explore. What we wanted to hear from them was about their sense of belonging. What did that mean? What did that look like? What did it have to do with the place in which they lived? And how was their heritage involved in this—if at all?

They told us some surprising things. I'm thinking in particular of two groups that were very specific about regeneration in their own communities. They defined 'their communities' as the larger urban centre, not as their own *local* communities. And what surfaced as important to them was their sense of well-being or, rather, their *lack* of well-being.

These were young people who felt they had no options; who felt that there was no future for them in the way that society works today; and who had no belief in their own opportunities and their ability to work within the existing social structure. One of the key questions they were invited to consider was what they wanted to know, and what they wanted to say, should they have an opportunity to question Tony Blair. What they came up with was:

Why aren't you spending the money to regenerate a part of the city that I belong to? When I have to step outside my door and know that I will always step outside this door or a door that looks like this, and find blood on the streets from a fight last night—what does that mean to me, and how do I fit into that society?

What we took out of that response was how it demonstrated a strong understanding on the part of the young people that merit wasn't what they were seeking, because they didn't believe there was going to be a place for them in society; in fact, what they were seeking was a whole new society. And what they wanted was an opportunity to be able to redefine themselves, and have society redefine them, as successful in whatever endeavours they undertook, knowing they would never, for example, manage to become a teacher, or get a Civil Service job. But they still wanted to be able to anticipate that they would gain respect, whatever jobs they were able to do, and be able to live with dignity in their own communities, knowing also that they probably wouldn't leave those communities.

One reason for my referring to this project was trying to conceptualise what positive action, affirmative action and positive discrimination might look like. It's easier to think about these in terms of what happens inside organisations, particularly if you want to look at them from the point of view of senior managers and people at board level.

What it means for people who are always going to be disconnected from that system, or very unlikely to ever be connected to it, is another matter altogether. This is where my own thinking gets more convoluted—but I'd like to look more closely at how ideas of meritocracy, equalities and human rights are being raised and debated as part of Runnymede's involvement as

94

a member of the Taskforce on the Commission for Equality and Human Rights.

Meritocracy and human rights

The rationale of the new Commission for Equalities and Human Rights, how its role gets interpreted by different communities and community groups, and what those interpretations mean for government policy on setting it up, raise exceedingly important issues for all the Commission participants on how to define equalities.

If individuals, young people in particular, are telling us that they want the opportunity just to be able to express themselves and exist, in whatever way they can, with some level of respect, then what does the term 'equalities' mean for the whole of society within that kind of framework?

And where does merit fit into that format? It doesn't! At least, not on the surface.

The battle that I see taking place around the Commission for Equalities and Human Rights is about recognition, again. Recognition is what people are requiring and demanding because of the level of exclusion based on racism that they continue to experience. So, on the one hand, I would argue that we need a single body such as this Commission, because I would like there to be an even-handed protection of rights and an equalised level of intervention in order to promote equalities. On the other hand, I see that we have communities of different kinds—thinking about race in particular, but also gender, sexuality and religion—who have different levels of protection at the moment, and who each want to ensure that they themselves reach the level of basic human dignity, before they can even start to think about offering that same courtesy to other people in similar positions to themselves.

This remains one of the big, perplexing problems for government to start thinking about more appropriately. So far, they don't seem to be doing it— and I'm not sure how they *should* be doing it. It's also a problem for researchers in organisations such as Runnymede to reflect on—while admitting to some uncertainty about how we will think our way into making recommendations to government on what should be done.[5]

Something that struck me in what Geoff Dench has written[6] is the idea that, somehow, multiculturalist policies are part of the striving by government for meritocracy, in order that this society can create itself as successful, multicultural and multi-ethnic, and that the reward structures would then be based around trying to ensure protection for that vision. But are minority communities likely to experience policy-making and the impact of policy in this way in this country? I don't think so—no more than they could sensibly anticipate experiencing meritocratic criteria as supportive of an openly multiculturalist and multi-ethnic society.

The situation in Britain now is very complex. One of the biggest problems is that we have very different types of minority community. We have different groups of classes within these communities. We have different understand-ings of class according to where we position ourselves in relation to class notions. And we have different interpretations of what a good society looks like and what it doesn't look like.

When you are at the top and find that you are still facing discrimination—racial discrimination—what you actually argue for is removal of the racial discrimination, but not a removal of social injustice in general. Conflict occurs as a result of this. Aspects of the debate on the proposed Commission on Equalities and Human Rights are now beginning to embody that conflict, and that contradiction.

Marginalised Young Men

YVONNE ROBERTS

Introduction

MERITOCRACY is defined by the *Concise Oxford English Dictionary* as 'Government by people selected on merit'. If meritocracy is the name of the game, then its fatal flaw remains what it has always been: the selectors predominantly come from a narrow and frequently inward-looking strand in society: white, male and middle class—a group that operates on the false premise that 'their' world is the only world, one to which they allow access to shamefully few who are not of their mould. As a result, in Britain, in spite of progress in some quarters, an unprecedented amount of talent and ability is lying fallow.

This process of exclusion is rotting into something that is toxic and damaging not only to individuals but also to society as a whole—as witnessed in the extremism of some young Muslim males and the waste of potential that could lift Britain from the bottom of so many European league tables for productivity and growth, not to mention well-being. Now more than ever, too many of our young people are disqualified from even attempting to rise through the ranks propelled by talent, because of the continually tightening constraints of class, poverty, racism and a universally appalling state education system—one that, too often, fails to bring out the holistic best in either the cerebral or the more practically inclined.

In these circumstances, how do young men at the very bottom of the pyramid give themselves a sense of worth at a time when society demonises and marginalises them to an extent unknown to their fathers and grandfathers? How do they find even a single footing on the ladder of opportunity when the capacity to learn a trade, earn a decent wage and find stability in a relationship has been so undermined?

Life at the bottom

In *Learning to Labour*, Paul Willis' seminal book on the marginalised working class, written thirty years ago, he begins the first chapter with the following words: 'The difficult thing to explain about how middle class kids get middle class jobs is why others let them. The difficult thing to explain about how working class kids get working class jobs is why they let themselves.'[1] Part of the answer to the latter question, perhaps, lies in the fact that 'working class jobs' were at the hub of what was to many an acceptable wheel of life—so much so that a number turned their backs on social mobility, sensing that it meant exile from a tribe they had no wish to leave. (Others, of course,

Published by Blackwell Publishing Ltd, 9600 Garsington Road, Oxford OX4 2DQ, UK and 350 Main Street, Malden, MA 02148, USA

including me, and many other newly educated young women, couldn't wait to say their farewells.)

The town in which I briefly lived as a teenager was dominated by the railway works, which built and maintained stock. At age 16, the boys would enter 'The Works' to begin an apprenticeship. Along with the status of learning a skill came entry to a brotherhood and the steadying hand of older men. An apprenticeship also provided a wage and—since that marked out a youth as good husband (and father) material—a wife would soon follow. The wife stayed at home and accepted the limitations on her life because, as part of the trade-off, her husband came home every week and put his money on the table.

In the past three or four decades, however, as has been well documented, the working class have lost a great deal—heavy industry, which provided employment; and trades that offered status and a sense of community, which acted as both a restraint on anti-social behaviour and an anchor. What has also come under threat are the long-term attachments that once gave incentives to the young and unruly to show responsibility and maturity and become men: attachments to wife, children and the extended family that gave a purpose, an identity, a sense of self-worth. A young working-class male mattered because he was a father/breadwinner/husband/mate. Now, the role of women has changed, influenced both by feminism and the economic pressure to earn a second wage. At the same time, many lads now drift into casual poorly paid work with few links to the more mature men who, in the past, provided guidance and support.

Research drawn, for instance, from the *National Child Development Study* shows that, over the past decade or so, depression, anxiety and a lack of attachments have become particularly prevalent among non-academic young males. While a fat slice of 16–24 year olds in Britain have never been better qualified or more affluent, a large and significant minority are seriously adrift. A study by the University of Glasgow, published in 2004, established that this disconnectedness had little to do with fecklessness and moral turpitude, but was caused by rotten schooling and the lack of unskilled jobs that once offered a degree of security. In spite of long periods out of work, most of the young men in the study were impressively committed to finding employment, often to the extent of taking work under intolerable conditions.

Typically, for these young men, few opportunities existed for training in short-term contract and casual work, while government programmes failed to provide entry into secure sectors of the labour market. The study also found that because benefits are so low, energies become focused 'on making ends meet rather than finding work'. In short, these young men were on the outside—and staying there. Inevitably, in an effort to swim with the current of contemporary affluence, many young men in these circumstances move into the black economy or petty crime. As a way of camouflaging their confusion, anger and sense of dislocation, some may slide into what Paul Willis originally termed, in the 1970s, 'valorised acts of insurrection'.

98

However, the cost exacted by society for such insurrection is far higher today than it was thirty years ago. The speed with which a young man may be catapulted from a minor offence to a prison sentence and recidivism— particularly if he is working class and/or from a black or ethnic minority— is striking. The Howard League for Penal Reform has been conducting a study of young offenders serving short terms of imprisonment. In *Out for Good*, it charts the devastation that a three-month sentence can cause—housing, girlfriend, child and hard-won job may all be lost.[2] Among 18–20 year olds, 70 per cent of those released from prison reconvict within two years.

One of the obsessions of today's middle class is happiness—Am I happy? How can I tell? How do I measure precisely how happy I am? If you talk to young marginalised men, their main concern isn't happiness—it's *respect*. In spite of Tony Blair's attempts to reclaim the word for middle England, for the dispossessed, the search for respect can manifest itself in extremely violent forms. Melvyn Davis helps to run a project, Coram Boys2Men, which is mostly for young Afro-Caribbean males. He tells the story of a young man who owned a pair of snakeskin shoes of which he was extremely proud, because they signalled—to him, at least—that he was a player. He would go with his friends to a club designed for a maximum of 200 people. Of course, twice as many would be jammed in. Inevitably, someone would inadvertently step on the highly prized shoes. A severe beating would be inflicted on the involuntary 'culprit'. His crime? Lack of respect. Everything the young man thought was important lay in those shoes. That code has an attraction when who you are and what you have to offer carries a rock bottom price in the mainstream marketplace. Reacting violently—to what should hardly matter at all—means that you count.

Camilla Batmangelidh heads Kids Company, a charity that supports almost 4,000 children in (and out of) twenty-one schools across London. The children suffer from severe behavioural, emotional and social difficul-ties arising from significant childhood trauma and or neglect. Often, this is to do with poverty and substance abuse by the adults in their lives. They are the children of the marginalised. Batmangelidh talks eloquently about how three and four year olds desperately want to change the situation at home, to end the unpredictability, violence and lovelessness. Gradually, they learn that they can't control the situation, so they cut themselves off from their own feelings. The more they cut themselves off from their own feelings, the quicker they lose empathy for others.

By the age of eleven or twelve, they are productive members of an economy trading in violence, with little understanding of how to make or keep relationships. They turn on the television set and see a society in which all that appears to matter is instant gratification—all that counts is 'bling-bling' and material possessions. On MTV music videos, the man who is Mr Big is a caricature—a gold-laden, overfed pimp who trades in sex and women. So some young men go out to acquire the props of this street-led definition of 'success'. They join an alternative 'meritocracy' in the fruitless hope that it will make them feel like somebody, before they lose their liberty, kill—as did the compassionless murderers of Mary Ann Leneghan, raped, tortured and stabbed to death—or are themselves killed.

Liberation to failure

Ask any charity working with young black teenagers, and they will tell you that it's relatively easy to raise money for a music project. The essentially racist assumption is that every black teenager wants to become the next Nellee or P. Diddy. Obtaining resources to encourage young males (and females) to acquire basic educational qualifications is very much more difficult. Black boys are up to fifteen times more likely than whites to be permanently excluded from school. A study by the Joseph Rowntree Foundation, published in 2005, measured the impact of exclusion on a sample of thirty-three Afro-Caribbean pupils. Even if they acknowledged that something they had done had led to their exclusion, the young people 'Generally expressed an overwhelming sense of injustice exacerbated by their belief that punishments were more severe for black pupils than for white.' The study continued, 'The experience made them conscious of the fact that race would affect the way they were seen by others . . . their experience of exclusion was very likely a foretaste of experiences they would have in a wider society.' While half had gained qualifications after exclusion and two-thirds were in further education, a number had spent time in 'educational limbo', doing nothing . . . and getting into trouble.

Shaftesbury Homes is a charity that runs several children's homes in South London. Its core belief is that you treat the child in a home as you would treat your own. Given the standards in some children's homes, this is a revolutionary philosophy. The charity employs teachers who give one-to-one support to each child. If required, the teacher will take the child to school to ensure attendance. Schools reluctant to accept potentially tricky pupils are taken to court and forced to fulfil their statutory duty. Young people are given financial rewards for good work—£10 for completing course work; £50 for completing GCSEs. The result is that while the majority of young people leave care with no qualifications at all, and well under 10 per cent have only a few GCSEs to their name, 45 per cent of Shaftesbury's young people achieve five or more GCSEs. In doing so, they crucially move a step closer to putting a value on themselves that the rest of society also rates. They begin to come in from the margins.

The scheme—which deserves to be rolled out across the country—costs £600,000 a year to run. It is in constant jeopardy, because government isn't prepared to allocate sufficient income on a permanent basis. This is what meritocracy means when you are at the bottom. It means that education becomes a luxury, not a right. Fifty years ago, education was the magic wand, facilitating social mobility no matter how deprived a child's background. Recent research tells us that this is no longer the case. On the contrary, in the unevenness of its delivery, it appears to be the cause of social exile for far too many of our young.

In the 1970s, Paul Willis wrote, 'The problem with education is that it is producing young people without any idea of what they need in terms of vocational guidance and education. Academic education is no good.' Those words still apply today, three decades later. Willis also pointed to the proliferation of worthless qualifications. Again, thousands of young people today are leaving school barely literate to be offered a pick 'n' mix counterfeit 'education', made up of courses lasting a matter of months, producing certificates of little real value. This is a waste of ability, opportunity, teaching skills and the taxpayer's money—all driven by the meritocrat's snobbish dismissal of practical learning. The tragedy for many is that at the end of this inauthentic period in 'higher' education, they find themselves back stacking shelves in their local supermarkets, thoroughly disillusioned.

A study of 100,000 inner-city children, published in 2005, established that a quarter skip school for up to a week a year. The worst offenders are absent for up to a term or more (according to teachers, a whole lot more). Tony Blair's mantra in his early years in power was 'education, education, education'. What he forgot to tell the electorate was that what he meant by this was nineteenth-century education, in which the academically adept (including his own sons) could be creamed off—while the rest attempted to catch up. Learning by doing, or 'vocational' study, has so long been associated with blighted secondary moderns that it now smacks unfairly of dullardism. The experience of education for so many young people is that it exacerbates the very sense of inferiority and marginalisation that fuels anti-social behaviour.

Changing attitudes to education

Whether absent from the classroom or half-heartedly present, the message coming from many pupils and their parents is 'We don't need no education'—at least, not of the kind that's on offer. Resourcefulness, creativity and a willingness to graft are assets that government ministers constantly tell us are much needed if Britain is to compete in the global economy. Yet when it comes to secondary education, government fails to capitalise on these assets. Instead, Tony Blair persists in shoring up a system that throttles more aspirations than it encourages.

The government has invested heavily in the early years in schemes such as Sure Start and the National Childcare Strategy, in the hope that generations of disadvantage can be halted. While such measures may have a positive impact, what continues to be ignored is the disastrously damaging sense of disconnectedness towards schooling that is prevalent among many British families today. The toughest educational challenge ahead isn't how we treat the academically brightest from the poorest backgrounds; it's how we trigger the hunger for knowledge and skills among the disadvantaged rest who don't shine so easily at exams. It's how we correct the corrosive sense of second best that is bestowed on so many school-leavers and holds them back from acquiring skills even in later years.

'The development of technical education is the greatest need for this country,' said Ramsay MacDonald in 1924. Almost every statistic, domestic and international, that measures Britain's productivity and skills in comparison with much of the rest of Europe tells us that we have failed to listen. In 2004, Sir Mike Tomlinson, former Chief Inspector of Schools, proposed scrapping A-levels and GCSEs in favour of a single diploma framework, offering vocational and academic options. He had widespread support, yet the government's White Paper instead opted to retain the destructive us-and-them theme in British education, keeping the alleged 'gold standard' of GCSEs and A-levels. The roots of learning for many young people are so shallow that the Confederation of Business Industry says that 47 per cent of employers are unhappy with the basic skills of reading, writing and arithmetic. The process of attending college, far from gaining entry to meritocracy, too often appears to be a time-filling charade, from which little will be gained except a low-paid, dead-end job.

Young people may start courses, but thousands fail to finish, arguably because it neither excites their passion nor fits with their interests and abilities. At the time of writing, only one in four teenagers who begin a modern apprenticeship completes the course. Britain comes twenty-fifth out of twenty-nine industrial countries for the percentage of 17 year olds in full-time education or training. Young people from disadvantaged families who do progress through higher education still find that the door to the meritocracy is barely ajar.

Andy Furlong and Fred Cartmel have been tracking students from disadvantaged families for several years. In a study published in 2005, they discovered that these less advantaged graduates had found that accent and area of residence had proved barriers to employment. In addition, while these students were positive about their long-term prospects, they owed a higher proportion of their debt to banks and credit card companies (and not, for instance, to parents). The need to service these debts hindered their career planning and had forced them to accept any job available, however underused their skills. For black and ethnic minority young men who do well academically, racism and white male tribalism often denies them their rightful opportunities to rise, to the detriment of the so-called meritocracy and social justice. Oxford, for instance, remains a pale-faced institution. In 2004, the university took in only twenty-four black undergraduates out of a total of 3,176—that's just 0.75 per cent. Fewer than 1 in 100 students at Oxford are black.

Does it get better once these marginalised black and ethnic young men move into management? Not really. The Runnymede Trust is an independent policy research organisation focusing on equality and justice through the promotion of a successful multi-ethnic society. Since 2000, it has published three reports, tracking progress towards equality and diversity (or the lack of

102

it) in FTSE 100 companies. It has found that while organisations talk the talk—97 per cent agree that promotion is entirely based on merit, for example—they fail to walk the walk. This is because of lack of leadership from the top; lack of monitoring; barriers in recruitment, retention and promotion; and the requirement on ethnic minority managers to provide an indefinable, and therefore often unobtainable, 'something extra' (a white skin?) to make it to the top means that discrimination is better disguised than thirty years ago and just as damaging.

Research shows that diverse workforces tend to have better problem-solving skills, are more creative and deal more effectively with complex challenges. Moreover, they reflect the globalised markets that companies are trying to reach. Yet, because the British meritocracy draws its recruits from such a small puddle of talent, many of these skills are under-exercised. Even wearing white collars and pinstripe suits, some young men are marginalised.

The meaning of success

How do young men find meaning—and merit—in their lives without the social capital so accessible to the middle classes? The answers are numerous and radical. Among them are a complete overhaul of the education system, resources targeted particularly at disadvantaged groups, cooperation rather than competition between schools, and alternative ways of encouraging skills and talent amongst those who may 'only' be 'good with their hands'.

What is also vital is for the white male Establishment to recognise that it is a major part of the problem. It needs to acknowledge that in others, 'different' doesn't mean less good. We need an imaginative and thoroughgoing over-haul of all discriminatory practices—Canada has plenty of examples in government and the public sector of how this might be done via contract compliance, pay audits and other measures. What also matters is a concerted attack on poverty and inadequate pay that offers less than benefits when combined with the cost of housing. As importantly, while a young man may find himself on the edge of society for a time, often through no fault of his own, there should always be the chance to come in from the cold and flourish.

John H. Laub is a professor of criminology at the University of Maryland. His colleague, Robert J. Sampson, is professor of sociology at Harvard. In *Shared Beginnings, Divergent Lives*, published in 2004, they concluded a study of 500 men who were remanded into reform school in the 1940s and have now reached (if still alive) the age of 70.[3] Initiated by Sheldon and Eleanor Glueck in the 1950s, this is the longest longitudinal study of childhood, age, crime and the life course. Laub and Sampson have combined rigorous data analysis and interviews with fifty of the men to reach a conclusion that is especially significant in an increasingly determinist society, eager to identify the evil seed.

They argue that there is no one 'type' who is more likely to commit crime than any other. Some of the men grew out of delinquency in their twenties but, among those who did continue to commit crimes long into adulthood, what gradually put a brake on their activities were the new connections in their lives—connections that physically removed them from their old environments and meant they had an investment of interest from others. So, many desisted almost by default—or because they had been offered a second chance to prove their worth. Women too had made a difference—the kind of women who set down boundaries and issued ultimatums: 'Shape up, or I ship out.' The importance of not failing others had a monitoring effect on their lives that, in turn, gradually had an impact on their perceptions of themselves.

Laub and Sampson argue that, somehow, we have to find ways of offering these points of reconnection all through an individual's life, so that the possibility of redemption is always a constant. The work of changing people's views of themselves, Laub and Sampson insist, requires long-term sustained support—including access to decent jobs, education and housing—if the lack of confidence is to be tackled, the inferiority complex that cripples eroded and the anger controlled. In contrast, Labour has a very managerial view to changing behaviour. Invest three years' seed-money, monitor a great deal (and, frequently, prematurely), establish targets, and then go away and expect the disillusioned and disregarded pupa to emerge from the chrysalis of social exclusion and turn into a modest middle-class butterfly.

What many marginalised young men seek is low key; a decent income from a job that offers some satisfaction and sufficient standing to attract a wife or partner who lasts the course. Sadly, too often, it's a dream that is impossible to realise. Others, given the chance, are the stuff of which leaders, shakers and movers are made. They are the new meritocrats-in-waiting—and they are growing increasingly angry that the Establishment's shoulder continues to be pushed so hard against the door while diversity and integration slogans are mouthed.

The Unmaking of the English Working Class

FERDINAND MOUNT

Introduction

MICHAEL Young's most famous book was *The Rise of the Meritocracy*: it was certainly his most famous unread book. Thousands of his non-readers automatically assumed from the title that it must be a celebration of this new class. After all, it is so often the case that commentators who identify an emerging new class rather approve of it. If they do not themselves already belong to it, they would like to do so. Ever since, this new word 'meritocracy', which Young coined for the purposes of the book has been widely used, mostly with a sense of approval, even admiration. After all, other words deriving from the same root—'meritorious', for example—had been terms of approval.

Class as personal success or failure

But *Meritocracy* is not like that at all. On the contrary, it is a satire, a slightly clumsy one perhaps (Young was not a creative writer by profession), but a satire that makes its point quite effectively. The book purports to be a history of English education between 1870 and 2033, told by a smug social historian of progressive views. In the latter year, he looks back on the steady advance of competition and promotion by merit in industry and in the Civil Service as a result of a stream of educational reforms from the Forster Act of 1870 onwards. Foreign competition demanded that we give up the old nepotism and promotion by seniority. In order to survive, we needed to reward and advance merit wherever it was found. As a result, a new elite was formed, and the lower classes were drained of their most talented members. In the old days,

... no class was homogeneous in brains: clever members of the upper classes had as much in common with clever members of the lower classes as they did with stupid members of their own. Now that people are classified by ability, the gap between the classes has inevitably become wider. The upper classes are, on the one hand, no longer weakened by self-doubt and self-criticism. Today the eminent know that success is just reward for their own capacity, for their own efforts, and for their own undeniable achievement. They deserve to belong to a superior class. They know, too, that not only are they of higher calibre to start with, but that a first-class education has been built upon their native gifts.[1]

Published by Blackwell Publishing Ltd, 9600 Garsington Road, Oxford OX4 2DQ, UK and 350 Main Street, Malden, MA 02148, USA

. . . What can they have in common with people whose education stopped at sixteen or seventeen, leaving them with the merest smattering of dog-science? How can they carry on a two-sided conversation with the lower classes when they speak another, richer, and more exact language? Today, the elite know that, except for a grave error in administration, which should at once be corrected if brought to light, their social inferiors are inferiors in other ways as well—that is, in the two vital qualities, of intelligence and education, which are given pride of place in the more consistent value system of the twenty-first century.[2]

And, as a corollary,

As for the lower classes, their situation is different too. Today all persons, however humble, know they have had every chance. They are tested again and again. If on one occasion they are off-colour, they have a second, a third, and fourth opportunity to demonstrate their ability. But if they have been labelled 'dunce' repeatedly they cannot any longer pretend; their image of themselves is more nearly a true, unflattering, reflection. Are they not bound to recognise that they have an inferior status—not as in the past because they were denied opportunity; but because they *are* inferior? For the first time in human history the inferior man has no ready buttress for his self-regard.[3]

Nor apparently is there now, in AD 2033, any way for the lower classes to remedy that inferiority. The ideal implicit in the comprehensive schools has been abandoned in favour of a revival of the old grammar schools. The historic mission of the Labour Movement is exhausted. The trade unions have changed their names to less confrontational, more technical-sounding titles. The Mineworkers became the Mine Technicians, 'worker' being now a taboo word, as indeed is 'Labour'. The Labour Party has been reborn as the modern Technicians Party and co-opted into the rule of the meritocratic elite. Protest is useless, the fatuous narrator opines, and the new underground movements— the Populists and the Chelsea Manifesto of 2009 in favour of a classless tolerant society, for example, and even the general strike that is about to happen—have no hope of success.

The redistribution of ability between the classes in society has ensured that 'the lower classes no longer have the power to make revolt effective . . . Without intelligence in their heads, the lower classes are never more menacing than a rabble, even if they are sometimes sullen, sometimes mercurial, not yet completely predictable.'[4] The book ends with a footnote recording that 'since the author of this essay was himself killed at Peterloo, the publishers regret that they were not able to submit to him the proofs of his manuscript'.[5]

Michael Young's warnings were not much heeded at the time and are not much heeded now. Yet a good deal of his prophecies have turned out pretty accurately: the trade unions have given themselves winsome new names such as Amicus and Unison, the Labour Party has become New Labour, antique barriers to promotion by merit (such as the 'glass ceiling' keeping down women) have disappeared, and comprehensive education is on the way out, at least in its unstreamed, idealistic form. Above all, we cannot help noticing that the old class system has been reconstituted into a more or less meritocratic upper tier and a lower tier, which is defined principally by its failure to qualify for the upper tier.

Removal of institutional props

But if that were the only damage inflicted on the self-esteem of the worst off in modern Britain, it might not by itself be so intolerable. After all, many people in all classes, perhaps most of us, go about the world with a sense of inferiority, suffering from the uneasy unawareness that we have not done brilliantly in life, either because we lacked the natural talents required or did not make the most of such opportunities as were available to us, or a combination of the two. There are other crutches and cushions that help us to struggle through. It is when these are kicked or whipped away from under us that demoralisation is liable to set in.

And that, I would argue, is what has happened to large parts of the working class in Britain, on a scale and with an intensity not experienced in other industrial nations. One support now missing—its disappearance well charted and much lamented by observers on the left—was formerly provided by the structures of the old industrial working class and the trade union network that underpinned them. The disappearance of the old heavy industries, it is generally agreed, has weakened the self-confidence and sense of identity of working-class men. Trade unionism in Britain is now largely confined to public-sector workers, who have their own ethos with or without trade union membership.

All this is true, but for me that is not the end of the lament. Other erosions of working-class self-confidence have been gathering pace at the same time, and these have often been deliberately accelerated rather than retarded or deplored by those same left-wing observers and ideologues. I would briefly offer, as examples, three that seem to me worth thinking about.

First, in time at any rate, has been the sustained assault by the intellectual establishment upon those dissenting churches that arose out of the lower classes and were predominantly patronised by them. It is not always appreciated today how virulent and prolonged this assault was, from Matthew Arnold and Dickens to E. P. Thompson and his followers. Secular historians have tended to minimise the importance of working-class religion, pointing to statistics (those of the 1851 census, for example) that showed that half the population—and at that, mostly the poorer half—did not go to church on Sunday. But that is vastly to underplay the reach of the Methodists, Baptists and Congregationalists into working-class districts through their schools and Sunday schools. In the late 1850s, it is reckoned that one chapel a week was being opened in Wales; by the 1990s, it is reckoned that one chapel a week was being closed down and turned into a bingo hall, squash club or furniture showroom. It is forgotten too that although the Church of England was constantly berated for its failure to convert the poor, it did provide a consecrating site for the hatching, matching and despatching of people of all classes. For all their failings, the churches together confirmed the poor in some sort of belief that they were equal members of society.

No less important were the unthinking assumptions of working-class patriotism. Proletarian celebrations of military victories and royal jubilees (and, indeed, the death of princesses) have always made intellectuals such as George Gissing, Virginia Woolf or Malcolm Muggeridge contemptuous or uneasy. Yet it is only in relatively recent years that intellectuals have concentrated quite so much firepower on these traditional loyalties, and tried so hard to dismiss them as childish infatuations that we ought by now to have grown out of. The critiques of Kingsley Martin and Tom Nairn are now refracted through the mass media—the Murdoch press and *The Guardian* here acting in an unadmitted alliance to root out any lingering reverence for the monarchy—while patriotism in the wider sense is depicted as a refuge for the simple-minded.

What then remains? What are the people at the bottom left with? With the disappearance of the great collective spaces, the only space that they can call their own is home and family, the only uncontaminated pleasures those of private life. Yet even these are under attack in a variety of ways: through the intrusions of the state, the sexualisation of everything and the shattering effect of divorce, which bears hardest on the poorest, for they have fewer counter-vailing compensations in life. What Christopher Lasch called 'a haven in a heartless world' is no longer the safe haven that it once was. There is no space here to argue these points in detail.[6] I want only to remark that with almost every liberty comes loss, and although the poorest enjoy the liberties as much as the better-off, they are likely to feel the losses even more intensely. I would only suggest that readers turn back to Michael Young and Peter Willmott's *Family and Kinship in East London*,[7] ponder the stabilities described there and question how much of all that survives in the Bethnal Green of today. It is also worth noting how alert Young and Willmott were to the role of the monarchy and patriotism as buttresses of life in working-class communities.

Glance for a minute at other European nations or at the United States. In all of them, the institutions of religion and patriotism are largely taken for granted, and the legal and fiscal structures are considerably more family-friendly. Although the usual processes of secular modernity are at work in these countries too, there is, I think, little positive effort to demolish the traditional social frameworks.

I am not undervaluing for an instant all the material gains, in health, life expectancy, comfort, leisure and travel, that the worst-off have made in the half-century since *The Rise of the Meritocracy* was published. But that searing tract has not lost its relevance, and its warning that the cumulative effect of modern society might be to demoralise those at the bottom of the heap has not lost its potency.

Age and Inequality

ERIC MIDWINTER

Equality and equilibrium

IN 1999, after I had just delivered a paper on 'Balanced communities', Michael Young told me that if he had been twenty years younger (that is, in his mid-sixties), he would have started a 'Society for the Advancement of Equality in Society'. Following his acronymic fashion, that might be construed as 'SAES'—'He who dares, wins.' It is worth considering what its arguments and campaigns would have embraced.

Shelving for the moment the moral and ethical deliberations, one could do worse than to rehearse the civic prospectus of such an organisation. The case for social equilibrium has a long heritage. Jeremy Bentham, arch proponent of self-interest, insisted that within his general concept of the greatest happiness for the greatest number, the two chief 'subsidiary ends of legislation' were 'security' and 'subsistence'. The government that failed to sustain the 'subsistence' of the more indigent members of the community placed at hazard the 'security' of those more plentifully endowed. To allow one's fellows to suffer hardship, deserving or undeserving, was not 'utilitarian'— that is, politically expedient—for it took the risk that the dispossessed might rise in assaults on the very private property Bentham was keen to protect.[1]

On the same tack, it is always worth recalling that the welfare state, far from being a red-blooded socialist device, was the coinage of the Oxford academic Alfred Zimmern in 1934, taken up by the economist Sir George Schuster in 1937 and then popularised by Archbishop William Temple. It was deliberately set against the 'warfare' or power state of Fascist and Soviet totalitarianism, whose advocates mocked the inability of the parliamentary democracies to protect their folk from economic slump.[2] Thus it was more about patriotism, and a solid and settled society with a common bond of fellowship. According to his biographer, Sir William Beveridge thought that the 'universalism' of the post-1945 settlement, with all paying that all might benefit, was 'desirable to foster social solidarity and feelings of identification'.

The disappearing middle

Conversely, a competitive meritocratic society is socially and culturally *un*balanced, arguably to the point at which most or all of its members suffer *dis*benefits to some degree. Crucially, it perceives the people as divided into winners and losers, with recipients of state benefits seen more as social casualties than citizens. The root causes of the ills of society are not difficult to

Published by Blackwell Publishing Ltd, 9600 Garsington Road, Oxford OX4 2DQ, UK and 350 Main Street, Malden, MA 02148, USA

detect but, because 'root' solutions would imperil the liberties that are so much cherished in such a society, there is only mild tinkering by way of remedy, barely consistent even with the Benthamite fail-safe, let alone the more noble concept of Beveridge. Many social problems touching us all are traceable to inequality, in the straightforward connotation of income and resources.

There is much talk in Britain of social exclusion. But there is little talk of the fact that social exclusion is two-edged: there are two groups who do not mix on equal terms with the rest of us. There is now a sizeable minority of very affluent people who are as far removed from the everyday norms as the haplessly impoverished. Over the past twenty or so years, the richest 10 per cent of the population has seen its income grow by a half, so that this fraction claim a quarter of all disposable income.[3] Conversely, the poorest 10 per cent has barely noticed any increase and can lay its hands on only 3 per cent of the whole. This has led to the curiosity of an average annual salary of over £20,000, but with two-thirds of the labour force earning less than that. The libertarian view that wealth 'trickles down' has been shown to be fallacious: wealth stays put and accumulates.

Thus a quarter of British households exist on less than the average income, and much stems from this. Those on good incomes own their own homes; they are able to save and engage in more favourable pension schemes; they tend to live in more salubrious and safer terrains; they may afford more luxurious leisure pursuits and—very significantly—they are able to provide better opportunities for their children. At a time when public services appear to be under pressure, a minority have bought their way out of trouble with commercialised schooling, health care and even security behind the increasing number of be-walled and secluded estates. The private security industry, covering business and domestic properties, involves 8,000 companies, with an annual turnover of £36 billion, employing 240,000 staff, far outnumbering the 160,000 in the police service.

Maybe it matters more now that a higher proportion of people are wealthy. In former days a bulk of the population, comprising the diligent middle classes and the respectable working classes, formed an 'integrated culture' at the core of society. Now, commentators speak of the advent of an 'hourglass society', with large elements of rich and poor, and relatively little in the middle. The gap is a wide one, all too redolent of the dystopian dichotomies of *Nineteen Eighty-Four* and *Brave New World*.

Inheritance of inequality

An important consideration in all this is that although such polarisation tends to be legitimised in terms of individual freedom, the resulting inequalities are transferred between generations. George Bernard Shaw reckoned that it did not matter if the Astronomer Royal and a docker did not wish to communicate, but that their children might wish so to do and social barriers prevented this. Children have always been the weakest link in the freedom chain. The children of the poorer do not compete fairly with the children of the richer groups. In truth, of course, they never did, but because ours was a class and not a caste-ridden society, there were always the social equivalents of blood transfusions to infuse the upper echelon with reviving plasma. Even in medieval times, Thomas Becket and Thomas Wolsey were not out of the top drawer. However, the meritocratic argument was that, by dint of an open education mechanism, this could be made more systematic, so that, at least, the rewards went to the ablest in society, irrespective of social rank.

For years the shibboleth of 'equality of opportunity' has served to justify this position. For all those years it has remained confused with 'uniformity of opportunity'. It is freedom to dine at the Ritz applied to schooling. Since the late 1950s, from soon after what seemed to be the establishment of a reasonably just educational process, evidence has piled ever higher that—to summarise that testimony with a quick fix—home and neighbourhood influences out-gun the school four to one. It is like a game of football between Manchester United and a team with its feet tied together.

Whereas four-fifths of the children of 'professional' parents obtain at least five good GCSE grades and go on to university, only a fifth of the children of 'unskilled manual' parents manage the first and only a seventh the second of those goals. The school is not an instrument of mobility; it is a 'consumer good', part of the reward for being in the right family in the right place at the right time. The school does not change frogs into princes wholesale: it is part of the endorsement process in either case, with precious few altering status in any significant manner.

The interaction of social factors is plain to see. There is health: infant mortality is twice as high in the poorest as opposed to the most affluent areas; on average, professional men live nine years longer than unskilled men, while—so much for the cheery workman and the stressed businessman—semi-skilled and unskilled workers suffer twice as much anxiety and depression as professional employees.[4] Children in the lowest social class are five times more likely to be hit by a car (chiefly because they don't get to ride in cars so often) as the children in the top social class. Recent American research suggests that the professional's child has, by the age of four, had 50 million words addressed to it, compared with 12 million to a 'welfare' child; while the former, by the age of three, will have had 700,000 'encouragements' and 80,000 'discouragements', set against the 60,000 and 160,000 equivalents, respectively, for the 'welfare' child.

Then there is crime, with much of the disorder concentrated on the 4,000 most deprived estates, within which 4 million people are resident. Moreover, health and crime are also interconnected. It has been persuasively said that 'death is now socially constructed', with the virulent 'epidemics' of the day socially derived. For example, alcohol is implicated in 33,000 deaths yearly in England and Wales and, at peak times, eight out of ten hospital casualty admissions are alcohol related; 40 per cent of violent crime and 88 per cent of criminal damage cases are drink related. Much of this, in turn, is class and area linked. One could take other unsavoury threads—drug-addiction, obesity, smoking—and similarly show their overall implications. All in all, the consequent mesh of social ingredients makes for a devil's brew of inequality that fails everyone, but especially the coming generation.

Imbalances between generations

Not that the outgoing generation fare much better—and here the demographic revolution kicks in. Radically improved survival rates, coupled with the phenomenon of retirement, have conspired to create Peter Laslett's 'Third Age', something that came to interest Michael Young very much. Of course, the collapse of work and the automation of the economy had, over time, also affected the 'First Age' of socialisation and the 'Second Age' of work and family raising.

In brief and rough summary, the position has changed thus over the past century and a half:

	Percentage of population in:		
Period	First Age	Second Age	Third Age
Early 1850s	14	84	2
Late 1990s	24	55	21

The notional worker, living seventy years in the conditions of the 1850s, would have worked one in three hours of his life; his equivalent in the 1990s would have worked one in thirteen hours.

This all puts a strange gloss on the meritocratic diktat, which is inexorably associated with the Second Age of work and the status and income it yields. Despite the incredible shrinkage of the Second Age, the increasingly lengthy other phases of the life-span remain governed by the 'merit' awarded during that Age. In other words, the more 'meritorious' people, with professional occupations and high incomes, are able to offer their children, on average, longer remission from and then preferred access to the Second Age. Furthermore, they are also able to enjoy a longer and richer Third Age themselves. We are now in a period when many retirements are as long as the working life; we are close to a time when, for some, retirement will make up half of life.

Thus the insidious tentacles of the meritocracy wrap themselves around older age. By accident or design, one takes up such and such a job at age 16, 18, 21 or thereafter. The die is cast. That event is destined, for good or ill, to determine one's income not only during the Second Age, but also throughout the Third Age. There is no 'equality of opportunity' to participate afresh in that long final spell of life with, it is estimated, a likely 44,000 centenarians in the 2031 census—it was 252 in 1951. As for today, it is claimed that 3 million older people are in rank poverty and 1.5 million are extremely well-to-do. Rather than continuing to fiddle here and there with child poverty and adult poverty and old-age poverty, there needs to be some genuine recognition that poverty is endemic, running, like a glacial geological slab, through society. Poor children often become poor workers and then poor pensioners.

The price of meddling with symptoms rather than dealing with causes is a high one. There are 70,000 people in prison, at a cost of some £30,000 each a year for a system recently described as 'an expensive way of increasing criminal behaviour', whilst the Audit Commission tell us that the chance of a police officer catching a burglar while walking the beat is less than once in every thirty years. Each young offender is kept in custody at an annual cost of £46,000; the average expenditure on the youth service is £59 per head, and it is as low as £19 in some areas. Research suggests that if 25 per cent of the pupils of a comprehensive school are well motivated and from supportive homes, then the peer-group pressure enables the management of a purposeful establishment. But divisive, unmixed housing complexes render that largely impossible. You cannot run a comprehensive system for very long in a selective society. Not for nothing did R. H. Tawney coruscatingly dismiss such a society as being based on a 'tadpole' philosophy, of allowing thousands to perish, socially speaking, that a few might emerge triumphant.[5]

Promoting solidarity

What would Michael Young's 'SAES' have offered as solutions? They might have come in two sorts, the one economic and the other more politically structural.

First, this would not be a strident shriek for strict egalitarianism. There was once an economist who argued that all the money in the country should be collected together and then distributed evenly amongst the populace—and then, when he had spent his share, it should be collected in again . . . No, there should be some recognition of incentives and responsibilities and differentials and enterprise and ambition. But there is no need for it to be open-ended. The campaign must begin with a frank acceptance that the yawning chasm between rich and poor is destructive of social equilibrium, and that this is threatening to everyone.

We have won the right to a (not very high) minimum wage that has steered 2 million workers (8 per cent of the labour force) out of the economic doldrums, without that rocking of the economic boat that was gloomily predicted. Now we should fight for the matching *maximum wage*.

It might be claimed, by way of illustration, that if £165 a week (£7,250 per annum) is regarded as the official minimum for an adult couple, then surely no one requires more than a £100,000 annual salary. One per cent of the workforce currently earn this amount, and recent research by Nick Isles demonstrates—not to mince words—that mega-pay has more to do with greed than competition; for example, there is very little global traffic either way in top executives, for all the hype about market forces pushing up executive salaries. There are, in any event, many oddities. For instance, the Bradford local authority recently advertised for a chief executive whom they were prepared to pay £200,000, although the Prime Minister only earns £179,000. (However, we should recollect the cautionary tale of W. S. Gilbert who, when he complained about his earnings and was told by Richard D'Oyly Carte that he received twice as much as the premier, curtly replied, 'I give more pleasure.')

Another approach, along the lines suggested by David Donnison many years ago, would be to introduce something like a *Ten to One* formula.[6] This would mean that, in any company or concern or on any salary scale, the top wage would never be more than ten times that of the bottom wage. Simply, there is no point in shoring up the lower incomes if the top ones are permitted to race madly away. There would be much else to do to the fabric of our society before it was anything like a socially egalitarian one. But an economic system that enables everyone, in the First, Second and Third Ages, to participate genuinely as fully fledged citizens in a compact and united community is an essential and imperative step.

Second, Michael Young was a Utopian Socialist. Indeed, in the quest for a more anocratic society, based on fraternal-cum-sororal principles, he was, by some criteria, perhaps more successful than his predecessors, such as Charles Fourier, Robert Owen and Saint-Simon. In pursuit of the self-mobilisation of the laity in mutual sharing, he was, of course, the ultimate social entrepreneur, with a long list of self-help organisations—a veritable spaghetti alphabet of acronyms—to his distinguished name. His other foe, besides the meritocracy, was its complement, giantism, the huge anonymous complex of state and commercial apparatus that beat down the ordinary man, woman and child with its blunt instrumentality. Michael Young faced and outwitted those ogres, his character akin to the tinker in all those folklore yarns, all the while seeking to find ways of arming the commonalty against this bulky, brooding enemy.

Possibly his tactical genius lay in the indirect thematic approach, whereby communitarianism was infiltrated at varied points—educational, retail, artistic, health care and so forth—into society. His predecessors had all tended to come a cropper by their attempts to found fully fledged 'harmony' communities that strove vainly to exist in an alien clime. The Rochdale Pioneers, whose venture enjoyed success for an extraordinarily long time compared with most 'utopian' schemes, were perhaps his more natural ancestors.

A pleasing example is the University of the Third Age, founded by Michael Young, Peter Laslett and myself in 1982, and now consisting of some 600 independent small-scale 'U3A's nationwide, with a joint membership of 160,000 and running approximately 14,000 interest groups and other activities. It satisfies three yardsticks. In the first place, it recognises that the older person should be accepted as a participative citizen: an active provider, not a passive recipient of services; the Svengali, not the Trilby, in the social equation; or—a more homely example—the Peter Brough, not the Archie Andrews. In the second place, through its dedication to shared learning circles, it immediately breaks the traditional hierarchy of professional tutor and lay student and evades the conventional competitiveness inherent in much mainstream education. In the third place, from the learning circle, via the local U3A, through its thirty-three regional networks to the central umbrella body, the mutual aid tenets of popular democracy prevail, producing what Kropotkin might have called 'a league of leagues'.[7]

Because the advance of equality and the retreat of meritocracy are dependent on cultural penetration as well as any legislative success, it would behove the Equality Society to practice what Michael Young preached. It should be on the constant watch for opportunities to establish popular, human scale, cooperative antidotes to the disease of inequality—practical expositions of ventures that might be preferred to what Tawney called 'the religion of inequality'. Michael Young always looked for chances to demonstrate in action the thoughts and visions he espoused. It would be wrong to renege on that aspect of his memory.

Ship of State in Peril

PEREGRINE WORSTHORNE

A leadership deficit

WITH the ship of state once again ploughing through turbulent waters, it has become frighteningly obvious that those with their hands on or near the helm are not up to the job; not up to the job, that is, of inspiring public trust and confidence. This, in my experience, is a new feeling. It has little to do with disagreements about policy, although these are profound. But then so were the disagreements over Suez profound, as were the differences over appeasement in 1939. Rather, it has to do this time with a feeling that we are entering an era of great danger, with a leadership deficit across the board. It is not just that one lot of leadership qualities—trustworthiness, truthfulness, courage and loyalty—and one lot of leadership characteristics—jutting jaws, steely blue eyes and stiff upper lips—have been devalued and have gone out of fashion, to be replaced by another lot; rather, it is that these old-fashioned qualities and characteristics have been trashed and *nothing* has been put in their place. Of course, fun used to be made of the old officer class, but even George Orwell was the first to thank God in 1940 for its continuing existence. For all his faults, Colonel Blimp, like Kipling's Tommy Atkins, was always there when the band began to play. Not any more, utterly in the case of Colonel Blimp and increasingly—truth to tell—in the case of the Tommy Atkinses, a significant number of whom are giving up the Queen's shilling for the richer pickings in the private sector.

For me, this realisation struck home last year while watching with dismay the performance of Sir Ian Blair, who had just been appointed Metropolitan Police Commissioner, at a press conference after the first of the July terrorist attacks, days before the tragic shoot-to-kill cock-up. He just did not seem or sound as a police chief should seem or sound: not so much a police chief, concerned to catch criminals, as a Blairite politician concerned to win votes. It was from him that we first heard all that guff about the heroically courageous reaction of the London public. Surely a chief of police worthy of the name ought to understand enough about heroism to know that while the London public fully merited that noblest of tributes after suffering weeks and months of full scale bombing in the wartime Blitz, having it bestowed after only one day's incomparably less widespread and ferocious attack was little short of insulting. We have come to expect soft soap from today's politicians, but it came as a shock to find Britain's chief policeman equally soft-centred.

To a degree, I admit, my rather contemptuous immediate reaction to Sir Ian Blair may be due to my age. What an octogenarian expects of that office is not necessarily what the younger generations expect. Indeed, it could well be that

 Published by Blackwell Publishing Ltd, 9600 Garsington Road, Oxford OX4 2DQ, UK and 350 Main Street, Malden, MA 02148, USA

younger generations, echoing the Prime Minister, expect a police commissioner not only to be tough on crime but also on the causes of crime. But this illustrates my point. For a police chief who sets out to be tough on the causes of crime is almost bound to have taken a university course in sociology—as Sir Ian Blair is proud of having done—and anyone who has taken a course in sociology is almost bound to spout its jargon, than which nothing could be more certain to arouse public suspicion and distrust.

Take, as another example, the infamous Lord Birt, who, very much in living memory, was put in charge of the BBC, Britain's main public service broadcasting organisation, the remit of which is to bring sweetness and light to the masses; to make the good popular and the popular good, as one great Welsh broadcaster put it not so long ago. That being its purpose, John Birt, whose only skills are managerial, was obviously a totally unsuitable man for the job. But, as has become all too clear in recent years, the BBC is no long primarily a public service institution. Prodded by Mrs Thatcher, it has become, like so much else, primarily a market-driven business and, as such, needs to be run not by mandarins but by managers; and if there is one form of jargon more off-putting to the public than the sociological, it is the managerial.

As it happens, Mark Thompson, the present Director-General, does have some of the traditionally human ingredients of leadership, as was beautifully demonstrated when earlier this year he refused to take up his entitlement to a large cash payment, for the very good reason that, as the head of a public service corporation engaged in laying off thousands of staff, it did not seem to him proper to be seen to be feathering his own nest. Just how abnormal, however, that basic leadership duty—a concern for those under your command—has become was horribly illustrated by the fact that all of Mark Thompson's senior colleagues pocketed their prizes as greedily and as insensitively as has become customary of late among the Titans of private industry.

Titans of industry my foot. If only they were. For the legendary nineteenth- and early twentieth-century robber barons of old did indeed command genuine admiration, if not trust. Pioneering the industrial revolution required men of action and courage, who built ships and railways, mined for gold and silver, drilled for oil and created giant new industrial empires—in short, genuine leaders. Nowadays, such types are conspicuous by their absence. In the post-industrial age the new money men are, for the most part, financiers with a gift for figures, for playing the market, for reading a balance sheet—nothing heroic or legendary about them, particularly when caught with their snouts in the trough. Yet, increasingly, these depressingly grey and greedy figures call the shots, not just in business but in almost every walk of life—academia, the professions, the museums, publishing, the media and even the Civil Service. Slowly but surely, their money-making priorities are draining from all these professional activities precisely the quality—that those involved were in it for motives that transcended financial gain—which gave them their authoritative status in the first place. Needless to say, money always came into it marginally, but not centrally, as is the case today, when altruists are made to feel as if they are letting the side down.

A tiny example. For years, family solicitors were able to 'waste' time exchanging family news with clients before getting down to 'business'. Now, I am told, this civilised practice has to be abandoned because the new young money partners insist that every minute 'wasted' should be charged for, lest the profit margins suffer. What I am drawing attention to is the extent to which market forces, while improving professional efficiency, detract from professional trust. The human touch is lacking. Just as police chiefs and BBC chiefs, for the most part, no longer look and sound right, nor do solicitors and doctors, museum directors or heads of Oxbridge houses, or even the ratings-driven editors of the so-called quality newspapers, because all of them now, even the very best, have to give the impression—if they value their jobs—of having their eyes not on the stars but on the bottom line.

Not even the armed forces have altogether escaped similar demeaning influences, although in their case it is technology, rather than market forces, that has done the damage. For the more they come to rely on superior technology, the less crucial becomes the role of human courage and endurance—again the very qualities that historically made the profession of arms so glorious. America's top brass are already suffering from this growing separation of war from the old martial virtues. When those great be-medalled hulks—than whom nothing in human shape could bear less resemblance to that *beau ideal* of chivalry, General Robert E. Lee—appear on television, I can hardly bear to look. Certainly their ability to unleash a wholly new order of advanced and ever more deadly firepower—always on relatively defenceless targets—is truly awesome, but, whereas in the old days it seemed possible to suppose that the great military leaders were the favourite of the Gods, nowadays a horrible suspicion has begun to dawn that their powers may come from below rather than above.

The wrong kind of merit

So, never has there been a time when what it takes to get to the top meritocratically has had so little connection with what it takes to inspire trust and confidence in human beings. This causes particular difficulties for Britain, because we are the only advanced Western country to have waited until the beginning of the twenty-first century before trying to develop a style of meritocracy that is authoritative in its own right, without the support of an aristocratic pedestal, for the very good reason that we already had our own system—with the supreme asset of the weight of history behind it—that was working well: a case, that is, of preferring to hang on to our aristocratic nurse for fear of getting something worse. By 'nurse', I mean our Whiggish aristocratic manner of governing, going back to the glorious revolution of 1688 and accepted over time because of the regular infusions of non-blue blood—of all parties and all classes—which, by successfully immunising us from the diseases of fascism and communism, put Britain in an incomparably better position in the twentieth century than those countries that had abolished aristocracy root and branch.

Of course, if this governing class had been rigid like that of Prussia, or caste-bound, like that of the French *ancien régime*, that would have been another matter. But thanks, as I say, to its Whiggish origins it was addicted to compromise and persuasion and allergic to coercion and extremism, succeeding to almost a miraculous degree in containing—not to be confused with repressing—both reactionary and revolutionary pressure from below. As a result Britain, unlike France, escaped the ding-dong of revolution and counter-revolution. Unquestionably, the preservation of these hierarchical continuities served the interests of the aristocracy, allowing them to retain some of their privileges long after these had been violently abolished elsewhere. But this tolerance of social inequality seemed a bargain price to pay for continuing to enjoy a governing class, uniquely civilised in the uses of power and with a long tradition of public service, that had banked up so much deserved credit in the past.

The firebrand socialist leader, Aneurin Bevan, for example, was thrilled when I told him, in the course of a silver tankard champagne-swilling interview at the Café Royal in the late 1940s, that he reminded me of the great eighteenth-century Whig orator and statesman, Charles James Fox. I believe most of his Old Labour colleagues then and later would have felt the same, since over and above their socialism was a deep understanding of the immeasurably valuable role played by this governing culture in safeguarding the freedom of the nation as a whole. Yes, it had without doubt meant tolerating essentially elitist political and social institutions—the monarchy, the public schools, Oxbridge, fox-hunting, titles and many other remnants of the old class divisions—but since the alternative in Britain meant pulling up by its roots an aristocratic tradition that had become part of our national heritage, this toleration seemed the commonsensical—in a word, Whiggish—thing to do.

Astonishingly, even the turbulent iconoclasm of the 1960s did not altogether change this. After all, Harold Macmillan, that veritable embodiment of the Whiggish tradition—whose government even included, among many other grandees, a Duke of Devonshire—was very much a central part of that decade. Nor should it be forgotten that had not Macmillan decided to impose the fourteenth Earl of Home as his successor to the leadership of the Conservative Party—a step too far—that tradition might have carried on regardless. What did for it eventually was not an excessive love of the upper class but, rather, excessive scrupulousness—wetness—in dealing ruthlessly with the trade union leaders of the working class. That dirty job, of course, was left to that embodiment of bourgeois triumphalism, Margaret Thatcher, who—seizing her opportunity—did not hesitate to use the body politic's mailed fist against Arthur Scargill's miners in a way long familiar in Ireland, but not seen on Britain's mainland in living memory. It worked like a charm, and that was the moment when the English bourgeoisie, who had previously been content to defer to the Whig political tradition, gained the courage 'to drop the pilot', and stand henceforth on their own two feet. Never again was the Whiggish tradition of *de haut en bas* paternalism going to be allowed to interfere with the unfettered freedom of market forces.

Only with the advent of New Labour, however, did the assault on the class system move into high gear, this time because Mr Blair, quite as much as Mrs Thatcher, has a good eye for the main chance. His opportunity came when the defeat of socialism worldwide left the Labour Party with no choice but to make its peace with capitalism. This meant abandoning the goal of *economic* equality and, instead, concentrating all the radical energies on *social* inequality—in other words, the old class system, and all the institutions and virtues that had supported it. And what a well-chosen enemy this has proved to be, bringing on side the Murdoch press and business generally. What a relief for the billionaires to find that the forces of radicalism no longer had them in their sights, unless they also happened to be Dukes, and even Dukes were excused so long as they did not give themselves any superior airs and graces—behave, that is, like gentlemen. Something very strange had taken place. With the collapse of socialism had come a transformation in the way the capitalist world saw the masses. Instead of fearing them as the breeding ground for revolutionaries, capitalists now began to welcome them as the breeding ground for profitable clients and consumers. So people's power was to be welcomed rather than resisted, and the governing order—behind the walls of which the bourgeoisie had previously been happy to shelter—could now be safely demolished, particularly as behind those walls would be found Tory patrician wets no less opposed to bourgeois triumphalism than they had been to socialism.

So between them—Thatcherite democratic capitalism that exalts money power and Blairite anti-elitism that exalts a peculiarly nasty combination of people's power and money power—the living daylights were squeezed out of the old Whiggish governing order. Perhaps this had to happen, but in the crucial matter of evolving a new governing order, the timing could not have been worse. Take France, for example. The French got rid of aristocracy 200 years ago, long before the current variety of anti-elitism had become all the rage. So in her case, as the aristocratic style of leadership sank, the bourgeois style rose. Here, however, in the course of the past 200 years they have slowly but surely merged into one, to the point at which it has become quite impossible in practice to get rid of the one without also getting rid of the other. Not that New Labour cares. For getting rid of both is central to the whole project, which is to consign to the dustbin of history the very concepts of exclusivity and superiority. The idea is that if you eliminate superiority, you will also eliminate inferiority: that is to say, if there are no more 'ins', there will be no more 'outs'; and if there are no more corridors of power, there will be no more corridors of impotence; and, most important of all, if there are no more proud leaders, there will be no more humiliated led. Aristocracy and meritocracy were, of course, always aspirations, not realities. Few nobles were really noble, just as few meritocrats actually have merit, as is well illustrated by the number of time servers and arse lickers who manage to get to the top of most of our corporations. But calling them noble and meritocratic expressed a public hope. Now not calling them such also expresses a hope—that nobility and merit will make themselves scarce, hide away in private places rather than flaunting themselves in public places.

This is plainly bad news indeed for the quintessentially elitist political institution of Parliament, not only for the noble Lords in the House of Lords, but also for the Right Honourable and Honourable gentlemen in the House of Commons, neither group having any place in the New Labour world, any more than do Royal Highnesses, let alone Majesties. Quite simply, anti-elitism makes a nonsense of the House of Commons, which has an essentially elitist function to fulfil. For most of the time, its 600 or so members enjoy the sole right to legitimise and ill-legitimise government. Only occasionally, on election day, do the people get a slice of the action. At other times (if the system is to work properly), the people have to put their trust—a very high degree of trust—in the 600 or so MPs who act on their behalf, which was why MPs were accorded these honorific titles in the first place—on the same principle that leads sensible owners who require a high standard from their dogs to give them a good name.

Here again, we have this baleful New Labour combination of democratic capitalism (Mrs Thatcher's contribution) and populist democracy (Mr Blair's contribution) wreaking havoc; the first by making it so hard for people at the top to develop leadership qualities, and the second by devaluing and therefore discouraging the very idea of leadership itself. (A politically correct public school headmaster told me recently that he had actually banned the use of the word.) If it was only the first, Parliament might stand a chance. For however little room the money men leave for high-flyers of quality to reach the top, national emergencies—such as the current terrorist threat—did seem to find ways for producing the right men for the hour, as happened during the two world wars of the twentieth century, which produced a formidably long list of honourable and gallant MPs—that is, members, largely but not exclusively on the Tory benches, who won their spurs and proved their mettle on the field of battle. Also during the twentieth century there was that other war, the class war, which produced a different lot of warrior heroes— largely, but not exclusively, for the Labour benches. And if in the old days coming from a privileged background—public school and Oxbridge—conferred authority mostly on Conservative MPs, having the guts to overcome the disadvantages of *not* coming from that background did the same for many Labour MPs.

PEREGRINE WORSTHORNE

Erosion of moral authority

In addition, the tradition of paternalistic public service requiring the privileged to go into politics 'to put something back', which was still operating in
those days, ensured the presence in Parliament of at least a few scions of the
great political families, some of whose forebears played important roles in
Shakespeare's Histories—the Percys, the Howards, the Cecils, the
Cavendishes, the Stanleys—and very many more no less historic Knights of
the shires. So at least the benches of the House of Commons, on both sides,
were filled with a respectable sprinkling of non-professional politicians
whose presence could be attributed to something more impressive than an
exceptional gift for telling the voters what they wanted to hear, or an
exceptional gift for writing amusingly about politics in the mostly Conservative public prints, or boringly about politics in think-tank publications, mostly
New Labour, which nobody reads.

The awkward truth, which it is time people faced, is that getting elected by
itself is not enough to confer authority—never was and never will be—since the
skills required have more to do with public relations than statecraft; more with
Max Clifford than Winston Churchill. Both aristocracy and meritocracy solved
this problem, the former rather more reliably than the latter, if only because the
supply of individual merit in the here and now is so much harder to guarantee
than class merit conferred by birth. When, just after being commissioned in the
army in 1943, my school and university friend Colin Welch and I presented
ourselves to his mother, she took one look before exclaiming, 'You two officers?
Heaven help us.' In one sense, she was right: no two more unmilitary figures
can have ever have existed. But in those days that did not matter because we
had the more important quality—class—and although this was not enough to
confer authority by itself, it was at least half the battle. In other words, authority
came much more easily in those days; the presence of pretty well anybody from
the middle or upper class was usually enough to prevent disorderly behaviour
in, say, a railway carriage. No need, for the most part, for ASBOs or policemen.
Of course, individual merit here and now counted, but not so much as did the
collective credit built up by the ruling class in the past. All avocations and
professions benefited from being able to recruit from this perpetually replen-
ished reserve of men and women born with acceptable habits of command, and
in today's democratic culture—where both aristocrats and meritocrats increasingly prefer to make money rather than history—none more so than Parliament. Like it or not, at least in Britain, without the underpinning of both the
aristocratic and meritocratic principles, the democratic principle by itself is not
strong enough to continue to uphold Parliament's central role in our affairs; its
sole right to legitimise or ill-legitimise government on behalf of the people,
rather than letting the people do the job directly for themselves. The pen has
always been mightier than the sword, but—judging by the disrespectful way in
which journalists treat MPs and even ministers today—it is fast becoming
mightier than the ballot box as well.

Until recently, of course, the replacement of parliamentary power by people's power was impracticable. The means did not exist. But they do now. Communications technology has made mass participation relatively easy. So the question today is not whether direct democracy, or people's power, is practicable, but whether it is desirable, and all the indications from the combined forces of democratic capitalism and populist democracy, under the joint command of Tony Blair and Rupert Murdoch, seem to have decided that it is. Indeed, for the very reason that our elitist Parliament was once so trusted by the capitalists—because of its effectiveness at containing envious social forces from below, stirred up by the *Daily Worker*—it is now distrusted because it might show the same skill at containing greedy capitalist forces from below, stirred up by *The Sun*. How much safer—more susceptible, that is, to market pressures—to have a people's Parliament and, by the same token, a people's monarchy, a people's judiciary, a people's media, a people's Oxbridge and even, in due course, a people's police force and a people's armed services. So just as anti-elitism has replaced anti-capitalism for New Labour, so has it replaced anti-socialism for the new capitalists; and this at a time when the people themselves show fewer signs of wanting to participate seriously in public affairs than ever before; at a time when the level of public discourse, as judged by discussions on TV and on the radio, is less serious than ever before; when the public prints cover politics less fully—except as theatre—than ever before; and, above all, when any true understanding of the continuities of British history and the traditions of British statecraft are less taught than ever before. It is true that in some areas—human relations in general and sexual relations in particular—the level of education has indeed risen, but in matters pertaining to any historic understanding of how to keep the British ship of state on a steady course, the level has never been lower, particularly among the intelligentsia.

Gaetano Mosca, in his great classic, *The Ruling Class*, warned 100 years ago that something like this might happen. 'At a certain stage of democratic development,' he wrote, 'a clique will detach itself from the middle classes and, in the rush to win the better post, try to seek leverage in the instincts and appetites of the most populous classes, telling them that political equality will mean almost nothing unless it goes hand in hand with economic equality.' As we know, that socialist moment came all too soon, and, thank Heaven, has passed—without doing much damage. Now, however, another middle-class clique, also in the rush to win the better posts, is seeking leverage in the instincts and appetites of the populous classes, telling them that political equality means almost nothing unless it goes hand in hand with social equality: a twenty-first-century variation on egalitarianism—this one backed by capitalism—even less likely than socialism to produce a better, still a less a re-moralised, social and political order.

Mao Tse-Tung once said that a fish rots from its head downwards. So—and this is what Conservatives should be shouting from the rooftops—does a body politic.

Analytical Value

The Moral Economy of Meritocracy: or, the Unanticipated Triumph of Reform and the Failure of Revolution in the West

IRVING LOUIS HOROWITZ

The argument of the book is that if the soil creates castes, the machine manufactures classes—classes to which people can be assigned by their achievement rather than ascribed by their birth.[1]

The ambivalent radical

IN my own experience, knowledge of the personal history of a scholar rarely explains his or her public contribution. But in the case of Michael Young his biography does help us understand the ambiguities of the theory with which he is most closely identified—the idea of meritocracy. In youth, in the mid-1940s, he authored *Let Us Face the Future*, which helped bring Clement Attlee's reform-oriented Labour Government to power in Britain. In his later years, in the mid-1990s, he was created Lord Dartington, doubtless commemorating his time at Dartington Hall, where he absorbed the Rousseaun credo that all children are born gifted. He was a confirmed non-believer and became involved in the Family Covenant Association to promote a secular form of baptism. He was a dedicated Fabian Socialist and friend to the down-trodden—as made evident in his brilliant ethnography *Family and Kinship in East London*, co-authored with Peter Willmott, who began a School for Social Entrepreneurs. His work made plain that formal education was the founda-tion of the meritocracy, yet he argued the case for students leaving school at any time after their primary learning, to work at tasks defined as socially useful. Little wonder, then, that *The Rise of the Meritocracy* should continue to evoke such contradictory and often critical responses.

In his directions to contributors to this enterprise (appropriately enough, issued on May Day 2005), some three years after the passing of Michael Young in 2002, Geoff Dench notes the ambiguous status of the concept of meritocracy and its author—even at this late date. His directive certainly adds a dash of spice to the ambiguous legacy of Michael Young. It merits direct citation: 'The collection arose because of the change of directorship here [Institute of Community Studies], and a feeling among fellows that it might be a good time to take stock of what was achieved under the old regime. The question which we asked ourselves first was why the Institute under Michael

Published by Blackwell Publishing Ltd, 9600 Garsington Road, Oxford OX4 2DQ, UK and 350 Main Street, Malden, MA 02148, USA 127

never really used meritocracy as a research idea, and from that we moved on to a series of questions (which now form the basis of the collection) concerning the context in which the book was written, how the idea was subsequently used by different groups, and what is there in it of relevance or value, or which could be developed into something valuable, for contemporary Britain.'

In so doing, Dench inevitably draws attention by the contributors to the question: Why should it be the case that the institute never used meritocracy as a research concept? My aim here is to explain the critical undercurrent of Young's legacy—namely, that the very notion of merit as a source of advancement undercuts the idea of revolution as an alternative to capitalism. However one addresses this issue, merit opens up a vast sea change of social change and stratification within the bowels of a free enterprise system, change that in strict socialist terms could not take place, without decimation of the present system as such. It is as if Young is reminding us that the Fabians turned out to be the realists, whilst the Marxians turned out to be the utopians.

The notion of merit is after all a measuring rod at the educational level and a way of life at the ethical level. It is intrinsically conservative in its presumptions as to policy options within existing British society in particular and Western capitalism in general. This view of stratification, set forth by a self-confessed radical and opponent of the establishment, did not go unnoticed—by the critics of the concept. For that matter, Michael Young himself sought, not without desperation, to portray the idea of meritocracy as fanning the flames of revolution—not as a function of oppression and exploitation, but in consequence of unmet expectations and unrelieved pressure for further upward mobility.

So my aim here is to make explicit those elements in the concept of merit that its progenitors prefer to leave implicit; namely, its propensity to create a schism, a rift, within the essential premises of socialism as a revolutionary option to gradualist improvements based on pedagogic advancement. Michael Young repeatedly made his contempt for old-fashioned socialism plain. He saw its soapbox, oratorical flourishes as resting on little more than the quicksand of factory labour and mining militancy. That the work of Young and his associates (to their own amazement, it would appear) caught on as a post-Second World War phenomenon did not elicit the usual happy response from the discoverer of a new idea, but the conflicted reaction of a confirmed radical in search of new ways to maintain a revolutionary posture in a volatile class environment that had outlived its utilitarian or moral outposts.

Michael Young's work is far more complex and sophisticated than its title or its use by others would indicate. His thinking is, at one and the same time, a bundle of estimates, observations and values. In my opinion, there is a core set of premises in *The Rise of the Meritocracy*, and I will focus on these in this statement. There is so much confusion about the notion of meritocracy as

128

such, concerns that Michael Young himself often expressed in his new introduction to his classic text, that before addressing the accuracies or inaccuracies of his forecasts, it might serve a useful purpose to state simply and clearly what the text is actually about.

Before doing that, let me say that the book is written with a light-hearted sense of humour. Even though at times it borders on the cynical, it is worthy of emulation by other social scientists. The text is anything but sombre. Young understands human foibles and frailties, and foolishness, and his book gives expression to all of these. He knows full well that education is not the same as intelligence and intelligence is not the same as creativity. Far more than the huge number of commentaries on the subject that followed, Young's book awakens us to the potential for charm and wit in looking at the human condition.

Michael Young's thesis

Young asserts, first, that the modern educational system brought about a huge shift from traditional forms of estimating merit, social class background being foremost, to an approach to employment based on schooling.

Second, he notes this shift did not represent a shift from ignorance to intelligence in the workplace or in the creative processes, but it did sort out those with educational backgrounds from those with raw physical skills.

Third, the explosion of educational facilities, aided and abetted by world wars and social demands, put an end to traditional forms of seniority as a mechanism of judgement of worth. This was replaced by educational attainment.

Fourth, the rise of this 'meritocracy' is not the same as an outburst in creative growth. Indeed, Young endlessly and pitilessly inveighs against the 'stupid', and the difficulties of mass education reform, in helping it distinguish intelligence from ignorance.

Fifth, Tories and socialists alike had been caught flat-footed by this shift from seniority to education in establishing the ground rules of a new workforce, and to a society based on egalitarian modes of thought.

Sixth, advancement through education—often simply identified as merit with misgivings by Young—knocks the props out from under both the pretences of the aristocratic elements (and their doctrines of deserved privilege) and those of the socialistic elements (and their own utterly confusing doctrines of hard labour as somehow superior to modernity as such).

Seventh, although traditional class systems and alignment are dead, little more than eccentrics at the top and rabble at the bottom, protest does not necessarily cease. Expectations rise exponentially among the educated classes, which now constitutes a majority. With this come new sources of unrest and social change.

These are Young's concepts, put forth with a minimum of embellishment or apologetics. Sociological examination's role with respect to the theory of meritocracy is to fix a place in the intellectual heavens for this concept in a new century—and away from the battles fought so long and gallantly by its inventor.

Arguably the most serious problem with the concept of meritocracy is its failure to distinguish merit from education or, for that matter, from cultural production as such. What was actually being advanced is little more than the outcome of Weber's notion of the bureaucratic–administrative apparatus— one that requires educated people rather than intelligent people, rule-makers rather than rule-breakers. Intellectual achievement is quite different from administrative achievement. That both of these often reside in a place called the university only blurs these essential differences. But it also creates serious crimp in the argument that the latter half of the twentieth century is somehow defined primarily (if not exclusively) by merit.

A parallel, and one might argue no less serious, concern is the increase rather than decrease in inequality in the advanced nations. While Young was careful to distinguish merit from equity, it is certainly the case that he did not envisage a situation in which (as in the United States), in the years between 1979 and 2000, real income of households in the lowest fifth, or the bottom 20 per cent of earners, grew by 6.4 per cent, while that of households in the top fifth grew by 70 per cent. Indeed, the family income of the top 1 per cent grew by 184 per cent. In 1979, the average income of the top 1 per cent was 133 times that of the bottom 20 per cent; by 2000, that income of the top 1 per cent had risen to 189 times that of the bottom fifth. But the significant issue for meritocracy is that this new rise in income inequality comes with a commensurate decline in mobility. What *The Economist*, in a review of 'Meritocracy in America', recently called 'social sclerosis'[2] is not only a decline in social mobility, but also the tenacity of elite controls in education and politics, or the very areas in which merit would seem to trump status.

There is little in Michael Young's work that allows us to understand how merit as such translates into the new class of administrators, bureaucrats, functionaries and even civil servants. In such societies, merit simply reflects the demands of the state, which becomes far more important than civil society. For that matter, the state and its needs become central to the economic performance of the workplace as such. In this scenario, meritocracy is a force that allows for change in the social composition of classes—away from industrial performance in the means of production: to cultural performance in the means of communication. Again, Young has nothing to say about the technological dimension of the very forces to which he draws our attention. This weakness was never overcome in Young's own writings, although a number of his followers and successors have made an effort to bridge this gap between economy and technology.

Since the concept of meritocracy is most often invoked in advanced industrial and presumptively democratic societies, a question arises as to the relation of advancement to merit, but also to such issues as justice and equity. A certain overlay of cynicism pervades the work of Young and his followers, so that the cultural or ideological formations of Western civilisation are not only blotted out, but also essentially denied. Given the existence of inequalities, favouritisms and the like, the idea that merit as such, or the educational system alone, can determine the course of stratification has a certain naive ring. Indeed, one might well argue that the educational ladder itself is not immune to status and hierarchy. One misses such nuance in the theory of advancement through merit.

A further serious deficiency in the ethical grounds of meritocracy is its virtual absence of discourse on what areas of 'merit' are most (or least) rewarded. To speak of advancement through merit does not do justice to vast differences in status, reward and power that accrue to people depending on their areas of expertise as in engineering or computer science *vis-à-vis* sociology or English literature. This is not a matter of what is intrinsically a better or more worthy field but, rather, what areas of the meritocracy receive stronger reinforcements and, for that matter, encouragement for the economic order or the political system. While the rise of the meritocracy is across the board, the rewards of this model in the social system do not necessarily follow suit. In short, stratification within fields of education, no less than the separation of those with education from those without education, becomes a touchstone and the measurement of the concept's practical utility. And this has still not taken place.

Young and his associates did take account of the revolt against merit through education at the end of his life. Yet the extent to which a 'hard core' (perhaps still a majority) still view education as pragmatic and task oriented at best, rather than as a stepping stone to broad economic and status advancement, plays much too small a part in the notion of meritocracy. Questions of value become central once again: the positive value of being plain spoken, rooted in hand-oriented (rather than head-oriented) tasks, and a concern, often inarticulate but plainly visible, that the asking price of entrance into the meritocracy may be too high in terms of matters of familial solidarity, marriage and love—in short, personal lifestyle as such. These notions are implicit in Young's personal scale of values, but less so in his intellectual definition of meritocracy.

Meritocracy as aspiration

A good deal of the debate over meritocracy derives less from issues of truth and error than from the built-in ambiguity of using merit as an explanation for both the evolution *and* the malaise of Western industrial societies. That said, the term does not easily go away. Merit summarises a good deal of the shift in society from struggles over the means of production to those of the means of education and communication. And in this subtle shift, meritocracy has spent a half-century in the shadows only to emerge as a core concept— perhaps less as an explanation of where we have been as much as a policy in the direction as to where we want the social order to go.

When we complete the process of addition and substitution for the notion of meritocracy, it becomes evident that it represents less an empirical description of advanced society than a policy prescription for those societies. In short, granting the weaknesses in meritocracy as history (it is more like a half-theory than a full-blown explanation of twentieth-century stratification), one is left with a choice of policies. The essential policy premise of meritocracy is individual choice and bottom-up decision-making in everything from career opportunity to lifestyle. The opponents of merit as the essential criterion must argue for some variation of liberal society as distributive justice; or, better yet, a top-down reorganisation of society that creates a levelling tendency, a *pari mutuel* machine whereby all horses at least start the race at the same starting gate and with the same weight, even if they may yet finish at different posts depending on personal qualities and aptitudes.

In this sense, as I noted at the outset, what Young and his associates presented to British and, indeed, other Western societies is the running sore within liberalism as an ideology and social democracy—as a third-stream way of life in places extending from Britain to Sweden. For neo-liberalism promises both freedom from statist tyranny and, at the same time, social regulation of the economy with the direct participation of the state. A sound current illustration of this is Stein Ringen's review essay entitled 'Poverty's history'.[3] 'If there is a small corner of the world in which poverty has been eradicated it is Scandinavia,' he writes. 'The lesson there is that development is necessary but that so also are forceful social policies for redistribution.' In this, Young—at first inadvertently but nonetheless emphatically—comes to certain conclusions that dismay his fellow liberals, who see the welfare state as a great invention in the world of action.

There is a flinty side to Young that proved irritating to his friends and foes alike. He argues that meritocracy is a fact of post-modern and post-welfare society—not a happy fact, not a free trip to paradise served up by the state, but a fact hard to ignore. It is possible that those expectancies will outrun realities, and that the rising tide of advancement through educational achievement will prove its own downfall. But for the moment at least, the alternatives—the notion of heavily managed policies emanating from the state apparatus—simply do not work, and indeed breed tremendous resentment. This is so to the point that even promulgators of the past, such as the Labour Party, have been compelled to abandon such heavy-handed thinking because it thwarts innovation and frustrates individual decisions. This appreciation and acknowledgement of the empirical situation is what elevated Young and his associates at the Institute of Community Studies from the dogmatisms of party ideologists and the interests of bourgeoisie trade unionists.

It is intriguing to note that what Young accepted with reluctance, Daniel Bell asserts with a certain pleasure.[4] Meritocracy is a fair, perhaps only, way open at the moment to produce a productive and a cultivated society. The institutions of the university, commerce and government each benefit from a system in which the most competent rise, and expand political leadership and economic productivity based on universalistic premises that, while imperfect and often biased, at least move beyond traditions vested in hoary antiquity or downright ruthless authority. As with the military, the merit system affords prospects for introducing equities of class, race and gender, unknown in the past. Further, these bootstrap efforts do not require a levelling off at the top or an incursion by the political system on the rights of individuals to move ahead.

It might well be correct that the claims about meritocracy and, even more, ambitions for it in the policy realm, are less than perfect, and filled with certain self-contradictory elements as well as the aforementioned partial sort of theorising that was characteristic of Young. But the alternatives appear far more mired in self-contradiction and, worse, carry the stigma of authoritarianism as a backdrop for the imposition of liberalism as an ideology and egalitarianism as a means of re-creating the myth of the classless society. And after a century that witnessed fascism, nazism, communism, and associated themes and variations in between, one has every right to claim that the merit system, however reluctantly put forth at one end, and however repelled at the other, is the best chance we have for a twenty-first century in which the sporting ideal that the best and the brightest trump what Young fiercely called the stupid and the coarse emerges victorious and democratic.

Japan at the Meritocracy Frontier: From Here, Where?

TAKEHIKO KARIYA and RONALD DORE

The background to Japanese meritocracy

LET us define a thorough-going meritocracy by means of two characteristics that Michael Young had chiefly in mind when he characterised the popular definition of merit in his dystopia as IQ plus effort. They are, first, the allocation of power, prestige and wealth in society largely on the basis of the educational credentials with which one enters the labour market and, second, a high degree of formal equality of the opportunity to acquire those credentials.

By that definition, Japan can well claim, still, to be the most thoroughly meritocratic of all the countries in the OECD, with the possible exception of Korea. It is also a country in which meritocracy as ideology in its full-blooded devil-take-the-hindmost form is gaining greater strength with the entrenchment of neo-liberal market individualism in government and private industry, and where—with the publication of books with titles such as *Inequality Signed and Sealed*—the awareness of the disastrously polarising consequences that Michael Young predicted are increasingly a matter of open concern.

Fertile soil

How Japan came to be at the meritocracy frontier is best explained by a comparison of Japan and Britain over the past 150 years. Britain experienced a slow growth of primary education, reaching more or less universal coverage by the beginning of the twentieth century. This was only partly thanks to the state. The weak role of the state reflected the ambiguous attitudes of the dominant classes, never quite sure whether mass literacy would create more dangerous disaffection than patriotic loyalty. Japan got to universal coverage at about the same time, but almost wholly thanks to the state and after much more rapid growth. It began to build a public system of primary education only after the Meiji Restoration of 1868, starting with the advantage of what was perhaps already something like 50 per cent male literacy, thanks to large numbers of private entrepreneurial and secular elementary schools, which were rapidly superseded by, or swallowed up in, the new public system. That school system was part of a wholesale remaking of the social and economic, as well as political, structure of society on a scale never experienced in Britain—a remaking in the name of a patriotic effort to 'import civilisation' (the word

 Published by Blackwell Publishing Ltd, 9600 Garsington Road, Oxford OX4 2DQ, UK and 350 Main Street, Malden, MA 02148, USA

'modernisation' had not then been invented) in order to make Japan capable of fending off the predatory colonisers of Europe.

The creation of a universal state education system was a part of that nationalist drive. There are, to simplify wildly, two notions of why the state should create schools: first, as part of its service to its citizens, giving them the opportunities for personal development; or, second, as a means of training its citizens to serve the state—to make the nation strong and successful in competition (military, economic and diplomatic) with other nations. In Britain, educational policy rhetoric has been predominantly the former, and in nineteenth-century Japan the latter, with fluctuations in both countries, as shown below.

That was one of five reasons why, when the first new secondary schools, teacher training schools, officer academies, colleges for the merchant marine and the arts and universities for the arts and sciences were created in late-nineteenth-century Japan, admission—in contrast to the situation in Britain—was strictly on the basis of academic achievement tests, plus the ability to pay fees. There was, that is to say, no disposition to waste the considerable expense the state incurred on any but the best available talent. The second reason was that the fee requirement, especially for the most prestigious schools, was set at relatively modest levels to allow the best talent to come forward. Hence, the level of popular aspiration for secondary and higher education was so high that objective achievement tests seemed like the only fair means of rationing. And third, Japan was still very much a particularistic and hierarchical society; personal obligations weighed heavily, especially obligations towards social superiors. The only way in which secondary school and university teachers could protect themselves from intolerable lobbying on behalf of their children from friends, acquaintances and patrons was by hiding behind rigid admission rules.

The fourth reason was that, in contrast to the continuity of dominant upper-class culture in Britain—which has made the transformation of the Oxbridge colleges into intellectual powerhouses such a gradual process that even today they retain some of the characteristics of their original role as finishing schools for the gentry—Japan's new secondary schools and universities were created *de novo* on the Western (after the 1880s, predominantly German) model. They purveyed the new brand of Western culture, not the culture of the old Japanese ruling class. That culture was by no means an unsophisticated one.

The core of it was the Confucian Chinese classical tradition—in a way, remarkably similar to the tradition of Greek and Roman classics in British nineteenth-century grammar schools—taught in the schools of that 5 per cent of the population who made up the *samurai* class. But the rejection of that culture in favour of the new knowledge coming from the West meant that, in the meritocratic competition for entry into the new prestige schools and universities, the comparative advantage of the children of that old upper class consisted only in the general 'training of the mind' that that old culture provided, not in possession of the specific intellectual content, aesthetic sensibilities or moral attitudes imparted by that training. Moreover, the entrance tests, being exclusively written examinations, not interviews, gave no opportunity for upper-class airs and graces and any sense of self-confidence to count—except in so far as they shaped habits of diligent study (which is not likely to have been very far, diligence not being anywhere a common ruling class virtue).

The last factor was that very cultural tradition. Japan's intellectual culture was 80 per cent Chinese. The Japanese knew all about the Chinese meritocratic mandarin system. Indeed, a basic question in the political science taught to advanced students in the fief schools was: What were the relative advantages of a feudal system that encouraged feudal lords to look after their fiefs for the long term, and a centralised meritocratic imperial system that avoided having dunderheads in power? And in China, as they knew, objective and fair judgement was so important that the candidates' examination papers were all transcribed before the examiners saw them, to avoid any suspicion of favouritism.

Dominant features

Two other features distinguished the system that had developed by the early decades of the twentieth century from that of Britain. The first was the hierarchy of institutions in the public system, which developed at each level. Tokyo Imperial University was the first modern university, built in 1886 on earlier more makeshift foundations. Those who passed its entrance examinations were considered the true elite. When the second university was created in Kyoto over a decade later, the general assumption was that only a few people with particular reasons for being in Kyoto would choose to go there if they were capable of getting into Tokyo University. Hence, the second university was assumed to be the university for the second-best, and so on down the line as, altogether, nine Imperial Universities (including two in the colonies of Korea and Taiwan) were created by 1940.

The same happened to the senior high schools, the 'order of foundation' ranking continuing, by and large, to coincide with the ranking in terms of the proportion of graduates who entered the top university. A similar hierarchy developed among junior high schools, but at this level the order of foundation was less important than the destination of their graduates. The more who were known to get into the elite senior high schools, the harder it was to score high enough in the entrance exams to gain a place.

There were also private colleges—the best of them allowed to assume the title of 'university' after 1918. They did not charge higher fees than the state universities but they were of lower prestige, and the option for students of lesser ability. The state universities produced the elite: civil servants, including those who went on to become statesmen, judges, professors, hospital consultants, engineers and managers of the established conglomerates. The private universities, together with a steadily growing number of state higher technical colleges, produced the lesser elite: businessmen, politicians, journalists and local government officials.

The other distinguishing feature was that, in Japan's 'new economy'—in 1900, say, the one-fifth of the population not engaged in family-based peasant agriculture, artisan production and commerce—educational credentials became the passport to career success in a much more definitive way than in Britain. One reason was that underlying the 'national utilitarianism' of the new economy, the old *samurai* values, which rated governing and fighting as much more prestigious occupations than producing and trading, still informed the ambitions of the young. The 'aristocracy' that had produced these values was now genuinely open to the talents. If you climbed the educational ladder to its peak—the law department of Tokyo University— you were (until meritocratic egalitarianism forbade it at the beginning of the twentieth century) automatically entitled to a job as civil servant in a prestige ministry. And precisely because that educational competition served as an elaborate IQ test, the large merchant houses were happy to recruit their managers from those who didn't quite make it on the road to that most glittering prize.

Two surveys in the 1950s document the consequences. In Japan, 70 per cent of managers had been to a university, or a specialist high school that by that time had acquired university status. In Britain, the proportion was 21 per cent, and among a sample of 200 top firms, 24 per cent.[1]

The infrastructure of meritocracy

These two features, 'credentialism' in the labour market and the hierarchical ranking of educational institutions, remain determining characteristics of Japan's educational system at the beginning of the twenty-first century, just as at the beginning of the twentieth century. Equally persistent are certain concomitant aspects:

- There is a clear link between the above two features: the levels of academic achievement of a university's entering classes are the measure that determines and sustains the hierarchical ranking of educational institutions. (As it has become in Britain. How many vice-chancellors have on their wall the UCAS chart showing A-level points scores of entrants to each university?) The validity of the ranking was reinforced in the first instance in the 1960s by the mock university examinations of the cram school chains, and then, after 1979, by a national common university entrance examination—a kind of ministry-run SAT. The result is that the ranking of the university from which one graduates has proved—or at least is generally thought to have proved—a sufficiently good proxy measure for IQ, and IQ is thought to have proved a sufficiently good proxy measure of future 'general ability' as engineer, manager, salesman or civil servant for the credential that matters most to be that ranking, rather than any record of performance in that university.

- Of great importance, also, was the development of the practice of lifetime-career recruiting. At first, it was largely confined, as in other countries, to public administration, but by the beginning of the twentieth century it was already spreading to the managerial ranks of the larger corporate sector—the big *zaibatsu* enterprises. The significance of this for meritocracy is, of course, that initial recruitment on entry to the labour market, when the only 'track record' is an educational record, determines ultimate occupational and social status.

- There is a flourishing industry of cram schools: (a) extracurricular, to improve children's performance; and (b) full-time, for those who take a year, or even two or three, at the crucial transition stages in order to get into an institution of higher rank.

- There is a heavy emphasis in the prevailing educational ideology on the effort part of the expanded 'IQ + effort + luck' recipe for success. Of the two automatically assumed reasons for lack of success—lack of effort, and lack of socio-economically structured opportunity—in contrast to Britain, the former is invoked more often than the latter, both in popular, political and educational–professional discussions. Effort is, of course, the most obviously variable ingredient. As for the IQ part, pills have never been quite so important in Japan as they currently seem to be in China, though the importance of diet is widely acknowledged and fills the women's magazines at examination time. As for the luck part of the equation, praying at shrines is about all one can do.

- The consequent, hard-driving, emphasis on memorisation, 'bucket theory of knowledge' style of school teaching, and criticism of its 'deplorably uneducational' consequences in killing curiosity and intellectual independence, have been consistently at the centre of educational debate. The new foundations in the 1920s of private schools for the moneyed professional middle class were inspired by Montessori, Bertrand Russell and A. S. Neill, but were also a reaction against the uninspired grind of the state system. (Especially on the part of parents of children who did not seem bright enough to have much chance of shining in the state competition. It also conferred on them a useful credential. The modern equivalent, especially for politicians, is to send their sons and daughters to American universities. Their American education helps in elections when they succeed their parents in the last remaining inherited occupation, and is one factor cementing Japan's position as America's satellite ally.) In the last three decades of the twentieth century, as shown below, the attack on unidimensional selection has centred on persuading high schools and universities to find alternative criteria for admission that allow for the acknowledgement of excellence in talents other than the ability to solve complex maths problems or remember arcane details of historical events.

138

The unfolding of the system in the twentieth century

From the beginning of the century to the point, in 1973, at which 90 per cent of each age group remained in school until age 18, there was a steady expansion of the catchment area for top elites—of the proportion of the population who consider their children to be candidates for the level of educational attainment (not just university, but the right university) that could claim the top jobs. This expansion was accelerated by the revamping of the system under American direction post-1945, which ended the grammar/elementary sort of two-tracking at the age of twelve, and continued compulsory, unselected and unstreamed junior secondary education to the age of 15, followed by non-compulsory high school.

Streaming within schools was generally branded as 'discriminatory education', but this did not prevent the development of clear streaming among schools within the state system beyond the age of 15. The academic high schools that led to the university (only a small proportion of these high schools were private in the 1950s and 1960s) selected by ability, and each area soon had its number one school, its number two school and so on down the line. At first, the limited nature of aspirations meant a good response to opportunities for vocational education; 40 per cent of high school pupils were in schools that gave them no chance of becoming a high court judge or an engineer, but did allow them to do better than dad, perhaps by becoming a court clerk or a lab technician.

So how can we assesses the current position? To do that, let us imagine a meritocracy score that, in principle, might actually be calculated. A 100 per cent score would go to a social system in which (a) educational credential attainment is determined only by IQ + effort and (b) career success is determined only by educational credentials. A zero score would go to a society in which either career success had absolutely nothing to do with educational credentials, or in which educational credentials had nothing to do with IQ + effort.

Acquiring educational credentials

Doing well at school

First, let us look at the first part of the equation: getting educational credentials. The meritocracy score was clearly increasing in the postwar period. Of the three variables whose interaction determines that score—opportunity (availability of schools and parental financial support), aspiration and ability—opportunity was increasingly equalised as the rise in incomes made it possible for more and more families to afford to send children to high school and university.

At the same time aspirations were also increasingly equalised, partly by the same increasing affluence and partly by the homogenisation of values brought, not only by radio and TV, but also by changes in educational organisation—the bringing together of parents in strong PTA organisations and the increased spread of aspirations by infection. That same equalisation of aspirations was an indicator of the increasing homogenisation of home cultural environments, of the sort of home reinforcement of schooling that produces maximum results from school education. That equalisation of opportunity and aspiration meant that the third element in the triad, ability—IQ, plus the propensity to put forth the effort to do well in school—was increasingly the major determinant of high educational attainment.

We have measures that show these effects. An extensive sequence of studies of social mobility in Japan allows us to compare patterns of social and educational mobility before and after the war. For the cohort that reached the age of 15 between 1925 and 1940, there is a stronger effect of family background in explaining high school than university education, but the correlation between university attendance and family income is much higher than for later cohorts.[2] For three later cohorts—the one reaching age 15 between 1940 and 1959, the one reaching that age between 1960 and 1974, and the one reaching it between 1975 and 1989—we can trace the extent to which a child's parental status, as measured by the father's and mother's years of education and the father's position in the occupational prestige scale, correlates with his or her getting a degree, from any university. For the youngest cohort, the correlation is much lower than for the earlier ones, and for boys it decreases steadily through all three cohorts.

For girls, for whom higher education was seen less as a road to occupational success than as a means of achieving the middle- and upper-class airs and graces required for marriage to the occupationally successful, the shift was in the opposite direction, though college attendance was so rare for the older cohorts that it is hard to attach any great meaning to this result. For girls, college attendance was originally less related to academic ability. (But not wholly unconnected. In the rural Japan of the 1960s, a girl's high school diploma would top the display of her trousseau at her wedding.) However, the correlation between junior high school grades and the likelihood of attending university was steadily increasing for the younger cohorts.[3]

At any rate, the chance of poor but bright boys and girls, but boys especially, wanting to go, being urged to go, being allowed to go, actually going, to a university, had greatly increased between the prewar and the postwar period.

Getting into higher education was still a function of many factors, but as the level of teenage academic achievement became increasingly important among those factors, so also did the earlier effects of family background on the growing child—the effect it had on a child's ability to profit from elementary and secondary education. For the three cohorts, we also have an indicator (retrospectively self-reported) of their level of achievement at the end of junior secondary school (at age 15), and of the extent to which it is affected by his or her socio-economic background (using the same combination of

140

measures—father's and mother's educational level and socio-economic class as measured by occupation). The correlations between reported attainment scores and background characteristics differ for men and women. For women, there is little change over the forty years. For men, however, the background characteristics clearly account for less—and presumably, therefore, 'IQ + effort' accounts for more—of the variance as one moves to the younger from the older groups.[4]

At the same time, there was a vast expansion of universities after the war, which had two notable effects. First, it made the hierarchical character of universities more apparent because the tail of low-prestige, low-intellectual-quality universities contrasted so sharply with those that produced the nation's elite. Second, they produced such large numbers of graduates that formerly largely uncredentialled white-collar occupations—local government, post office and so on—became university-credential-access occupations, and this in turn served to change aspirations. We characterised the vocational schools that 40 per cent of high school children attended in 1955 as schools that did not prepare you for being a high court judge or an engineer, but could promise a future as a court clerk or a lab technician. By 1970, even the aspiration to be a court clerk or a lab technician was beginning to mean having to go to a university. And as the proportion of the age group getting a university education expanded from the 5 per cent at mid-century to nearly 45 per cent by 1980, aiming for university came to be more and more the normal thing to do. Consequently, the demand for 'dead-end' vocational education dropped. By 1985, the vocational schools were taking not 40 per cent but 28 per cent of high school students; they were generally considered as the home for children who could not succeed in getting entry to a decent academic school, and were constantly diluting and re-diluting the vocational content of their education in order to offer their pupils the fig-leaf of a possibility that they could get back on the university track.

Thus the educational system became more and more a unified pyramid, through which children progressed according to the single criterion of academic test scores. Let us define the 'race for the top' or 'the race to enter the meritocratic elite' as competition for the chance of entering the 5 per cent of the population at the peak of the income, power and prestige hierarchies. The proportion of children whose parents had reason to think of them as realistically taking part in that race (realistically in the sense both of being able to afford it and of considering their children to be bright enough) increased greatly in the forty years after the war. There are a number of studies of parents' aspirations for their children, but changes over time are difficult to pin down because of differences in the wording of questions: however, the story seems to be as follows. For boys, the proportion of parents hoping to get their son into a university was already around 60 per cent by the 1960s and has remained at that level. For girls, however, there is clear evidence of more recent change; the proportion aiming for university was only half that for boys in the 1960s, and gradually crept up to parity by 1990.[5]

TAKEHIKO KARIYA AND RONALD DORE

The demands of the labour market

The postwar period was turbulent in two senses. First, there was a great deal of entrepreneurial activity, which saw the disappearance of established firms and the birth of new ones such as Honda and Sony: a good deal of shuffling of the managerial cards. Second, there was a militant labour movement, which only slowly settled down into a pattern of enterprise unions embedded in firms as a sort of constitutional opposition. That period of turbulence had pretty much ended by 1960. Thereafter, the identity and scale rankings of the major corporations changed only slowly, and the spread of the lifetime employment guarantee (made possible by the high rate of growth and made necessary as a means of taming trade union militancy) led to an enormous extension of the power of the educational credential. It was not just that getting to the right university became a dominant determinant of whether one could become a manager of a high-prestige Mitsui firm or only of a small struggling provincial firm. The recruitment networks of the major corporations incorporated schoolteachers (in junior high schools until the early 1960s, senior high schools thereafter), so that whether one got a well-paid, secure lifetime job on the shop floor of a high-prestige large firm or a less well-paid less secure job in a small firm depended very much on one's school record.

There was another aspect to the settling down of labour relations in the late 1950s. Egalitarians can be crudely divided into communal egalitarians who are concerned about differences in outcomes—in income and power—and meritocratic egalitarians who are interested primarily in equality of opportunity to compete for outcomes that may be vastly unequal. Communal egalitarian sentiments were strong in the Japan of the 1960s, and served to mitigate income disparities between managers and public officials on the one hand and lower-paid workers on the other. Still, CEO salaries are between fifteen and twenty times the average pay in the firm. The prizes for which the meritocrats compete are not so glittering as in many other countries. Income and wealth distributions are not as skewed as power and prestige distributions.

The wartime wiping out of concentrations of wealth, plus the postwar wealth tax and inheritance taxes justified by the exigencies of reconstruction, also helped to create a more equal society with a more egalitarian ethos. Inheritance taxes continue to be quite heavy by international standards and still limit the extent of hereditary transmission of economic advantage. Increasingly, though, as private wealth has accumulated in spite of the inheritance tax barriers, the inequality of its distribution is becoming an important political factor. The drive over the past fifteen years to transform the Japanese employee-dominated corporation into a shareholder-dominated corporation is led by a political and intellectual elite who have a strong personal interest in the returns to capital. The primary interest of that same elite as it approaches educational issues is in making sure that Japan

142

continues to benefit from the inestimable advantage of being run by people like themselves, and of making it possible for their own children to follow in their footsteps.

Social mobility slowing down

There are clear signs, recently, that social mobility rates are declining, and hereditary transmission of class status is increasing. Japan is now seeing the operation of all those complex factors that in Britain have produced the result that, for all the covert affirmative action that socially conscious college admissions committees can somehow reconcile with meritocratic principles, Oxbridge still can't get more than half of their pupils from state schools.

One major factor in this is the steady growth of private secondary education. The most well-documented and analysed of what are still the routes into the narrow top elite is the entering cohort of students at Tokyo University. Over the past two decades, one can clearly trace the effects of what has become the new twelve-plus—an uncovenanted, unintended, private-sector twelve-plus. Ninety per cent or so of the age group still get to the third year of high school at age 18. Of these, 70 per cent are still educated in the state system—unstreamed secondary schools until the age of 15 (though there has been a considerable increase in broad band 'setting' for mathematics in both elementary and junior high schools) and then selective upper secondary schools. In the remoter agricultural areas, the top public secondary school still has considerable prestige and has little competition from private schools for the brightest pupils. For eleven of the most rural of the forty-five prefectures, all those who were admitted to Tokyo University came from such schools, though they made up only 4 per cent of the total admitted.

In the metropolitan areas, however, almost any family that can afford it tries to send its children to one of the all-through schools—junior and senior secondary combined—which select their pupils at the age of twelve by stiff entrance examinations. These are of two kinds: the attached experimental schools of the education departments of national universities, and private schools. The former, with some 3,000 pupils, take 0.02 per cent of the age group; the proportion going to the latter is difficult to calculate, but the proportion going to all private high schools from age 16 to age 18 is nearly 30 per cent. Not all these private secondary schools, not even all those that recruit chiefly at age 12 rather than age 15, are renowned for success in academic examinations. There are some, particularly for girls, that ensure a good ladylike atmosphere and cultivate the feminine arts of flower arrangement and so on, and some that help not so bright children, who might be lost in a public school, to achieve a reasonable competence. Nevertheless, overall, the 30 per cent of the age group who go to these private schools have nearly four times the chance of getting into Tokyo University compared with the 70 per cent from the public system.

However, if you go to one of the national experimental schools, you have 1,000 times the chance of a public school pupil. And if you go to one of the top ten private schools (top, as measured by the number of entrants to Tokyo University), you have 2,000 times the chance. The national experimental schools have the advantage over the top private schools of lower fees: their pupils' 'chance ratio' would be better than 1,000 were it not for the fact that Tokyo University's attached school has refused to select by ability. (The excuse of the other attached schools—rarely challenged—for spending extra taxpayers' money on the *crème de la crème* is that experimental schools' experiments don't always work, and bright children are less likely to be damaged when they go wrong than the not so bright.)

Those 1,000 times or 2,000 times odds are reasonably well known, if not with any numerical precision, and families whose children are in the race for the top (the fees are modest by British standards, but still quite stiff—ranging from the equivalent of one month's to two months' income for the average family) expend enormous efforts on their eight, nine and ten year olds—after-school and weekend cram schools, private tutors—to prepare them for the highly selective entrance examinations of those national experimental and top private schools. Entrance to these privileged schools not surprisingly correlates well with class, though, as one might expect from the fact that private schools take 30 per cent rather than 8 per cent of the age group, not quite so much as British public schools. One study of students at a selection of high schools—some in Tokyo, some in rural districts—looked at the occupations of pupils' parents. In the private high schools with a good reputation as university preparatory schools, 76 per cent had professional and managerial and 6 per cent had manual worker parents. At schools in the bottom-most of five grades (vocational schools with almost zero admission barriers), the proportions were 35 per cent and 22 per cent, respectively.[6]

One of the odd ironies of the Japan meritocracy story is that the growth of elite private secondary education was enormously accelerated by reform efforts in the Tokyo heart of the system—drastic changes in the examination competition for public high school entrance that were in fact designed to liberate the junior secondary schools from the incubus of examination cramming and promote genuine education for all abilities. Until 1970, the elite public high schools, the chief of which was Hibiya, Alma Mater of a large proportion of top people now in their fifties and sixties, were open to the top academic performers from the whole of Tokyo. The buses and trains were full of high school children commuting across the sprawling city in order to claim their hard-won place at number three school or number four school, rather than go to number five school or number seven school nearer their home. But what was worse, from the point of view of those who cared about education, was that the junior secondary schools were rated, by themselves and by parents, according to the proportion of their pupils who succeeded in getting to the top high schools. At first the last year, then later the last two years of junior high school, came to centre around preparation for the high school entrance examinations—to the neglect of lower-ability pupils, who had little chance of getting into a high school that counted for much. The solution was a drastic revamping of the admission system: by grouping high schools and distributing pupils among them in very broad ability bands, how good an education one got, and with classmates of what ability level, became something of a lottery. Outraged at the loss of its 'good schools', the middle class voted with its feet and the enormous growth of private secondary schools was the result.

When the military government of Seoul undertook exactly the same reform for exactly the same reasons a few years later, it rode roughshod over any scrupulous distinction between public and private. The private secondary schools were forced into the same admissions system as the public. In Korea, the middle class adopted the British defence—they moved house to be near a 'good' school.

Recently, a similar policy effect has occurred. As is discussed below, the recent shift in official education philosophies and policies in favour of 'relaxed education' (reduced curriculum content, fewer school hours and so on) has, it is generally agreed, led to declining levels of educational achievement in the public system. This has once again led to a further acceleration of the 'flight of the bright' to the private sector.[7]

Factors beyond the economic

The importance—the growing importance—of parental ability to buy educational privilege in explaining the decline in social mobility via education is clear. But what about the other two factors? First, there is the 'cultural capital' factor—the extent to which growing disparities in home environments, the aspirations imparted, the TV programmes watched and the breakfast table conversation is responsible for different levels of achievement. Second, there is the genetic factor—the possible effect of several generations of meritocratic selection in skewing the cross-class distribution of the hard-wired ingredients of educational achievement.

The two are difficult to sort out, but two studies conducted by one of us gives some hints. A repetition, in 1997, of a study of eleven high schools carried out in 1979 shows up the direction of change in the correlation of school performance and social class. The schools were public schools representing the whole of the ability-ranked spectrum of high schools in two prefectures where there were no private high schools of any note, and only the exceptional family sent children to metropolitan high schools. The increase in the class/achievement-score correlation was clear when the students were grouped into three achievement levels and three socio-economic levels by a combined measure of parental education and father's occupation. In 1979, 49 per cent of the lowest socio-economic group were in the highest achievement grade, along with 71 per cent of the top group. In 1997, the figures were 45 per cent and 77 per cent, respectively.[8]

Another 2001 study tried to get at the underlying attitude and perception dimensions. It collected data on almost 1,000 fifth-grade students and over 1,000 eighth-grade students. The sixteen public elementary and twelve junior secondary schools from which they came had been the subject of a similar study in 1989. A score of 'students' learning skills' was constructed, using their answers to questions about whether they always took notes in classes, whether they often raised their hands and offered opinions when teachers asked for them, whether they asked their teachers when they didn't fully understand what they were supposed to have learned, whether they took the lead in group activities, whether they did research on their own, whether they corrected what they had got wrong in tests, and so on. Another score rated the children's home backgrounds as culturally rich or culturally poor using such measures as whether their parents watched the news on TV, whether they had a lot of books and a computer at home, whether they were ever taken to museums or had their parents read to them when they were young, whether their parents did any home baking, and so on. The correlation between the two scores was strong. Children with a high 'ability to learn' came disproportionately from culturally rich homes.[9]

Japan has long been known as an 'all middle class' society. Opinion surveys asking people to identify themselves as upper, middle or lower class have regularly found large percentages opting for 'middle', and a large measure of cultural homogeneity—tastes in food, clothing and entertainment—was a matter of measurable fact. But the polarisation is becoming clearer. In a 1974 survey, 61 per cent of respondents put themselves in the middle middle class, and only 28 per cent in the lower middle or lower class. By 2004, the figures had become 53 per cent and 37 per cent, respectively.[10] In the 'learning environment' survey mentioned above, another possible comparison between 1989 and 2001 is between the answers of children to a series of questions, asked in both years, about their daily habits and relations with family members—what one might call a 'fecklessness/self-discipline' score. (Do you have breakfast/brush your teeth every morning? Do you use the conventional 'tadaima' greeting to your parents when you go home? Do you arrange your school satchel the night before? Do you have a fixed bedtime?)

The distribution of the scores was just perceptibly more polarised in 2001 than in 1989 (to a degree that might have been due to measurement error), but the correlation of the scores with maths achievement was much higher. In other words, differences in 'cultural capital' seem to be growing, and (one presumes because more 'relaxed' primary and junior secondary education means that the school's pressure on the slow learners to learn is reduced, and therefore the family's role becomes more important) those differences have a greater effect on school achievement.

And, of course, there is a material, income distribution, dimension to this polarisation of 'cultural capital', one indicator of which is the proportion of children receiving public assistance (in Japan, not just free school meals but an 'education allowance' for books and stationery). In 2000, it was 8 per cent, but by 2004 it had increased to 13 per cent. In the poorest borough of Tokyo, the proportion increased in those four years from 31 per cent to 43 per cent.[11]

Converting credentials into career success

The current state of play

It is hard to give more than an impressionistic account of the other half of the equation: the extent to which there are changes in the degree to which entry into the elite levels of the income, power and prestige dimensions depends on educational credentials, rather than family connections, entrepreneurial flair, talents other than intellectual, or sheer luck.

First, family connections. There is no evidence that they have in any way come in recent years to count for more in the public sector than they have done for the last 100 years: the fact that quite a lot of diplomats' children become diplomats is more evidence of the direction of aspirations than of any deviation from meritocratic selection. And in the private sector, the family firm is still on the decline. A Toyota great-grandson may be promoted to the board ten years earlier than his peers, but unlike scions of the Agnelli family in Italy, he would not get to run an important part of the family empire unless he proved eventually to have exceptional talents.

As for the balance between what the American sociologist Ralph Turner once called 'sponsored' and 'contest' mobility, there has been a lot of talk about wholesale change in Japanese employment practices—the ending of lifetime employment, and so on. It is quite true that, whereas in the 1980s 95 per cent of school-leavers had the prospect of a full-time job, with at least the possibility of lifetime employment, this has ceased to be the case. The problem of youth unemployment, and casual employment (the so-called freeters—free arbeiters), with no real chance of acquiring skills on the job, is a source of much public concern.

But this has brought little change to those in the higher reaches of the ability spectrum. The Civil Service, the judiciary and the major corporations still recruit as they have always done, from people who have proved their intellectual ability in school and university. And, the norm is still, both in the public and the private sector, lifetime employment. The wage survey covers male employees in all establishments with more than ten workers. It shows the relation between education, age and length of service in present job. The proportion of 30–34-year-old university graduate male employees in manufacturing who had less than one year's service with their current employer was 3 per cent in 1985. It rose with the increasing mobility of the bubble period to 4 per cent in 1990. In 2002, when jobs were harder to get and you clung to what you had, it was back to 2 per cent—lower than in 1985.

Many argue, however, that the situation is becoming much more fluid. In the first place, 'the top' is a much more pluralistic place. The media create sports stars, newscasters and the miscellaneous performers who in Japanese are called *tarento*. These people have celebrity. They also make a great deal of wealth, but their influence in the power structure is limited, though they can sometimes translate their celebrity into positions of power as politicians or prefectural governors. There is also an increase in the voluntary mobility of people in their twenties out of the traditional elite cadres of the Civil Service and the major corporations (to foreign banks or to start their own companies). Those who start new companies associated with the Internet—the so-called net entrepreneurs—are prominent in the media, especially because of their spectacular attempts at takeovers of established companies. They are sometimes portrayed as breaking the mould—*heroes* breaking the mould, in fact—until in January 2006 one of the three most prominent (Horie, Mikitani and Murakami) was accused of breaking the legal mould too and his company collapsed. All three, incidentally, entered elite universities. (Horie, the one who got his comeuppance, did a Bill Gates and left before graduating.)

But Japan is also a democracy. The top of the power dimension is occupied by politicians whose credentials consist of getting elected rather than going to a good university. But there are two respects in which the relation between democracy and meritocracy in Japan is different from that in most other industrial societies.

The first is that, as the epigram 'politicians reign but bureaucrats rule' puts it, in terms of real power, if not in prestige and authority, bureaucrats rank on a par with, if not on occasion above, politicians. It is still largely the case that politicians, however well endowed with charisma, do not have to be very bright. The 'Yes, Minister' syndrome is even more a Japanese than a British phenomenon. A British minister introducing legislation to the House of Commons will not survive long if he cannot master his brief and answer the most detailed questions. In Japan, fielding such questions is usually the job of civil servants. Once, this happened as a matter of course. A 1995 law tried to stop the practice, in the interests of forcing an improvement in the intellectual quality of ministers. It went too much against the grain to succeed. Top civil servants continue to play the key role when Diet committees examine legislation, but now that has to be legitimated by a special resolution calling for 'civil servant witnesses' at the beginning of each committee session.

Second, in the conservative parties that have long dominated Japanese politics, politician is the last remaining largely hereditary profession. Some 170 MPs (out of 622) are sons, daughters or nephews of former MPs. However, the mechanisms that account for the ability of parents or uncles to hand on their seats to the next generation—careful cultivation of constituencies, and personal loyalty voting—are of diminishing effectiveness as media performance comes to count for more and more in elections. The September 2005 election was symptomatic. A number of traditionalists were thrown out of the Liberal Democratic Party for their revolt against the Prime Minister and replaced by younger people with no family political background—economist women, media stars, former civil servants and others who had made their way to occupational prominence through academic achievement.

Moves towards gender equality

Hitherto, the discussion has been mostly about boys' education and men's careers, and there is some justification for this in that, until recently, women's involvement in occupations that carry power, prestige and high income has been quite small. The predominant characteristic of women's labour market participation was the M-shape one—high in the early and mid-twenties, falling sharply as most women left when their first child was born, and rising again as women took (mostly part-time and mostly low-level) jobs when their youngest child reached its teens.

Slowly, the situation is changing in Japan as it has changed in other industrial societies. In the universities more women have been competing—successfully—with men for places in the elite universities (Tokyo University students are now 20 per cent female) and the popularity of the elite women's universities that produced ladylike wives for older generations has declined. (One consequence is that there is an increase in marriages of fellow-students guaranteed by the selection examinations to be of comparable intellectual power, thus increasing the assortative character of mating and accelerating genetic—and cultural—stratification.)

There has been a similar slow increase in the number of women seeking professional and managerial career jobs. Marriage is increasingly postponed, many double-income couples remain childless, and those who have children are gradually finding ways (grandmothers, day-care services and very rarely professional live-in nannies) to combine a career and having a family (though much more gradually in Japan, where motherhood out of wedlock is far less easily accepted than in other countries, with the consequence that increasing female participation has meant a more precipitous decline in the birth rate). In the 2002 occupational survey,[12] women were represented in almost equal numbers in professional occupations (schoolteachers and social workers predominating) but in managerial occupations men outnumbered women by more than eight to one. A government committee—the Council for Gender Equality—recently announced a target to raise the proportion of women among entrants to the career civil service from its present 22 per cent to 30 per cent.[13]

The routes to the top for women, however, are no different from those that must be taken by men. A change in the gender composition of the elites may alter its character in other ways, but not alter the mechanisms of meritocracy. The feminist movement is not strong in Japan. There seems little prospect that women will come to share the 'passing delusions of a section of the upper classes' that would lead them into an alliance with the rebels in Michael Young's dystopia.

The educational policy debate

Interaction of pedagogic theory and political concerns

Recall what we said near the beginning of this chapter:

There are, to simplify wildly, two notions of why the state should create schools: first, as part of its service to its citizens, giving them the opportunities for personal development; or, second, as a means of training its citizens to serve the state—to make the nation strong and successful in competition (military, economic and diplomatic) with other nations.

To be sure, there are—under either head—a vast range of educational theories or concerns: the advocates of 'child-centred' and the advocates of 'subject-centred' education have widely differing views of what is meant by 'personal development'; and the 'education for national strength' strategists may emphasise knowledge, or creativity or patriotism. But the overall balance between the two aims or groups of aims is important, and over the last century and a half—as a result of its late catch-up development and its war history—that balance has shifted in Japan more markedly than in most countries. One might chart a rough, impressionistic assessment of those shifts as in the following table:

Era	Drive	
	Individual	Nation
1870s	10	90
1920s	30	70
1940	0	100
1945–50	90	10
1960s	80	20
1980s	60	40
1990s	70	30
2000s	60	40

The drive to 'enrich the nation and strengthen the army' was the keynote of the early efforts to establish a national education system. The 1920s was a period in which liberal individualism began to gain ground with universal franchise, the growth of trade unions, the loss of popularity of the army after the fiasco of the Siberian expedition and a reformist national education commission. The run-up to the war reversed all that, and the new education introduced by the American-inspired reforms after the war reversed it all yet again.

Since then, the balance has become far more complicated. The emphasis on manpower planning, and the development of 'human resources' for economic growth, became a dominant concern in the 1960s and led to extra resources for scientific and vocational education. The further reassertion of national purpose in the 1980s took the form of a rejection of uniform curriculum-bound instruction in favour of an emphasis on the national need for individuality and 'creativity'. Japan had finished its 'catch-up phase' of growth, and was enjoying not only its new affluence but its growing international reputation for economic efficiency. But Japan did not get many Nobel Prizes. There were many in the business world who pointed out—and a grand education commission, the so-called Ad Hoc Council on Education, 1984–6, made a point of emphasising it—that now Japan was at world technological frontiers, its future prosperity depended on the ability of its most gifted individuals to push the frontiers forward.

Promoting 'creativity'

Not only did affluence make the rigours of traditional schooling seem less necessary, and so give a fair wind to proposals for a five-day school week (partially implemented in 1992), but those rigours—and the standardisation and emphasis on rote memorisation—were also blamed for killing creativity. This advocacy of a more relaxed form of education with emphasis on individuality suited the mood of the 1980s, the decade of prosperity that ended with the bubble, when economists were busy talking up the 'leisure industry'. The whole syndrome of changes subsequently introduced (reduced curriculum content, five-day weeks, shorter hours, 'life-style classes') came to be known by the slogan phrase '*yutori no kyoiku*' (variously translated as 'room for growth' or 'more relaxed educational style' or—an official translation—'liberal, flexible and comfortable school life').

Few people raised the issue of the possible inegalitarian implications of this for the education of slow learners. The trouble was the problem that one so often finds in educational debates, especially in Japan, where political correctness is of more compelling force even than in the United States—a reluctance to face up to the fact that some children are bright and some are dull. Both the individualists and the nationalists claimed to be providing universal recipes for the average child—a reduction of the compulsory curriculum load, more child-centred learning, discovery learning, self-starting learning tailored to individual needs and lifelong learning to counter the obsession with the initial school-leaving credential.

For the nationalists, most concerned to make sure that the brightest children had an improved chance of developing their nationally useful mental faculties in the company of their peers, this avoidance of the knotty question of ability differences had great advantages. They could avoid doing anything to hinder the growth of elite private schools, and work gradually towards selection at age twelve for the best of the public schools by turning former junior and senior high schools into all-through schools.

The 'individual personal developmentists', for their part, were indeed concerned with the slower learners. The rigid drilling of traditional pedagogy that got 90 per cent of children up to a reasonable 3-R competence (not a bad achievement given the complications of the Japanese script) still left 10 per cent branded as failures, and a major concern was the damage to self-esteem and alienation of that 10 per cent. The doctrines that prevailed in the egalitarian Britain of the 1950s and 1960s—'child-centred learning', 'self-starting learning based on children's own choices', 'knowledge for life, not just for academe', 'there are all kinds of valuable abilities, besides the meretricious tricks required to pass exams'—were seen in Japan, too, to be possible means of avoiding stigmatising failure. Sometimes they were dressed up as 'a new technological age with fuzzy logic etc. requires a New Kind of Learning'. Some of the former high school vocational streams have been transformed into 'Comprehensive Learning Streams'. A new subject, a hybrid of the old social studies, ethics and science classes called 'Learning for Life' (introduced in the first two grades of elementary schools in 1992), followed later (in 2002) for all schools—including high schools—through 'Integrated Cross Disciplinary Study', consisting of various kinds of discovery learning. Sometimes this can produce exciting and effective learning, but success depends very much on the efforts and quality of teachers, especially when confronted with large classes—the maximum permitted remains forty.

The mid-1990s had a dual character. On the one hand, the inertia of the move towards '*yutori no kyoiku*' of the previous decade continued. At the same time the economic bubble had burst, and it was obvious that the era of spectacular growth rates was over. In the 1980s, no one had been very conscious of a trade-off between promoting the creativity of the most able, and equality of opportunity. People spoke as though everyone could be creative in his or her own way. But in the 1990s the trade-off became more apparent and the division of opinion became sharper, especially as a result of the growing strength of the advocates of the neo-liberal agenda, pressing for wholesale reform of the pension system and the welfare state, reduction in the progressivity of income taxes and educational reform. One heard more and more denunciations of 'false egalitarianism'—a supposed preoccupation with 'equality of outcomes' rather than with equality of opportunity. Competition, said the neo-liberal reformers, was what brought progress—and competition had to be for reasonably substantial rewards. The welfare of society as a whole was secured not by the state, but by the invisible hand. Matters of distribution could be taken care of by 'trickle down', which needed no planning. (Hence the rating in the above chart of the 1990s as more individualistic than the 1980s.)

But this argument for equality of opportunity rather than equality of outcome also borrowed from the 'left-wing egalitarian' notion that there should be recognition of human diversity; everyone has different individual abilities, interests and aptitudes, and what was wrong hitherto was the notion that the only opportunity of any importance was the opportunity to get into the top universities. This last 'anti-unidimensionality' interpretation of equality of opportunity went hand in hand with an attempt to change admission criteria. Universities were urged to vary their methods; using essay-type exams as well as the usual multiple choice tests, interviews and high school recommendations—especially the latter. This has made minimal difference to the nature of the road into the elite, but has had a bigger effect in universities lower down in the university ranking, where high school recommendations have been used more freely. One reason for this is the contraction of the 18-year-old age group and increased competition from the lesser universities for students. But it has not much altered the tendency for university teachers, whatever the means of selection, to try to get the brightest students available. Hence the correlation between academic attainment at the high school level and the prestige rank of university entered has been little changed.

Similarly, there was a change in the first selection barrier—admission to high school. The ministry banned the use of mock tests and the ranking of students by their 'standardised scores'—the major criterion used for allocating junior high graduates among high schools—and urged the substitution of teachers' recommendations. At the same time, high schools were encouraged to develop their 'individual school character'—in other words, develop subject specialties and recruit their pupils according to their aptitudes and interests rather than the single criterion of examinations marks. All of this did little to change the relation between academic achievement and the chance of entering the top public high schools (top in the sense that they had the best records for getting students into good universities), but it did, by modifying the unidimensionality of the criteria by which students lower down in the ability range were admitted, blur the clarity of the prestige hierarchy in the tail of the prestige distribution—that is, make for fewer clearly defined 'sink schools'—and, eventually, modify the criteria by which employers recruited the graduates from those schools.

At the turn of the century, however, the recognition grew that the changes both in education and in the occupational system were having polarising consequences. There was a spate of books with titles such as *Inequality Signed and Sealed, The Educational Crisis of an Increasingly Stratified Japan, Japan: the Unequal Society* and *Society of Stratified Hopes.*[14] The reinforcement of a national perspective indicated in the above table had two aspects: a growing concern for the quality of life as the gap between rich and poor widened and society became more polarised, and concern at the loss of prestige as the international scholastic achievement surveys showed Japan losing its position as a 'model education nation'. Officialdom began to show its concern: the Ministry of Finance with the prospects of an increasing welfare burden, growth in the black economy and a lowered tax base; the Ministry of Labour, Health and Welfare with the implications for social security and the pension system, the Ministry of Economy, Trade and Industry with the general question of levels of competition, the provision of safety nets—which is always mentioned as an afterthought by the gung-ho reformers who want ever more competition—and the income distribution implications of 'socially useful' cartels. Each of these ministries has mobilised a number of academics into working groups on stratification (bureaucratic initiatives, with which politicians have had little to do). The Ministry of Finance's working group has already published a volume entitled *Income Differentials and Social Stratification in Japan.*[15]

The last ministry to show some recognition that there was a problem about equality was the Ministry of Education, Culture, Sports, Science and Technology (shortened in English to MEXT). Another aspect of the advance of neo-liberalism besides the emphasis on individualistic competition is the ideology of the 'small state'. Proposals, backed by the current Prime Minister, Koizumi, for a large measure of decentralisation of educational budgets raised the prospect not only of reduced power for the ministry, which was a concern of some officials, but also of accelerated inequality between richer and poorer prefectures, which was a genuine concern. Their battle was lost: the argument about growing inequality failed to cut much ice with the much more powerful economic ministries that had all the weight of the Koizumi reformers behind them, and decentralisation went ahead.

The problem of educational polarisation

One consequence of all these developments—the new challenge that the media and politicians throw at the educational world, the educational hot topic *par excellence*—is the much discussed 'decline in educational standards', which is in fact, though rarely recognised as such, a *polarisation* of educational standards.

The fall-off in achievement standards is clear from the international comparison scores. It was apparent also at the micro-level in the study quoted earlier of the same schools in 1989 and 2001. The distribution of scores in an identical grade 8 maths test was skewed in a similar way in both years, but not only had the peak of the distribution, which had been in the top percentile, moved to the second percentile, but the standard deviation of the distribution had increased, both for mathematics and literacy.

The clearest evidence of polarisation, however, comes from a comparison of the OECD's PISA (Programme for International Student Assessment) studies in 2000 and 2003. The mathematics scores showed a startling change in the lower part of the distribution. In 2003, the Japanese 95th percentile scorer was still thirty points above the OECD average for 95th percentile scorers, dropping only two points or so from the 2000 score. The 5th percentile scorer, however, had dropped from being seventy-five points above the average 5th percentile scorers of other countries to being a mere thirty points above, and the 25th percentile scorer had similarly dropped from being nearly seventy points above children in the same ranking percentile to being only thirty-five points above.[16]

Reactions were varied. Egalitarians were concerned with ways to reduce this obvious polarisation by policies to 'equalise starting positions'. Those who were less bothered about inequality, and particularly those who were identified with the *'yutori no kyoiku'* policies, tended to dismiss these results on the grounds that they were mere test results, which failed to reflect the new 'whole person development' aims of the new education. Others, and this was perhaps the majority view in politically dominant circles, were more concerned with the fact that there was relative decline even in the top-decile students (economists were complaining about the mathematical competence of entering students) and proposed special classes in science or English for gifted children.

Conclusion: meritocracy for ever?

The general picture, then, is of a society in which the meritocratic mechanisms of advancement seem stably established. The encroachment of democratic mechanisms—a shift in power from those who get to the top by diplomas to those who get there by votes—is slow and uncertain. (There is no hint of Japan following the American practice of replacing 3,000 top civil servants with each presidential election, nor even of the British proliferation of special advisors.) But the ability to travel those routes to the top is becoming ever more restricted as the hereditary transmission of class status seems to grow clearer.

What light does the Japanese experience throw on the crucial question: In so far as this seems to confirm Michael Young's prediction that meritocracies tend to become hereditary, what does it tell us about the mechanisms involved? To what extent is it a matter of transmission of economic privilege—which social policy can, in theory, do a lot about—or of cultural privilege—which social policy can do something about—or of genetic privilege, which social policy can do nothing about, short of eugenic policies (for example, control over marriage, which does seem to be increasingly assortative) that no democracy could even contemplate?

Given the complexities of the interrelation between nature and nurture, the last two—the cultural and the genetic mechanisms—are extremely difficult to disentangle. It is particularly difficult in Japan, because the avoidance of the study of inheritance has been even more complete than in the Anglo-Saxon world. Tokyo University's attached school which, as mentioned earlier, is one of a small number that have not deliberately selected for ability, has for many years had a special intake of twins, but few studies have been carried out on any but physical characteristics. One generalisation, which is in fact a tautology, is that the more homogeneous family environments are with respect to their tendency to promote intellectual development, the greater is the amount of the variance in ability that can be attributed to genes. Hitherto—and this is what people had in mind when they talked of Japan as an 'all middle class' society—the homogeneity of family environments has been much greater than, say, in Britain. But some of the studies quoted above suggest that this is changing rapidly: not only is economic advantage counting for more, but also differences in the family cultural environment are adding to genetic mechanisms to produce ever less real equality of opportunity.

This is the challenge for Japanese policy. Maybe there is a genetic motor that is responsible for increasing class rigidity, and policy may not be able to stop it. But it can apply the brake or the accelerator, and at the moment it is the accelerator that is being pressed.

Just Rewards: *Meritocracy* Fifty Years Later

PETER MARRIS

The fairness dilemma

ALMOST fifty years ago, Michael Young dropped a draft of *The Rise of the Meritocracy* on my desk. Re-reading it now, I don't know quite what to make of it. It sets out, with wit and prescience, a dilemma that we now confront more obviously than in 1958: the fairer the opportunity structure of society becomes, the more it seems to legitimate a hierarchy of privilege, and the more entrenched are the class divisions it justifies. Yet the future it describes doesn't seem at all to resemble the world I see around me. How can it be at once so right, and so quaintly wrong?

Michael's story, like Edward Bellamy's *Looking Backward*, uses a historian of the future to imagine the evolution of an ideal. But Michael's future society, unlike Bellamy's, is a nightmare—a complacent hierarchy of privilege, where intelligence has become the sole arbiter of status. As intelligence testing is progressively refined, everyone is directed more and more exactly into the occupation that best fits their abilities, leaving no need or justification for social mobility. Intelligence, status, occupation and power have become so perfectly correlated that democracy itself dwindles into an unnecessary encumbrance to the rational order of society. This prophetic vision seems unreal, in part because few still believe that intelligence is a single, genetically determined trait. Yet it also seems to predict, shrewdly, a competition for academic credentials that has intensified, as it becomes more open. Does the striving for equality of opportunity in the end make inequality more tolerable, and the right to power and privilege less easy to challenge?

Yale, for instance, rejects nine out of ten of those who apply, who are already a largely self-selected group of high achievers. And it recruits from the whole population, without regard for ability to pay. When Michael wrote *Meritocracy*, Yale students were all men, mostly from well-to-do families, whose fathers had often been there before them. Now half of them are women, and some of the students I have taught there have grown up in public housing projects, the children of single mothers struggling to survive on welfare benefits. Many universities are now even repudiating the claims of 'legacies', an admissions office term for the children of alumni. And this puts the squeeze on middle-class parents, who push their children into summer school maths programmes, SAT tutoring, and adventures building latrines in rural Paraguay, in an increasingly frantic effort to enhance their résumés.

Published by Blackwell Publishing Ltd, 9600 Garsington Road, Oxford OX4 2DQ, UK and 350 Main Street, Malden, MA 02148, USA

The strategies are evidently successful, especially when parents are rich enough to back them to the hilt. On 22 April 2004, *The New York Times* reported that 'At prestigious universities around the country, from flagship state colleges to the Ivy League, more and more students from upper-income families are edging out those from the middle class, according to university data. . . . Experts say the change in the student population is a result of both steep tuition increases and the phenomenal efforts many wealthy parents put into preparing their children to apply to the best schools.' Lawrence Summers, the president of Harvard, was appropriately shocked. 'It's very much an issue of fundamental fairness,' he is quoted as saying: 'An important purpose of institutions like Harvard is to give everybody a shot at the American dream.'

The competition begins to reach younger and younger children. Some of the most sought-after nursery schools in Los Angeles now require letters of reference from their applicants. Parents are bringing their six-month-old babies to specialists in cognitive enhancement. Homes are full of books on how to outwit the college application process. Doesn't all this frantic emphasis on academic credentials sound just like the meritocracy Michael foresaw?

There is a fundamental difference. Michael was directing his satire, I believe, primarily at Anthony Crosland and others in the leadership of the Labour Party, who represented a strand of scientific rationalism in socialist thinking that threads back to Saint-Simon. This conception of socialism envisions the rational ordering of society according to scientific principles—five-year plans, a social science research council, nationalised industry and the eleven-plus intelligence test to track entry into secondary school. Michael's meritocracy is a society run by technocrats with an empirically confirmed faith in the perfectibility of intelligence testing. But the meritocracy of America and Britain today is a capitalist meritocracy, whose intellectual roots are in Adam Smith, not Saint-Simon. It draws on the principle that the efficient distribution of labour, like any other productive resource, requires a competitive market, through which ability is allocated where it becomes most productive. Monopolistic practices, such as restricting entry into professions to a privileged class, or to white men only, are inherently inefficient. In principle, any restriction on the free marketing of ability inhibits the potential wealth of nations.

Capitalist meritocracy

Michael's meritocrats struggle with fairness. The society they create is so repulsive partly because they deal with the issue so hypocritically. If merit equals intelligence plus effort, as his meritocrats define it, and intelligence is a genetic endowment, as he imagines, then it is not clear why an intelligent person should be paid more than a stupid one who works just as hard, since the intelligence is not earned but given. Eventually, therefore, in Michael's imaginary state, everyone is formally paid the same. But the privileges of the meritocrats—their servants, comforts, holidays and luxuries—are then justified as the necessary conditions for the fulfilment of their responsibilities, much as communist states awarded cars, country cottages and access to capitalist luxuries to their nomenclatura.

The ideal of a capitalist meritocracy is more honest. You are rewarded according to your market value, and that price is ultimately determined by your contribution to productivity, and so to the realisation of profit. The university professor is not well paid because she or he has a beautiful mind, which needs to be cosseted, but because, by research and teaching, she or he supposedly ultimately contributes more than most to the growth of the national economy. Those who are not part of the market economy, such as mothers without paid employment, benefit only indirectly, whatever the merits of their contribution.

This capitalist conception of a meritocracy seems to have so much in common with Michael's, only because employers use educational attainment as a convenient surrogate for the ability to produce profit. Why has it become necessary to have a college degree, even to get a job as a sales clerk? Not because a demonstrated skill at writing term papers about French literature or the war of 1812 is in any way useful, nor even because it shows how smart you are. A college degree confirms that the graduate is a responsible, diligent member of society, who knows how to conform to its requirements. If the degree is granted by a prestigious institution, it confirms that the graduate is a potential member of the elite. It opens the way to graduate school, to medicine and the law. Correspondingly, without a degree, occupational choices will be, for the most part, restricted and poorly paid. The educational system sorts young people out so as to save employers a great deal of time and trouble finding out the qualities of potential employees for themselves. A capitalist meritocracy institutionalises a sequence of entry thresholds into the labour market, and offers only contempt for those who fail. Even amongst their peers, young African Americans in Harlem, struggling to make an honest living serving in fast food restaurants—not as easy or unskilled a task as you might imagine—are despised as 'hamburger flippers'.[1]

The tensions these inequalities create are compounded by changes that Michael did not foresee. Just as, first, manufacturing employment and then clerical processing were shifted overseas to countries with cheaper labour, so now British and American employers are finding accountants, software designers, engineers and radiologists in Bangalore or Manila, who will do the job for half the pay of their British or American counterparts. The United States is becoming a nation with a small, very wealthy elite, a growing population of working poor, and a shrinking middle class, with the highest rates of poverty, the widest inequalities of income and the least social mobility of any of the world's richest nations. Yet the nation still prides itself on its egalitarian culture and its commitment to equality of opportunity. And the more it tries to realise that ideal of equal opportunity, the more it seems to justify the gross inequality of the outcome.

Michael's meritocracy is a nightmare of scientific positivism, rather than of unbridled capitalism. It institutionalises a hierarchy of intelligence, and tries to condition its citizens (unsuccessfully, we learn on the last page) to accept it. But does the pursuit of equality of opportunity, whether under a capitalist or rationalist system, necessarily lead to a meritocracy? Must we assume that occupation, status, power and privilege are inextricably linked? And if they are, what is the alternative? Not, surely, *inequality* of opportunity. His satire offers one hint of the kind of society he wanted. Towards the end of the book, his imaginary author quotes, with patronising contempt, the last paragraph of a dissident manifesto:

Were we to evaluate people, not only according to their intelligence and their education, their occupation, and their power, but according to their kindliness and their courage, their imagination and sensitivity, their sympathy and generosity, there could be no classes. Who would then be able to say that the scientist was superior to the porter with admirable qualities as a father, the civil servant with unusual skill at gaining prizes superior to the lorry driver with unusual skill at growing roses . . . The classless society would also be the tolerant society, in which individual differences were actively encouraged as well as passively tolerated, in which full meaning was at last given to the dignity of man. Every human being would then have equal opportunity . . . to develop his [or her] own special capacities for leading a rich life.[2]

The inspiration for this paragraph is, surprisingly, not Marx, but Matthew Arnold, and I think it represents what Michael himself believed. It is an eloquent answer to a meritocracy obsessed with intelligence testing, but it doesn't offer an alternative to a capitalist meritocracy, because a capitalist meritocracy does not pretend to evaluate people's intrinsic worth, only the market value of their skills. American newspapers are full of stories that celebrate the courage, kindliness and devotion of ordinary citizens and the dignity of humble occupations, just as Michael's manifesto would wish. American culture is deeply ambivalent about its own meritocratic assumptions. It has no answer to inequality except to pursue yet more equality of opportunity. But it pretends that the ensuing class divisions do not exist, or represent some fair return for effort.

Salvaging social justice

Let us assume that we are all equally deserving of respect. How *should* the rewards be distributed, in a society with a complex, highly differentiated occupational structure, drawing on a wide range of skills? Should we all be paid the same, making allowance for the number of our dependants, so long as we all work equally hard to the best of our abilities? If that is too simplistic, should we diverge from absolute equality only when it is to the benefit of all of us to do so—to provide incentives, for instance, to recruit applicants for work that is dangerous, burdened with responsibility or requires long and arduous training? John Rawls argues for this ethical rationalisation in his *A Theory of Justice*.[3] But what if, as neo-liberal economists would argue, society benefits most from a competitive, free market in labour?

In practice, I doubt whether either theories of justice or utilitarian rationality can be much of a guide to the pursuit of fairness. In the real world of the contemporary US or Britain, wages are determined by an incoherent competition between incompatible principles: the tug of supply and demand; residual notions of fairness; conventional assumptions of status; discrimination by gender or race; and the balance of power. Minimum wage laws, redistributive taxation, social security, universal health insurance and subsidised housing all imply limits to the inequalities society should tolerate. Within those limits, most societies also seem to acknowledge a hierarchy of occupational status, which legitimises unequal rewards. I remember how shocked my mother was, in the days when the coal miners' union could still hold the country to ransom, at the idea that a coal miner might be paid as much as a schoolteacher. Institutionalised traditions have established distinctions and equivalencies between and within classes of occupations, which largely govern the gradations of reward. University teachers are paid more than schoolteachers, and teachers in high school more than those in nursery school. Doctors are paid more than nurses, surgeons more than general practitioners (though in the days when cutting off hair and cutting off limbs were seen to be much alike, surgeons were paid like barbers). These hierarchies of reward and prestige most resemble Michael's meritocracy, because they are closely tied to educational qualifications, and because the surgeon who saves your life, or the professor whose work inspired your career, do seem to possess extraordinary merit, and to have trained long and hard to achieve it.

But neither profession leaves this reward structure in the hands of a grateful society. Each tightly controls entry, limiting the number of medical schools, restricting the size of the incoming class of trainees, enforcing accreditation systems and legal bans on competition from outsiders. Power, as much or more than merit, determines wages. The outrageous rewards paid to the CEOs of American corporations are not really a reflection of the returns a charismatic leader can generate. Some of the most highly paid have driven their companies into bankruptcy, or faked the profits. They earn so much because the consulting firms who advise on corporate salaries are made up of the same corporate elite, and share the same exaggerated estimate of their value. Conversely, the wages of American workers are scarcely any higher, and the minimum wage is worth less, than in the 1970s, despite the spectacular growth of the economy, because the decline of manufacturing occupations has undermined the power of the trade unions.

Yet, rigged as the labour market is, both by the occupational power structure and by national control over the entry of foreign workers, supply and demand still exert their pull, sometimes indirectly. Although history departments turn out far more PhDs than universities can absorb, academic salaries do not fall in response to this glut. Instead, universities exploit it by hiring few assistant professors, and meeting many of their teaching commitments with part-time lecturers, and even graduate students, paid at piecework rates. The market will trump the institutionalised power of occupational privilege, if supply and demand diverge too widely.

So long as power and privilege, gender and racial discrimination, unionisation, supply and demand, norms of occupational status, and some residual sense of social justice jostle to determine the distribution of rewards, we don't have to confront the dilemma that Michael sets out in *The Rise of the Meritocracy*. The interplay of factors is too incoherent ever to produce an outcome consistent enough to legitimate a hierarchy of rewards by any principle of necessity or fairness. So I do not believe we need worry that by advocating greater equality of opportunity, we will rationalise an unchallengeable class structure. But I do worry that, at least in the US, urging more education and vocational training is virtually the only strategy for raising people out of poverty with widespread support. For any one young man or woman growing up in a poor city neighbourhood or a rural backwater, graduating from high school and going on to college or to professional training is the surest way out of the neighbourhood and out of poverty. But for the age group as a whole, the strategy is less convincing, because there aren't enough better jobs to go round. If everyone becomes better qualified, the qualification is devalued. So we need, above all, to increase respect for the most humdrum occupations, and ensure that everyone, no matter what they do, has a decent place to live, enough to eat, good, prompt and friendly health care, and a school where their children are encouraged and enabled to learn. It doesn't sound a great deal to ask of a very rich country. But in the context of the present United States, it is an almost utopian demand.

What Do We Mean by Talent?

RICHARD SENNETT

Merit in the New Economy

WHAT I want to do is to raise a question about what we mean when we talk about talent, in relation to meritocracy. There is a particular incident that got me thinking about this. My research programme in London and New York has been studying changes in the workplace over the past twelve years—it has been mostly ethnographic work with people in the so-called New Economy, which is a misnomer. We have been studying people who have been working in financial services, the new technology and to some degree media services. Amongst that work was a study with forty-six personnel managers of investment banks in both New York and Chicago, and what I want to describe is something that really surprised us.

One of the questions we asked these personnel managers was obviously about what kind of talent they looked for in people they were hiring, about their criteria for promotion in banks and so on. What surprised us was that the words 'aggressive', 'hungry' and 'ambitious' didn't figure very much in these personnel managers' descriptions of middle-level employees. It's a dog-eat-dog world, and it's a nightmare at the top—but when you get down to the middle ranks of companies such as Goldman Sachs or Lehman Brothers, where these personnel managers operate, then it's very different.

What they said was that they were looking for people who were capable of—as they put it—surrendering their competence over any particular task. What that meant was they were looking for workers who were not so much good at one thing, but capable of learning new tasks as the institutions themselves took on new kinds of work. When they hired young people, that translated very concretely into looking, for instance, not at people who had great quantitative skills (though they had to have some background in economics): they were more interested in people who were capable of learning foreign languages, as indeed are the top business schools in the United States. If you study Greek as an undergraduate, for example, that's a very good entrée into a business school, because your choice indicates that you are capable of changing, getting out of normal contexts, and learning something that is strange and foreign. And in a highly mobile business world this is seen as an ability that counts more than mastering some particular skill—such as money leveraging—and then practising that skill year upon year.

This seemed reasonable to us, although not quite what we had imagined. We then took a look at the promotion fix, and we were told that if someone is not promoted fairly rapidly within the organisation, particularly in their first

Published by Blackwell Publishing Ltd, 9600 Garsington Road, Oxford OX4 2DQ, UK and 350 Main Street, Malden, MA 02148, USA

five years, they are doomed. Similarly, when they hire people from outside the bank, if they see that someone has been in a particular job for more than four or five years, that counts as a negative mark against them. The notion is that they have become institutionally ingrown and attached to a particular skill. So if the business climate changes in a such a way that the skill in question is no longer so valuable, then they will have too much investment in their old abilities, and in doing that particular thing, to move on.

A disappearing ladder

Leaving aside for the moment the framework of the banks, which is what our research mostly considers, the same phenomenon turned up when we carried out a study of personnel managers at IBM. Before 1993, IBM used to be an extremely paternalistic company, in which people spent their whole working lives. They learned how to do one thing; and on the basis of doing that one thing well, they were promoted and so on. After 1993, that kind of skill ladder disappeared and, for instance, people who were skilled at mainframe programming in the 1980s—which was a very profitable time for the industry—became rather negative presences in the corporation, because they knew how to do IBM's 'old' business. Simply the fact that they had developed those skills was held against them as a negative. Unfortunately, in firms with this kind of mindset, if you don't move your kit—that is, the notion that you do one thing, just stay with one thing and stay with it stably—it is viewed as a negative, quite literally. It is a bureaucratised negative. People who stay in the same job for four or five years are very vulnerable to being let go.

This bears not on Michael Young's version of meritocracy, but on Daniel Bell's version. What happens is that such employees slowly become down-wardly mobile within the company. You can do anything with them. They will hang around—it doesn't matter. So, over the course of time, they actually become deskilled. In media companies, this is a very rapid phenomenon indeed—so much so that people in their late forties and fifties, unless they become really mogul-like, and even though they've done long service in the firm, will end up working at an inferior skill level compared to young people who have just come in. There's a presumption that the modal efficient age in media companies is between 32 and 38. Sometimes they quit; it depends on the firm. But if they're kept, they gradually become deskilled. That's why we're in a different world of talent, certainly compared with Michael's book. There's no question of criticising him; after all, why should he have perceived this happening? But, nevertheless, we are living in a different world.

Our recently published study identifies a twofold significance to this phenomenon. One aspect is that in these leading-sector kinds of businesses, the notion of developing craftsmanship is a negative. It comes back to the complaint about the way in which people do things in the US. The notion that acquisition of a specialised skill is seen as being a positive in a corporation such as IBM is very ambiguous. Because you may commit yourself to respect from other people on the basis of that skill, you may invest too much in it. It correlates with the diminution, in the high-tech industries, the high-finance sector and the media industries, of the notion that seniority is a climb, and a reward. This is rapidly changing.

So, then, the second issue is this. If craftsmanship, with its vibrant tradition of service to the organisation—of mastery of a particular skill—doesn't constitute merit, then, under these changing conditions, what *is* merit? As we began to probe this in some detail in our study, we found that merit has been redefined by these managers—as with the example of learning Greek—as a *potential*, rather than practice. And when they look for employees to hire, they are trying—using all the gobbledegook of most human relations gurus, and also various testing methods—to find measures that represent a condition in which merit is a capacity, as it were, to dramatise one's own potential. The idea is that people who are capable of disinvesting themselves in particular activities, who are good at dealing with changing circumstances and who don't claim ownership of skills, have more potential than people who commit.

When we are talking about meritocracy, it seems to me that, for the future, this is a large issue that social analysts need to study in depth. If the ability, in such a corporation, to walk away from something—to take a distant stance; to not get too ingrown; that is, not to develop too much corporate loyalty—is seen not as negative but as a positive, and means that you are flexible, then it means that when business conditions change, you can change with them. Under those conditions, the notion of self-development becomes something extremely problematical. You are constantly, as it were, walking away from your own commitments. The aspect of this that interests me the most is the notion, based on my own presuppositions about what work does for people's long-term self-organisation, that you do have to have a feeling of accumulation and a narrative flow; that you don't just have serial experience, one job after another. In some way, you do need to accrete—to glue together—your experiences.

We currently have a study under way that involves some 28 year olds who have gone into a set of these high-flyer firms. We are making comparisons with a study of young people of about a similar age that was carried out at Harvard's Murray Center thirty years ago. The exercise is about a sense of strategy for the future, orientations about how long young people want to use the skills that they acquired at university, their education, their life networks and so on. To summarise, what we are finding is that under these new kinds of business conditions what you get is people who have no work narratives— that is, they can't project into the future. They are well adapted to a world of work in which there are no long-term career narratives. They have a great deal of trouble thinking about where they want to be in five or ten years' time. Even though many of these young people went to very expensive business schools, the meaning of their education is very opaque to them. They say, 'Well, they didn't really teach me anything, because the firm can buy most of the skills abroad, from people who are even younger than me.' These young people have a sense of a kind of self-consumption.

Skills in the global economy

The framework for the old system of meritocracy—not so much, perhaps, Michael Young's approach, but more the one that Daniel Bell and Alain Touraine developed in their versions—was a skill-based society in which skills were concrete practices, and the more skilled you got, and the more experienced you became in exercising these skills, the more value you had and the higher up you rose. But that kind of post-industrial world has been dispensed with in flexible capitalism, because the institutions—at least, the kind of institutions that we've been studying—no longer operate in that way. They don't draw on the accretion of human capital. They don't reward people who have become very attached to doing one thing.

All of this is tied up with the emergence of the global economy. The people who have been the subjects of our studies are not at the very top—that's a kind of nightmare that I can't consider here—but they're the upper-to-middle level managers. At this level, the market is causing a shift towards a more generalist style of working, which can cope flexibly with changes in very unstable circumstances. This shift is taking place in firms—especially high-tech firms in the financial sector and types of media firms—that are extremely attractive to investors who want short-term, shape-up price returns from them, rather than long-term profits. This is the position in the high-tech sector, and it is equally true for those banking or financial services firms that have gone into the market to raise capital.

Since 1976, globalised investors who hold shares for relatively short periods of time have been looking for factors that can boost the share price rapidly, which means changing business plans and a sense of dynamism. The crucial point is that a firm is dynamic—that there is something unknown about it—because you can sell this to someone who is prepared to take a punt on the fact that change is going to mean that share prices go up even more.

I think the analysis offered by economist Bennett Harrison—that what we are seeing is a whole change in the structure of work, driven by the way in which firms are financed in this global stock market—is a very persuasive argument. We looked, for example, at the case of the Sunbeam organisation, which is an amazing story. Sunbeam made toasters, blenders and so forth, and they made a lot of money out of them. Then, in 1996, after a decree by a new company president that Sunbeam was no longer actually going to make toasters or blenders, there was a public offering of new stocks. The idea was to sell off this profitable business and use the resulting windfall to finance the debt for a new public offering, and Sunbeam would then move into owning credit card companies.

Following this, the company's share price went up forty-six times—not 46 per cent, but forty-six *times*. Meanwhile, its profitability fell to zero. For a year, the sheer drama of what might happen to this firm meant that the stock price continued to go up and up and up. And then, of course, it crashed—leaving about 14,000 employees without work and the company unable to produce any profits, because it had sold off all of its profitable sectors in order to finance the IPO. This is the story of a great many companies in this realm. When I come to think about it, it has become the norm, not the exception—and that's very hard for us to understand.

The effects of globalisation have been different lower down in companies, and in less advanced or leading-edge firms. This is evident in the way in which modern capitalism deals with outsourcing, for instance—relatively semi-skilled activities such as rendering accounts, preparing accounts and so on. It isn't just that there's a race to the bottom in terms of the global labour market, but the notion is that if you pay overqualified young people in other countries poorer wages, you get higher-quality work, and run a more efficient organisation, than you can by developing those same skills within your own corporation. So the logic of a lot of this outsourcing is actually to seek people abroad. Indian call centres are a great example of this; even *more* so are Indian centres for software programming—where you have people who are getting high-quality wages by their standards, but awful wages by Western standards. Such people are overqualified intellectually for the work, and they do it well.

And this is where the issue broadens out. That kind of economics of merit is more attractive to corporations in the West than investing in skills, and the development of skills, amongst people here. So the dilemma posed by the skill component of meritocracy is something that, I think, presents us with a real time bomb. What our research group has found is not just indicative of the way in which Lehman Brothers is, of course, not a model for running a dairy or building train parts. It could not do that sort of thing. But more than that, the focus on privileging flexibility within the organisation, defining skills as potentials and exporting the old-fashioned notions of merit—as competences, intellectual craftsmanship or mental ability—seems to me to create a situation in which meritocracy loses all the moorings you usually associate with it.

Therefore, when I listened to Tony Blair in 1996, giving his famous meritocracy speech, it seemed to me one of the most nostalgic pieces of political rhetoric I have heard. It is about a form of investment in human capital that in Britain, as in the US, is rapidly disappearing. People who actually get good work on the basis of their education, because they know how to do something, because they have specialised skills—that kind of world is dying out. It is being replaced by something much more complicated in terms of the global economy. We need to have this in our minds, and to reconsider what we mean by skill and ability, whenever we discuss meritocracy.

Resolving the Conflict between the Family and Meritocracy

BELINDA BROWN

Introduction

THE concept of meritocracy as Michael Young proposed it and we have come to understand it exists in opposition to the family. I would suggest, however, that this is less about the inevitable nature of meritocracy, and more about the way in which the family has been perceived. Not only does this view of the family undermine it, but it may actually be threatening to meritocracy too: a system that cannot properly include such a fundamental social institution cannot be sustained. What I would like to do here is show that there are other ways of conceiving the family that are far less threatening to a meritocracy. Viewed from a different standpoint, the family could actually be an essential support for a meritocracy, but for one that is less hierarchical, broader and more inclusive than the idea that we currently have. In order to understand this, we need to examine how notions of family and meritocracy have been developed in relation to each other, and the assumptions on which the relationship between them is based.

As the word is generally used, 'meritocracy' conveys a number of related ideas. People are rewarded in terms of status and power—financial or otherwise—and socially valued goods are distributed, according to some deserving attributes of the individual—however these are conceived. The word is also used to impute fairness. Rewards may be unequal, but that is all right as long as people get what they deserve. This view assumes a particular understanding of the adult individual, which has become so taken for granted that it is seldom spelt out. In this, the individual and his bundle of attributes are seen as separable from his environment, particularly the family. He is *sui generis*, complete within himself. Consequently, the individual has no need of the family, and neither does the meritocracy. On the contrary, because it distributes rewards according to—apparently arbitrary—kin relations, rather than according to merit, the family throws a spanner into the works.

A whole host of policy assumptions follow from this. Since the family is operating according to its own independent and non-meritocratic distributory mechanisms, the state needs to reduce its influence so that individuals are given a fair chance. This calls for various forms of intervention and mediation between the individual and the family, as well as a range of other mechanisms aimed at reducing the extent to which privilege can be transmitted through lines of descent. Another way in which the state has tried to limit the influence of the family is by protecting individuals from it by giving them an alternative

 Published by Blackwell Publishing Ltd, 9600 Garsington Road, Oxford OX4 2DQ, UK and 350 Main Street, Malden, MA 02148, USA

membership as citizens within the state. In this way the state is able to *liberate* individuals from family interference, so that they are all given equal chances to thrive on the basis of their merit. Meritocracy requires restrictions on the relationship between the individual and the family, and this calls for increasing intervention by the state.

The alternative idea that I would like to explore here is that far from being independent and separable from his or her family, the individual is intimately constituted by it, so that it necessarily plays a crucial role in the creation of merit. Policies that weaken the role of the family will undermine the creation of merit, and this is as responsible for decline in standards of education as anything that has been happening in schools. In fact, if we really want to understand the creation of merit and its distribution within society, we should look at structures, relations and roles within a family—rather than issues of discrimination or levels of social deprivation. This will tell us more about what has been going on.

The Rise of the Meritocracy: fact, fiction or bad joke?

I am going to explore these issues by looking at the way in which the family, state and meritocracy were conceptualised by Michael in *The Rise of the Meritocracy*. However, first we need to consider the appropriateness of launching such a critique on this basis. On one hand, *Meritocracy* provides one of the clearest expositions of this ideal, and encapsulates many of the assumptions that came to be held subsequently or were already prevalent at the time. On the other hand, it is after all a work of fiction rather than political theory or manifesto; it is also highly satirical, which suggests that it is after all a joke. It may also seem hardly fair play to examine meritocracy critically through a book that sets out to reveal its problems; over half of my job would appear to be done. However, what I would like to suggest is that it acts far more effectively as a template for meritocracy than as a cautionary tale, *and was intended to do so*. In this opening section, I will examine how this was done.

First of all, it should be remembered that Michael was very much in favour of meritocratic principles. Although he often declared how valuable the family was, he also believed that the power of the family to influence social position should be dismantled, so that some people would not be able to benefit disproportionately. Michael is quite explicit about his dislike of inherited privilege, and in the introduction to the 1994 edition, he tells us that 'Nobody should be born with a silver spoon in his mouth, or, if he is it should choke him.' Likewise, in his *Rita Hinden Memorial Lecture* twenty years earlier, he describes any society that allows for hereditary privilege as being 'no more than just a casino'. He suggests in this same lecture that he might have developed these principles even further had he known at that time just how influential the family was:

I imagine I would have made more of the point in the *Meritocracy* book if more of the research studies had been published which have since shown how much more important is the influence on academic achievement of the home than that of the school.[1]

Michael's views on several issues were ambivalent, if not actually contradictory. Thus, while he intimated that his ideal social system would be diverse and pluralistic, he didn't seem to realise that the inequality against which he was fighting was in part an expression of just that. It was often precisely because people had different, alternative values that they accepted inequality; whereas for him these attitudes were something that had to be overcome:

The acceptance of differentials in wages, prestige and power, especially when related to competence, goes very deep and although it may change it won't do so quickly.[2]

And alongside believing in equality he also supported the meritocratic justification for the unequal distribution of wealth:

On the other hand we nearly all, in some part of our minds, also take almost as axiomatic the other principle I mentioned, . . . in short a greater contribution to the sum of goods and services . . . deserves a greater reward.[3]

Likewise his support for comprehensive schooling, which some might cite as concrete proof of his resistance to meritocracy, was actually more likely to be a product of his dislike of the way in which children were excluded from the meritocratic race from such a young age.

The story itself unfolds directly from the clash of these principles. It starts by recording how, in order to prevent the distribution of status and wealth being dependent on kinship, an alternative set of principles has to be constructed—that is, meritocratic ones. And these need to be promoted and protected by the state. Accordingly, the state gets rid of all forms of inheritance, and becomes responsible for assessing what contributions individuals will make to the overall sum of productivity, through intelligence tests that are administered at an increasingly early age. Children are then removed as far as practicably possible from their families in order to ensure equal access to education (dependent on their abilities) at school. They are sifted and sorted into jobs that reflect those abilities, and appropriate rewards follow from that.

Much has been made of Michael's espousal of pluralism—that is, the emphasis on the social value of non-elite contributions—which he repeats in his Rita Hinden lecture. But in fact this has only a passing, perfunctory role in his story. These ideals are set out in the Chelsea Manifesto, the document of his rebellious class:

The classless society would be one which both possessed and acted upon plural values. Were we to evaluate people, not only according to their intelligence and their education, their occupation, and their power, but according to their kindliness and their courage, their imagination and sensitivity, their sympathy and generosity, there

170

could be no classes. Who would be able to say that the scientist was superior to the porter with admirable qualities as a father [etc.].[4]

Fine as these ideals may be, they are not allowed to structure his story in any way, nor given any real context. They provide no viable challenge to meritocracy and never actually take root. Only the very end of the story hints that they may have any power at all.

What we do have instead in the story is a clear exposition of the justification, logic and structure of meritocracy. Whether in doing this he was simply reflecting and expressing the views of those around him, or actually forming them, is debatable. But there is no doubt that these ideas were remarkably prescient and that they anticipated, even if in a caricatured form, many of the features of British society today. First, Michael's meritocracy is based on a very one-dimensional understanding of merit as involving intelligence that can be tested and used to rank everyone. In real life we can see this reflected in the prioritisation of the academic skills over technical or vocational, and in the creation of an education system that reflects these values. So, for example, rather than emphasising the ways in which polytechnics were different from universities, the system has assimilated them to the university system and ranked them hierarchically within it. School qualifications have become standardised—even the content of practical subjects such as art has become more academic—and, in order to be perceived as having any value, GNVQs have had to be given an equivalent academic grade. Intelligence tests to get into university may be imminent and even IQ tests for six month olds have been proposed.[5] It is these sorts of academic qualifications rather than skills or experience which provide a passport for a job.

All this is very reminiscent of the meritocracy story in which the narrator explains that 'all subjective judgements about the status of different jobs were assimilated to the one national model'.[6] These actual policies serve to remind us how pluralism is receding into the distance.

Meritocracy also describes how education needs to start earlier and earlier in order to release clever children from the disadvantages that might accrue to them if they come from less privileged families. We learn that

The social ladder was so long—the gap between the styles of life of upper and lower classes so wide—that promising children had to begin their climb through the schools at the earliest age possible.[7]

In later years schools become such a crucial aspect of the children's lives that 'their homes have become simply hotels, to the great benefit of the children'. In real life, under New Labour children are being encouraged to attend nursery schools earlier and earlier, and all forms of early childcare are increasingly assessed in terms of explicit educational aims. Within government, responsibility for childcare has moved into the department that deals with education. Homes may not yet have become simply hotels, but schools are already feeling that they increasingly bear the burden for a child's welfare and well-being.

Another way in which Michael was remarkably far-sighted was in his anticipation of a massive service industry. In his story, the problem of widespread unemployment is resolved when intelligent people stop performing menial domestic tasks and the previously unemployed army of floating labour provides personal services in the home. While it is not, of course, the less intelligent who do this work, there are now a host of agencies providing services from cleaning and dog walking to cooking and a range of other domestic duties—as well as an army of new migrants who will do the same for much less money.

These are just a few of the things that Michael anticipated accurately. Others include giving fancy names to straightforward jobs, the cult of sport, the increasing class gap, the fact that age (often along with experience) is not just disregarded but seen almost as a handicap when looking for someone to do a particular job, and paying young people to stay on at their studies, all on top of the more obvious things such as inheritance tax and the banning of hereditary peerages. Michael could hardly have predicted the future with more acuity even if that had been his main aim.

The book was also intended to act as a warning about the downsides of meritocracy, and this aspect of the book was important to Michael. He explains in his 1994 introduction that 'if the book is not seen to be counter-argument as well as argument the point of it (or at least a good half point) will be lost'. The Achilles' heel of meritocracy is seen as its tendency to promote social polarisation and the creation of a bitter, excluded underclass. But this is not spelt out, only hinted at. So while acting as a warning, the outcome does not undermine the model in any more fundamental way. Many casual readers may miss the alarm. This may be helped by the way in which the whole story is delivered through a fictional narrator, an alternative Michael or *alter ego* rather than Michael himself. This serves to distance the outcomes from the exposition of meritocracy, and means that we do not take it too seriously ourselves.

However, while meritocratic values clearly structure our society, we do appear to have heeded these warnings as well. Michael's overall aim was to show that a society that was structured according to individual intelligence would be more unpleasant to live in than anything we had ever known. In real life, we have tried to ensure that differing levels of ability do not have too much impact on the system of rewards, by inhibiting them from being expressed. So, for example, children in primary school frequently do not receive marks for their work that would enable them to distinguish their own ability from that of their peers. Sports days have become a team activity, where nobody loses or wins. Access to higher-level qualifications and education has been broadened out to the point at which A-levels have become all but meaningless, and university staff now have few means for sorting the wheat from the chaff. And if particular groups of people are falling behind, they are given an extra boost so as not to feel alienated from the meritocratic process.

When Michael explained that the counter-argument was included with the argument, the implication was that they both had equal weight. This was disingenuous. By presenting the *contra* along with the *pro* arguments, he protected meritocracy from too much analysis, and so left it firmly in place. As a result, the message of the book seems to be that meritocracy should be aspired to, but that precautions need to be taken against its potentially negative outcomes. In the event, this is more or less as things have worked out in Britain. Michael was far-sighted enough to anticipate the direction in which things were moving, and he may also have had a hand in determining the direction they followed.

But this message is, I think, wrong. I believe that the problems of meritocracy to which Michael alluded were not simply side-effects, which could be combated. They were actually symptoms of a much more fundamental flaw. This was his assumption that there was an essentially antagonistic relationship between the family and effective meritocracy. His assumption not only had negative outcomes for ideas about the family, but was responsible for the more unattractive features of the meritocracy that he portrays as well. In the following sections I will explore how he conceptualised this relationship in a way that was damaging for both parties to it, and then conclude by suggesting an alternative way in which things could be understood.

Weakening the power of the family from above

In Michael's model, the institutional power of the family has to be reduced in order to allow for the flowering of meritocratic ideals. I will outline the process by which this was done. First, it is important to note that in the story the primary focus of the state is not inward, on 'the greatest happiness for the greatest number' of its citizens, or some other legitimising formula. It is outwards, on the threat posed by other countries and the need to maintain a competitive position in relation to them. There are constant reminders of this throughout the book:

But Britain could not be [remain] a caste society if it was to survive as a great nation, great that is, in comparison with others. To withstand international competition the country had to make better use of its human material, above all, of the talent which was even in England, one might say always and everywhere, too scarce . . . the sanction for such folly [not doing so] would be sharp. China and Africa would draw ahead in productivity. British and European influence would fade as our science became cluttered up by the second-rate. We should once again be 'over-matched in the competition of the world'.[8]

This need to maintain a competitive position provides a justification for subordinating those institutions that appear to work against efficiency, and that means the family. For at the start of Michael's analysis we learn that Britain is in the grip of a kinship system that structures the public world of production and the government to people's personal advantage. Jobs and businesses are inherited through nepotism. As he explains, 'even in business job succession was quite common enough to be a very serious impediment to productivity'.[9]

By paying for a private education, the wealthy are able to pass their privilege on. The workplace imitates the age structure of the family, in a gerontocracy that requires that the most able have to retire in their turn, while seniority is reached regardless of a person's ability to do the job. Aristocracy ensures that position as well as wealth is inherited. And far from such privilege endowing people with a sense of responsibility and duty, as Peregrine Worsthorne has lately reminded us,[10] Michael argued that it takes away their motivation to do the job. Laziness is not only a feature of the property-owning classes: it is emulated by the labourers, who expect tea breaks and suchlike and who strike when they cannot have them. Production suffers greatly as a result—not simply because people are lazy, but because the absence of competition means that the best person is seldom in the important job.

In order to obtain greater efficiency, all forms of social advancement and promotion based on the family have to be discouraged, to ensure that it is only on the basis of personal ability that people get ahead. So family influences are gradually removed from production, government and other aspects of public life. The hereditary House of Lords is abolished. The young gradually usurp the elderly by claiming that their more up-to-date education means that they are better suited to the job. People are no longer able to pass jobs on to their children, and the creation of larger companies through nationalisation of industry means that one is less able to transmit jobs to others simply because of knowing them. Death duties and capital gains tax are also introduced. And for those who do somehow manage to retain part of their wealth, this cannot be used any longer to purchase a privileged education for their children, since there are no longer fee-paying schools worth paying for.

The power of the family is considerably weakened as a result of this, with the most powerful—the aristocracy—being the greatest victims, and the main beneficiary being the state. After this, the family can no longer provide a guide to orient people's actions, or an alternative value system. This leaves the state free to determine the agenda and set the criteria by which people are to be judged. The narrator explains what these criteria should be:

Since the country is dedicated to the one overriding purpose of economic expansion, people are judged according to the single test of how much they increase production, or the knowledge that will, directly or indirectly, lead to that consummation.[11]

This provides the justification for hierarchy and the uneven allocation of rewards. But in retrospect the case does not seem as compelling as it might

174

have been. If Michael had really been against the hierarchical organisation that follows on from state power, he surely would not have been so ready to dismiss the role of the family in social organisation. He might have thought more carefully about ways in which there could have been cooperation between the family and state.

Weakening the power of the family from below

The family is weakened not just through limitations on its public, institutional role, but also by having attention drawn to the importance of the individual. This works at two levels. Michael's narrator focuses first on the importance of achieving fairness between individuals—this is a central aim of the meritocracy:

On the strength of sheer individual merit they could rise up the social ladder as far as their ability would stretch. This was a boon to them and a boon as well to their parents.[12]

This provides the state with an obvious justification for attacking the power of the family. But on top of this, the family is seen as trapping the individual:

The ordinary parent . . . wanted to hand on his money to his child rather than to outsiders or to the state; the child was part of himself and by bequeathing property to him the father assured a kind of immortality to himself: the hereditary father never died. . . . Parents, by controlling property, also controlled their children; a threat to cut a child out of a will was almost as effective an assertion of power in industrial as it had been in agricultural Britain.[13]

By concentrating on the way in which the state *liberates* the individual from the family, Michael obscures the self-interested motives of the state and the ways in which it might benefit from what is going on.

The role of the family is also pushed into insignificance by the way in which individual merit is constructed. On a first reading, the concept of merit sounds eminently reasonable. Merit is defined as the sum of effort plus intelligence. The component intelligence does not appear to be just some kind of abstraction, but an operational concept that can be measured to see whether one has the qualities to benefit from a higher education. Thus as well as intelligence in conventional terms, one would imagine that it could include the ability to work hard, good communication and social skills, originality of thought, powers of concentration and a whole range of other things. If merit were really understood as effort plus all these things, there would be plenty of room for acknowledging the role of the social in its formation.

Initially, the narrator seems to do this. For example, he draws attention to the range of environmental influences that can affect intelligence:

They realised the brain was no more separable than the sexual organs from the biochemical economy of the individual, and the individual no more separable than his lungs from the environment, social as well as physical, in which he lived.[14]

Likewise, he seems to be aware that the family has a very important role too, and mentions its influence a number of times:

the champions of the family have argued that for raising children there has not yet been any adequate substitute for the device which has served mankind so far . . . steady affection from the same parents—this has been generally accepted since the experiments in the late 1980s—is necessary for the full glandular development of the infant. Love is biochemistry's chief assistant.[15]

However, when we look at the subsequent things he says about intelligence, and the way in which he discusses the meritocratic society, the earlier comments appear to be simply lip service. His equation doesn't add up. So, for example, rather than being able to include the broad range of qualities that some of his previous references suggest, intelligence becomes just 'the ability to raise production, directly or indirectly . . . this iron measure is the judgement of society upon its members'.[16] Even more damningly, he persistently refers to the role of Nature (always spelt, unlike nurture, with a capital 'N') in determining intelligence, suggesting that it is an absolute that can be predicted, a property an *individual* is endowed with, rather than something that the family plays a role in constituting. Either you are a member of what Michael describes in his new introduction as the 'lucky sperm club' or you are not. And there is nothing that any amount of nurture can do. As for effort, this is never mentioned again.

So, in the narrative the family is neither allowed a role in providing the individual with a direction in life nor credited with any important influence on who the individual becomes. The structure of early education prevents parents from having much input into their child, and as he or she becomes an adult they are not allowed to use their own resources to help the child along. Family is reduced to a shadow of its former self, left without any apparent levers—until the Women's Movement comes along later in the story. This insignificance of the family is reflected in the generally powerless position of the private realm, which I shall examine next.

The place of the private realm

Since the family does not play a role in the creation of merit, it cannot be seen as contributing to production, and therefore is accorded very little value in the greater scheme of things. So, for example, whereas teachers are paid as much as industrial scientists, those who do childcare are regarded as 'persons of low intelligence' and are very poorly paid. Childcare is not accorded any particular value, but seen as something that would be best taken over by schools. So women receive no rewards for their mothering work.

The subordination of the private realm is reinforced by the fact that there are no take-home wages. The home is instead regarded as an extension of the workplace, and receives money in the form of expenses, sufficient to ensure that the employee can perform to maximum efficiency at work. This results in

176

a situation in which the home has no independent status of its own, but is entirely dependent on the public sphere.

All of this engenders a particular tension for women, whose source of identity has always been lodged more securely in the private sphere. A devalued private sphere can no longer provide this. Work can, and so women are far more eager to participate, and participate equally, in the public sphere. At the same time they recognise that the care of their children is essential. Indeed, as childcare is now so devalued, there are likely to be fewer people of suitable quality who can take their role. So it is even more essential than before:

But they cannot, if they take any notice of the teaching of psychology, entrust the entire care of their offspring to a person of low intelligence. Infants need the love of a mother; they also need her intellectual stimulation, her tender introduction to a high culture, her diligent preparation for a dedicated life. She will neglect her motherly duties only at the peril of her children, not to speak of the displeasure of her husband.[17]

This puts women in the position of having to do childcare as well as work outside the home. As they derive no real recognition for the former, and cannot participate equally in the latter, they now occupy a far more subordinate status than when the family had a central institutional role.

Thus the meritocracy evolves in opposition to the family. These are two opposing principles that cannot coexist:

A sort of egalitarianism flourished then because two contradictory principles for legitimizing power were struggling for mastery—the principle of kinship and the principle of merit . . .[18]

When merit triumphs, it is no longer possible for the principle of kinship to survive. We can see this if we look carefully at the construction of the meritocratic state. For within a meritocracy it would not be possible to attach value to care and nurturing, as this would set up an alternative basis for merit, a potential for pluralism, and the hierarchy so fundamental to meritocracy would be undermined. Alternatively, if the state were to value childcare in terms of its role in social reproduction, and reward mothers accordingly, the process of child rearing would become entirely an extension of the public realm and the family as we know it would not survive.

The family is a fundamental social institution, and meritocracy's inability to accommodate it sets up the fault line along which the whole thing breaks down. This is established right at the beginning of the story, in the presaging statement that hints at the eventual outcome:

We underestimated the resistance of the family. The home is still the most fertile seed-bed for reaction.[19]

And so it proves. Women, who cannot participate equally in the public realm, end up feeling, rightly, that the system is very much structured to favour men. In response to their dissatisfaction, they join forces with other categories who also feel exploited by it—including the less intelligent and less articulate working classes and those older men who feel they haven't received the seniority appropriate to their age. Together they form an uprising, which appears eventually to lead to the collapse of meritocracy.

Alternative ways in which the family could fit in

The meritocracy and some of its underlying principles have never really been challenged. This is possibly, as argued earlier, to do with the way in which the book has been constructed. If Michael had really wanted to promote debate, he would have done better to place a utopian argument in favour of meritocracy on the table and let the critics have their say. With his satire he beat them to it: consequently, a really thorough analysis has not occurred. While he deals with one major problem of meritocracy, he does not, I think, tackle the central flaw, which is the idea that the family is a source of inequality, inefficiency, individual repression and all the other bad things against which his meritocracy fought. What I would like to suggest, however, is that it is possible to make completely the opposite case for the family; that is, to see it as the source of equality and efficiency and merit. Once we realise that Michael's suspect is in fact innocent, many other problems can be resolved.

Far from being opposing principles, the family and merit are in fact very closely linked. Even within his story, Michael has difficulty maintaining a convincing separation, and the narrator makes frequent reference to the advantages that accrue to children when they come from a nurturing home:

These clever people were in a sense only half educated, in school but not home. When they graduated they had not the same self-assurance as those who had the support and stimulus of their families from the beginning.[20]

It is also apparent that for people to contribute to production they need a lot more than raw IQ in order to be effective. However, he never allows such observations to impinge on the structure of his story, but returns to merit as a narrow and measurable form of intelligence, which is genetically determined and cultivated in schools but is not a social product in any more fundamental way.

Following on from *Meritocracy*, the dominant thinking in Britain on individual attainment has emphasised the role of schools. If only all young people accessed a good education, their full potential would be achieved. This type of thinking is exemplified by David Miliband, who thinks that parents do have a role to play in terms of their level of expectations, but apart from that outcomes are very much a product of education in schools.[21] For other commentators, though, schools are only part of the answer, and increasing attention is being given to the family and home. For Harry Brighouse, the increasing impact of class on social mobility occurs because so many of the qualities that employers are really looking for (such as physical and psycho-

178

logical characteristics, social skills and dress sense) are not something that children learn at school. They are transmitted through their family, community and peer group socialisation.[22] Neil MacIntosh too suggests that parental commitment is the single most important resource for social mobility, and that this can be undermined where the state becomes too involved:

The ability of education to contribute to social mobility is heavily influenced by the capacity of the family to prepare, enable and support children to succeed in learning.[23]

The idea that the family has a role in constituting who their children *are* in a far more fundamental sense is explored by Adam Swift. He explains that what families do to or with or for their children may simply influence them *extrinsically*; 'things without which their children would be better or worse off'.[24] This might include things such as direct transmission of property, and the use of economic resources to procure competitive advantage for them: the sorts of things which, as he points out, are turning out to be much less important than many had believed.

Other factors, he explains, seem more *in*strinsic—change these and what you have are different people:

We should understand parental influence primarily to occur through other mechanisms, mechanisms that, I will suggest, can helpfully be regarded as constitutive of the family, or of the children raised in them (or of both) . . .[25]

He considers three ways in which this intrinsic type of constitution might work. First, parents affect the well-being of their children by constituting them genetically. Second, parents do things that are constitutive of their personalities:

Some of the variation in personality traits is due to variation in what parents do to or with or for their children. These personality traits help to explain how people fare in life and many regard this as entirely appropriate; they properly count as desert bases.[26]

Finally, parents can 'influence their children's identities: their understandings of who they are, and what matters to them'. He quotes Brian Barry on this:

The details of upbringing that make for a greater or lesser thirst for educational attainment and a greater or lesser capacity to give educational institutions what they want are a part of the constituents of people's personal identity—they are not necessarily to be repudiated as something that merely 'happened to them'.[27]

'Happened', for example, as a member of the 'lucky sperm club'—a view that Michael certainly took.

Once we recognise the strong connections between merit and family, whole new vistas of understanding and opportunity open up. If the impact of education is only secondary, this helps to explain why education detached from family support is now having a declining effect on class mobility. The influence of the parents will not be so easily undone, or made up for. It helps to explain the persistently lower achievement rates of those who come from single-parent homes, even where other indicators such as economic or educational background suggest that they ought to do very well. If family is significant to achievement, then family breakdown will affect it.

The possibility that family is one of the most important variables in understanding merit is also helpful in understanding differences in achievement that occur between different ethnic groups. For some migrants, one of the most direct consequences of migration is a breakdown in family ties. Other migrant groups, including many Asians, come from backgrounds where families would appear to be much stronger—and where somehow they manage to keep these ties going in the country of settlement. An exploration of the different family structures of migrant groups may offer greater insight into variations in achievement than currently conventional explanations around racial discrimination ever could.

If we question *Meritocracy*'s essentially negative view of the family, we realise that most of the other arguments can be turned on their heads. Far from being a *source* of inequality, the family may provide one of the most effective institutions through which it can be overcome. This can work in different ways. First, if the family and processes of socialisation produce individual merit, rather than genetic inheritance and economic resources, this means that our own economic and educational circumstances do not condition our offspring's achievements in the way that we often assume. Parents may be in a position to develop merit in their children regardless of their own economic limitations.

When we look at societies studied by anthropologists, we can see some of the ways in which families can act to reduce inequality between individuals. The family is effectively a network of individuals bound together by recognition of long-term common identity and mutual obligations. As such, it provides a ready-made framework for relations of reciprocity and exchange, in which poorer members can get access to contacts, jobs and money. The effect is redistributive. Families can also provide a mechanism for pooling resources. These can be used to buy education for an individual child, or accommodation for a newly formed family. With a larger number of people to call upon, differences of opportunity between individuals become evened out.

As families provide individuals with more secure support networks, they also enable pluralism to be sustained. So, for example, an individual who knows that he or she has the backing of his or her family is more able to hold values and beliefs that differ from those of the mainstream, because he or she is not dependent on it for support. In fact, it may be because some people do have different values that what appears to one person to be inequality may not be perceived or experienced as such by another. Families act as alternative institutions to the state, sustaining their own values and beliefs. It may only be through the existence of strong alternative institutions like this that scarce but essential skills and abilities are perpetuated.

Families also act as a vital nexus between the individual and the state. As Michael recognises in *Meritocracy*, individuals do not readily subordinate their own interests and destinies to something as abstract as the state or the nation. If required to do so, they are likely to rebel. However, they are capable of great hard work and sacrifice if it will benefit their children, and it is the future of their offspring that in large part motivates individuals to produce. Michael, both as narrator and author, was alert to this, but tended to regard it either as an atavistic tendency or as something that was only appropriate to an agricultural system:

Agriculture demanded hard unremitting exertion, and, in the prevailing mental climate, this was best secured when men knew they were working for children and grandchildren who would benefit from improvement as they would suffer from neglect . . . Inheritance at once prompted exertion, instilled responsibility, and preserved continuity.[28]

The assumption is that in an industrial society with a meritocratic system, such instincts on the whole need to be subdued. But no convincing replacement for the family is offered.

A more powerful family system not only contributes towards social equality and pluralism, but could lead to improvements in the status of women as well. For the family to become a more influential institution again, both in the life of the individual and in mediating his or her relationship with the state, would require a reallocation of economic resources and status in the direction of the private sphere. This is of particular benefit to all those who have compromised their possibilities in the public realm by choosing to prioritise their caring role.

Implications

A lasting legacy of Michael's book, I believe, is that the family is conventionally seen as the enemy of social mobility and justice. This is far from my own view, though. I think that in reality the family could be a very useful instrument in promoting a genuinely open society, in which a much wider range of abilities is appreciated than at present.

Many politicians are aware of the family's invaluable role as a mechanism of support. At the same time they are afraid of promoting it, because there is a belief—which perhaps *Meritocracy* itself helped to spread—that it is a threat to equality of opportunity. This is clear from Stephen Aldridge's report:

Indeed, the dilemma for policymakers is that it is highly desirable in a civilised society that parents should do this but the consequence may be to reinforce inequalities of opportunity.[29]

Part of the reason for these misplaced worries may be that family solidarity has different implications in different sectors of society. When Michael made an association between family and perpetuation of inequality, he was extrapolating from the aristocracy and property-owning classes for whom, at a superficial level, family is all about transmission of titles and wealth.

What he did not take into consideration was the role that families played for poorer people, not only in potentially instilling them with social and cultural capital, but also through providing them with a range of support mechanisms enabling them to get on. Ironically, this is something that he did express in his other work. But it seems to be forgotten in *Meritocracy*.

The capacity of the family to act in this positive way has become obscured over the years. *Meritocracy* was written at a time of great policy changes, which the book was designed to encourage and justify, if not to affect. As previously mentioned, these were in part to do with reducing the role of inheritance. But they were also concerned with establishing non-family supports, in the welfare state. It is becoming increasingly evident that some of these changes have had unintended consequences which, moreover, have affected the worst off disproportionately. By providing a public source of social support, the welfare state has contributed to a weakening of the family, the institution on which people would otherwise depend. This means that not only do the less well off lack economic resources, but they also now lack the support and social capital that the family, in different circumstances, would be more likely to provide.

Similarly, it can be argued that the introduction of comprehensive schools has meant that there are no more grammar schools to act as a means of escape for the working class—'escalators for the gifted'. All this has resulted in an intensifying relationship between poverty and lack of social mobility. There is a vicious circle here, to which the usual response is simply to call for more intervention from the state—which ignores the ways in which state control may give new elites the means to *hold back* the working class from rising and competing against them.[30]

Growing recognition of the failure of state action does, however, mean that people are starting again to look to families. A strengthened family could help to even out inequalities, and support a plural value system. Far from conflicting, it could provide opportunity and mobility with an institutional basis. But this new meritocracy would look very different from the one that Michael conceived.

Meritocracy and Popular Legitimacy

PETER SAUNDERS

Introduction

IN this chapter, I explore two simple questions: Do we live in a meritocratic society and, if so, is this something to be celebrated or deplored?

On the first question, the evidence suggests that contemporary Britain is, broadly, a meritocratic country. If you are bright, and you work hard, you will probably succeed. You may not get to the very top, for there are many other bright, hard-working people competing with you for the top positions, and factors such as a supportive family or good schooling will give some people additional advantages over others. Sheer luck also often plays a key part in shaping people's careers. But those who enjoy the happy combination of ability plus effort (Michael Young's definition of 'merit') generally achieve a reasonable degree of educational and career success in modern Britain, whatever social background they start out from.

Most of the obstacles to success that used to confront able individuals from lower-class origins have been removed since the end of the Second World War. Access to education has been opened up, credentialism has become much more important than personal networks when it comes to job recruitment, and it is easier to borrow capital if you want to start your own business. These and other changes mean that talented, hard-working people now tend to end up in relatively high-status, well-remunerated 'middle-class' positions, even if they start out from humble origins.

This does not mean that Britain is a perfect meritocracy, for accident of birth still plays some part in shaping occupational outcomes. But class origins now operate more as a brake on people sliding down the snakes than as a barrier to those seeking to climb up the ladders. The days when a working-class background set tight limits on the kind of work to which you could realistically aspire have long gone, but well-off, well-connected middle-class parents can still to some degree help their less able children to avoid failure by sending them to the best independent schools, by passing on values of personal success and ambition, and by bequeathing them various forms of cultural and economic capital.

The main factor preventing full realisation of the meritocratic ideal today, therefore, is not the obstacles in the path of those moving upwards, but the capacity of those near the top to limit their children's chances of falling. These limitations on downward mobility pose interesting dilemmas for politicians (like Mr Blair) who say they are committed to extending meritocracy.

If we really wanted to take the final step towards achieving the meritocratic ideal, the problem we would have to overcome is how (and whether) to pare

Published by Blackwell Publishing Ltd, 9600 Garsington Road, Oxford OX4 2DQ, UK and 350 Main Street, Malden, MA 02148, USA

back the safety net for those at the top. This is a very different agenda from the one that drove so much social and educational policy reform after 1945, and it is a lot more problematic. It is a lot easier politically to promote policies intended to help bright lower-class children to succeed (e.g. by improving state education) than it is to set out deliberately to ensure that dull middle-class children fail (e.g. by abolishing private education). It is also questionable whether it is sensible, or even ethical, for governments to use their power to try to prevent 'good' parents from doing all they can to benefit their children, even if the aim is to make competition 'fairer' among their offspring.

Given these considerations, pursuit of an ever more perfect meritocracy is not an agenda that is likely to appeal to many elected politicians in the future, although recent attempts to bias university selection procedures against applicants from private schools indicate that New Labour is still flirting with the dream of turning a middle-class background into an educational disadvantage. Short of abolishing the family, however, it is difficult to envisage how any government could make serious inroads into limiting the transmission of cultural and educational capital from one generation to the next, even if it were thought this was a good idea.

Sixty years after the end of the Second World War, we have probably therefore gone as far as we can realistically expect to go in pursuing the meritocratic ideal. But is this a blessing or a curse?

Reflecting on the growing importance of talent and brains in determining people's positions in contemporary America, Charles Murray and Richard Herrnstein suggest that meritocracy has led to a system of 'cognitive stratification', in which talented people rise into a well-paid and respected 'cognitive elite', while those of lower intelligence gravitate to a low-skilled, low-paid and increasingly disaffected 'cognitive underclass'.[1] This, of course, was precisely Michael Young's nightmare scenario for a meritocratic Britain—a growing social division between a high-IQ leadership stratum and a low-IQ substratum.

What Young found so objectionable about the shift to meritocracy is that it leaves no hiding place for those who end up at the bottom. In a meritocracy based on the principle of 'just desserts', those at the bottom seem 'rightfully' to belong there, and there are no excuses or rationalisations with which they might salvage a sense of dignity and self-worth. It is for this reason that he came to question whether meritocracy really is such a good ideal to aim for after all.

In denial over meritocracy

British empirical sociology has for many decades had as a core focus the analysis of class inequalities. This partly reflects what Peter Bauer has called a 'British obsession' with class—the popular idea that Britain is in some way uniquely crippled by class divisions.[2] But it also reflects the traditionally close links in this country between academic sociology and social democratic or socialist politics. A staggering 84 per cent of British sociology professors identify themselves as politically on the 'left', while just 2 per cent say they are on the 'right'.[3] Given this skewed pattern of political sympathies, it is little wonder that British sociology has been obsessed with analysing class, for this reflects a strong commitment within the discipline to exposing, modifying and overturning what are seen as the iniquities of free market capitalism.

Because of the centrality of class analysis to their political philosophy as well as their discipline, sociologists in Britain have always been suspicious of arguments claiming that the country is moving towards meritocracy, for this implies a weakening of the class system that they are reluctant to contemplate. There has always been resistance to claims that social class origins no longer weigh heavily on individuals' life chances. For years, prominent sociologists such as Tom Bottomore, Ralph Miliband, Peter Worsley and Anthony Giddens were happy to promote and recycle an orthodox view that social mobility chances in Britain are severely limited, and that opportunities for working-class children are stunted, even though the evidence for these propositions was very shaky.[4]

This orthodoxy was grounded in a rather uncritical reading of just one very old study (David Glass' analysis of male social mobility rates). But this study was based on research carried out in the 1940s, on people who had been born as long ago as the nineteenth century, and its data were clearly flawed (though it was not until 1987 that any sociologist thought to investigate some of the glaring weaknesses).[5] Generations of students were therefore taught that top positions in Britain are self-recruiting, that any movement that does occur takes place across very short distances, and that opportunities for working-class advancement are sorely restricted—yet none of this was actually true.

This sociological orthodoxy was finally challenged (albeit only partially) in 1980, when John Goldthorpe published the results of a major survey conducted eight years earlier. Dividing the population into three broad classes, Goldthorpe found (much to his own surprise) that mobility between them was common and extensive. Half of all the adult men in his sample had gravitated to a different class position from the one they had been born into, and long-distance movement both up and down the occupational class system was remarkably common (more than 40 per cent of sons born into the upper class had fallen to a lower class, and getting on for half of working-class sons had risen to a higher one).

Later research confirmed and even strengthened these results. Surveys in the 1980s found that one-third of those entering professional and managerial positions had been born to manual working-class parents, and that rates of downward mobility (the toughest test of the openness of a class system) were higher in Britain than in almost any other developed Western nation.[6]

But having scuppered the prevailing sociological belief that Britain was a closed society, Goldthorpe promptly resurrected it. He did this by arguing that although absolute rates of social mobility were much higher than anyone had expected, 'relative mobility chances' were still heavily skewed against those born into the working class.

What he meant by this was that working-class children had less chance of succeeding (and a higher chance of failing) than middle-class children. Despite all the movement up and down the class system, a child born to professional parents was still three or four times more likely to end up in the middle class than a child born to semi- or unskilled manual worker parents. Goldthorpe deduced from this that working-class children must still be facing barriers that middle-class children were not having to confront—which meant that Britain was still a long way short of being a meritocracy.

There was, however, a fallacy in Goldthorpe's reasoning, and it is a fallacy that repeatedly surfaces in British sociological research on social inequality, be it inequality of class, gender or race. It is the consequentialist fallacy of deriving causes from looking at outcomes.

When comparing different social groups, social researchers commonly find patterns of differential outcomes. They might find, for example, that blacks are over-represented in prison populations compared with whites, or that females are under-represented in top management positions as compared with males. In Goldthorpe's case, he found that working-class children are under-represented in the professional and managerial grades as compared with middle-class children.

Armed with such findings, the temptation is to assume that they indicate the operation of systematic 'social exclusion', rather than telling us anything about the individuals who comprise the different groups in question. The possibility that the prison population is disproportionately black because blacks commit more crimes than whites is, for example, often resisted in favour of the idea that the police and courts must be 'institutionally racist', disproportionately arresting and convicting more black people than white people. Similarly, the possibility that more women than men may choose to spend time with their children at the expense of pursuing their careers is discounted in favour of exclusionary theories based on the idea that a 'glass ceiling' is blocking women from gaining the promotions they seek. And in Goldthorpe's case, the possibility that middle-class children outperform working-class children because they are on average more motivated or more intelligent was ruled out from the outset in favour of an assumption that institutional blockages and class biases must be to blame for their differential rate of performance.

The problem with consequentialist explanations such as these is that they substitute circular reasoning for evidence. An unequal outcome is taken as sufficient grounds for establishing the operation of some process of 'social exclusion', and social exclusion is in turn assumed to be the only possible cause of an unequal outcome.

Goldthorpe, for example, made no attempt to investigate whether the differences in relative mobility chances that he found could be explained wholly or in part by differing average levels of ability between children from different class backgrounds. He simply assumed (and asserted) that they could not. Having defined away the only competing hypothesis, he was then able to locate his research findings in a long tradition of Fabian-inspired sociological studies designed to show how an unequal 'social structure' (which could get expressed in all sorts of ways, including overcrowded housing conditions, inadequate parenting in lower-class families, anti-school subcultures in working-class peer groups, poor schools in poorer areas, class-biased selection procedures and examinations, a class-based curriculum, negative labelling of working-class students by middle-class teachers, or class-based linguistic codes in academic learning) conspired to block working-class advancement. The unequal outcome itself thus became the evidence of its own cause, and the disturbing question of intelligence could be put to one side and ignored.

Michael Young's belief that it is intelligence more than any other factor that is increasingly driving occupational attainment was, therefore, never actually tested by British sociologists. It was simply assumed to be wrong, and the question of intelligence was dismissed from the sociological agenda.

How meritocratic is Britain?

Defining something out of existence is not, however, the same as disproving it, and trying to explain patterns of occupational recruitment without analysing individual ability levels was like staging Hamlet without the Prince. It was inevitable that, sooner or later, the question of ability would have to resurface in the social mobility debate.

Although it may be unpalatable for many sociologists to accept, it is quite plausible that the scale of difference in mobility patterns discovered by Goldthorpe could be due to differences in average ability levels among children from different social class origins. To see why, we need to perform a mental experiment.

In a perfectly meritocratic society, each generation would be recruited to different class positions on the basis of individual intelligence. In such a society, people composing the middle class would therefore be more intelligent than those in the lower class. This in turn would mean that we should expect the people in the middle class to produce children who would be intellectually brighter on average than working-class children, because their parents would be brighter (psychological research on the transmission of intelligence predicts a correlation of around 0.5 between parents' IQ scores and those of their children). In a meritocracy, therefore, bright individuals who end up in higher-class locations will tend to produce bright children, who will then often emulate their parents' success. Far from demonstrating a lack of meritocratic selection, as Goldthorpe assumed, differential relative mobility rates are exactly what we would find in a meritocracy.

Elsewhere,[7] I have shown that Goldthorpe's mobility data correspond fairly closely to the pattern that would be predicted had the parents and children in his survey been living in a perfect meritocracy. We need only assume that ability is normally distributed in each generation, and that it correlates at 0.5 between parents and their children. Goldthorpe's reported rates of upward mobility then fit the predicted perfect meritocracy model almost exactly, although his rates of downward mobility are somewhat less than the model predicts that they should be. Overall, Goldthorpe's evidence on occupational selection is broadly consistent with what would occur if Britain were a perfect meritocracy.

Goldthorpe himself never included data on intelligence in his survey, but there is survey evidence that allows us directly to measure the influence that ability has had on individuals' social mobility patterns. One week in 1958, all the children born in England and Wales were included in a survey that has continued at regular intervals ever since (about 11,000 people are still in the sample). Over the years, an enormous amount of information has accumulated about these individuals, including various measures of their intellectual ability (e.g. their reading and numeracy test scores from the age of seven and IQ scores at eleven) and their work motivation (e.g. their school attendance records, teachers' assessments and their attitudes about work during adulthood). The survey also records many different indicators of the social advantages or disadvantages these people may have experienced since they were born (e.g. their parents' social class, the type of schools they attended, their parents' interest and involvement in their early years, and so on). Using multivariate analysis, it is possible to compare the impact of all these different factors on people's subsequent educational and occupational achievements, and when we do this, one factor stands out over and above all the others—their intellectual ability.

Nothing else comes close. This one factor alone accounts for half of all the variance we can explain in people's occupational outcomes. If you had to predict the occupational status achieved by any one of these individuals in adulthood, the single most useful item of information you could ask for would be their IQ test score at age eleven. Taken together, their measured intelligence and motivation when they were at school (or in Michael Young's terminology, their 'ability plus effort') predict nearly two-thirds of the total explained variance in their social class destinations as adults (when the qualifications they have gained are also taken into account, this increases to around 80 per cent). The remaining 20 per cent of explained variance is predicted by their class origins and all the other factors associated with the social advantages or disadvantages to which they were exposed (e.g. the type of schools they attended and the degree to which their parents showed an interest in their education when they were growing up).[8]

This evidence is unambiguous and compelling. It shows that, while Britain is not a perfect meritocracy, individual ability and effort ('merit') are far more important in shaping occupational destinies than the social class origins or the socio-economic conditions in which people grow up. Modern Britain is a society in which talent and determination count for much more than class origins, and where bright and hard-working children enjoy the realistic prospect of occupational success no matter where they start out from in life. This is a strongly meritocratic society.

The trouble with meritocracy

If Michael Young's outline of a meritocratic society has, to most intents and purposes, been realised, this raises the question of whether it is bringing in its wake the personal unhappiness and social dislocation that Young foresaw in *The Rise of the Meritocracy*.

Young's was an unusually gloomy prognosis. For much of the twentieth century, sociologists believed that meritocracy would contribute to social cohesion rather than undermining it. The classic statement of this idea was by Emile Durkheim, who warned in the 1890s of the socially disruptive effects that would follow if talented people were prevented from rising to the social positions to which they are best suited (what Durkheim called a 'forced division of labour'). In Durkheim's view, social solidarity is only possible when 'the distribution of social functions' corresponds to 'the distribution of natural talents' such that 'social inequalities exactly express natural inequalities'.[9] In other words, individuals will only be happy, and society will only function harmoniously, if social positions are allocated strictly on the basis of individual merit.

Much the same view was elaborated fifty years later by the American sociologists Kingsley Davis and Wilbert Moore, who famously proposed that societies function most coherently when they are able to fill the most important social positions with the most talented individuals. In their view, this was achieved in market societies by economic inducements, which meant that far from tearing a society apart, social and economic inequality actually helps stitch it together by ensuring that the 'best' people get to fill the key positions.[10]

Against arguments such as these, however, Young seemed to be predicting that meritocracy would bring discord, not harmony. He suggested that, by stripping the lower classes of their naturally most gifted leaders, a meritocracy would create an increasingly marginalised and sullen underclass, which would feel little attachment to the core norms and values of mainstream society, and which would eventually rebel against its subordination.

In the fifty years since his book was published, there is certainly evidence for the deterioration in traditional working-class urban neighbourhoods that Young was predicting. Labour MP Frank Field, for example, detects a breakdown in respect and civility that he believes has followed from the collapse of leadership in traditional working-class communities (although he traces this collapse more to de-industrialisation and the growth of welfare dependency than to the rise of the meritocracy). The churches and mutual societies that, together with civic leaders, used to enforce rules of behaviour and standards of common decency have largely disappeared, and coupled with the corrosive effects of widespread reliance on unconditional state welfare, this has, in Field's view, undermined personal responsibility and led to widespread disorder and disengagement from the norms of acceptable behaviour.[11]

This is a long way from Young's predicted populist revolt, but it does suggest that 'anomie' may be much more prevalent today than a century ago. Despite all the opportunities open to them, many young Britons seem dangerously disaffected. While Durkheim was almost certainly right in saying that when people are prevented from competing for access to privileged positions, the response is likely to be resentment and intensified levels of conflict, this suggests that he may have been wrong to assume that when these barriers are removed, the resentment and conflict will necessarily subside.

One hundred years ago, if you failed to rise up the social scale, you had the compensation of knowing that virtually nobody else around you was rising either. But when social mobility becomes commonplace, failure is likely to be that much more difficult to bear. In his celebrated analysis of promotion prospects in the American military, Robert Merton showed that career satisfaction was higher in the units with low promotion rates than in those with high rates, for soldiers in the former compared their progress with others who had been passed over, while in the latter the comparison was with those who had been elevated.[12] If there is one thing worse than being blocked, it is seeing others succeed where you have failed.

Dissatisfaction and withdrawal are not, however, limited to those who fail. Success too seems today to offer few safeguards against disaffection. The young people who today are turning away from politics and civic engagement are not just the failures—they are the successes too. The explanation may relate to what economists call 'positional goods'—things that only have value in so far as others are denied access to them.

The more opportunity there is for people to succeed in society, the less value such success is likely to have for them. The expansion of the universities offers one obvious example. The positional advantages to be gained from higher education decline the more the number of university places expands, for when everyone is a graduate, a degree ceases to be a passport to status and prosperity. More generally, in a meritocracy with a burgeoning middle class, a middle-class destiny is no more than many people expect, and the respect and sense of self-esteem that used to come with a rise into the middle classes is gradually attenuated. Success therefore affords little satisfaction or joy—it is already factored into people's expectations.

Is meritocracy fair?

Young predicted that meritocracy would not survive these sorts of strains and tensions. In his sociological satire, the meritocracy is overthrown in the year 2033 by a populist uprising, which puts in its place an egalitarian, classless society in which every individual is held in equal regard irrespective of his or her talent.

But what happens next? Young's book is silent on this, but the reality is that a post-meritocratic, egalitarian society would be likely to suffer even greater problems in ensuring social cohesion than a meritocratic one does. This is because ignoring hard work and ability is much more unfair than rewarding it.

The moral case put against meritocracy by egalitarians is that there is no clear ethical reason why talented people should be rewarded more highly than others. Their point is not simply that meritocracy strips the less able of their esteem and self-respect by marooning them at the bottom of the money, authority and prestige pecking orders (although this is an important aspect of their concern). It is also that meritocracy rewards those with greater ability for something they have done nothing to 'deserve'. Whether ability is a genetic or a social endowment inherited from one's parents, there seems no compelling ethical reason why the lucky recipients should be rewarded with social and economic privileges. As Young himself put it, why should the members of the 'lucky sperm club' be treated more favourably than anybody else?[13]

This might be a powerful argument if it really were the case that rewards in society got allocated on the basis of some sort of talent contest. But this is not what meritocracy entails. There is no board or committee allocating rewards on the basis of people's talents. We do not live in a society in which bright children are guaranteed elite entry, or where the best jobs, the highest salaries or the most prestigious residential addresses get allocated to adults on the basis of national IQ test results. Mere talent entitles you to nothing in a meritocracy, for to get the rewards, you have to mobilise your talents in a way that other people find useful.

Individual IQ scores correlate quite highly with occupational status (in the United States, for example, accountants have average scores of 128, compared with 122 for teachers, 109 for electricians, 96 for truck drivers and 91 for farmhands).[14] But this is not because jobs have been handed out according to an intelligence ranking. It is rather because, in the market competition for jobs, bright people are generally more able to supply the sorts of tasks that are in high demand, and which are therefore more highly rewarded and regarded.

Michael Young emphasised that merit equals ability *plus effort*. Merit therefore lies in making use of your talent, not in mere possession of it. Talented people only get rewarded when they develop their talents and successfully sell them in a competitive market. Talented artists do not get rewarded unless they produce canvasses that collectors want to buy; talented entrepreneurs do not make fortunes unless they develop new commodities or services that meet many other people's needs; and talented lawyers, architects and computer programmers will not earn high wages unless they get out of bed each morning and put their skills to good use.

Meritocracy, therefore, operates in harness with the marketplace. It is the interplay of supply and demand that generally (but by no means always) results in the most talented people getting the highest rewards, and this comes about only because the market tends to reward talent that is developed and offered in a form that others find useful. The ethical justification for meritocracy is not that people should be rewarded for their genes or their upbringing; it is that everyone benefits when the talented are induced to hone their abilities to what other people demand in the marketplace.

This, however, poses a second ethical difficulty with the meritocratic ideal, which is that the market does not always reward talented people, even when they work hard and try to provide other people with what they want. You might apply years of geological training and experience by working day and night fruitlessly test drilling in an effort to find oil, only for a complete amateur to strike oil while he or she is digging up rhubarb in his or her back garden. You might show real talent as a roof thatcher, a wheelwright or a typesetter, honing this talent through years of training and practical experience, only to find all this skill and effort rendered worthless by technological innovation. Sheer luck plays a major part in determining people's social class destinies (well over half of the variance in the occupational destinations achieved by the 1958 birth cohort discussed earlier remains unexplained by any combination of individual and social factors that can be measured, and much of this unexplained variance has to be put down to the vagaries of chance).

Precisely because there is no committee handing out rewards on the basis of talent and effort, the meritocratic virtues can easily be overlooked or disregarded in a modern market society, and people who lack 'merit' can find themselves rewarded more highly than those who exhibit it. But this does not necessarily undermine the moral case for meritocracy.

The huge role often played by luck in people's lives need not erode the legitimacy of a meritocracy provided that people see that everyone has had the opportunity to share in it. This is why nepotism poses potential dangers for legitimacy while lotteries do not. People resent nepotism because it closes off opportunities, privileging some people at the expense of others. By contrast, we do not generally begrudge the good fortune of lottery winners, for although they have done nothing to 'deserve' their winnings, anybody could have bought a ticket. We can live with luck, provided that we can trust that the draw has not been rigged.

But where does this leave inheritance? Not everyone has an opportunity of being born to wealthy parents, so isn't inheritance the Achilles' heel of modern market-driven meritocracies?

Emile Durkheim certainly thought so. He believed that harmonious functioning of the division of labour required not only that everyone have access to education (so that 'natural talents' would gravitate to the most rewarding 'social functions'), but also that nobody should get an unfair advantage by inheriting wealth from their parents. Over a century later, however, inheritance arguably poses less of a legitimacy problem than it did in Durkheim's time, simply because it has become so much more 'normal'. With widespread home ownership, the majority of people can now expect to inherit capital of significant value, and (rather like the lottery) this takes the sting out of the sense of unfairness that surrounded inheritance when it was limited to a small elite. While the right to do what one wishes with one's own property still sits uncomfortably with the right to compete on a more-or-less equal footing with one's peers, the tension between inheritance and meritocracy seems to get more manageable, the more property ownership spreads through our society.

While we all know there are talented people who will work hard all their lives and never accumulate a fraction of the amount showered upon the lucky lottery winner or the beneficiary of a large family bequest, this does not necessarily offend us, for commitment to the meritocratic ideal does not demand that all rewards be allocated on the basis of merit. All that we ask is that there should be a fair opportunity to compete.

Meritocracy and popular legitimacy

Michael Young was clearly right that life in a meritocracy can be a bruising experience for those who fail. What he overlooked, however, was that meritocracy resonates powerfully with deeply held ethical values about *fairness*, and these are broadly shared throughout the population.

Young's egalitarian alternative to meritocracy, a society in which individual talent is regarded as a pooled resource and where everyone is accorded equal standing, is not simply unrealistic; it is also deeply unappealing to the great majority of the population. There will be no populist revolt against meritocracy, because open competition on the basis of ability and hard work is widely endorsed (by failures as well as successes) as the fairest system for determining social and economic outcomes.

Evidence for this comes from surveys of public attitudes which I have run in both Britain and Australia. In both countries, people were asked if they agreed or disagreed with three different propositions about material inequalities, and although these surveys were conducted fifteen years apart, at opposite ends of the world, the results were remarkably consistent. They show that the meritocratic ideal is deeply embedded in popular consciousness—at least in the Anglocentric world of liberal capitalism.

The first proposition on which opinions were solicited was a simple free market argument that people are entitled to whatever wealth or income they can lawfully accumulate by means of free exchanges. In both countries, around one-half of people agreed with this principle, and around one-third disagreed.

A second proposition corresponded to the egalitarian ideal according to which tax policy is used to redistribute incomes so that nobody ends up with a lot more or a lot less than anybody else. Again, the Australian and British responses were very similar, with about one-third in each country agreeing and a half disagreeing.

The third proposition represented the meritocratic principle that incomes should reflect hard work and talent. In both countries, support for this principle was overwhelming, with almost nine out of ten agreeing and fewer than one in ten disagreeing.[15]

The generally weak level of support for egalitarianism, coupled with the overwhelming endorsement of meritocracy, indicates that Young was wrong to believe that meritocracy is ultimately incompatible with popular legitimacy. Elsewhere in this volume, Irving Louis Horowitz suggests that 'Meritocracy is a fair, perhaps only, way open at the moment, to produce a productive and cultivated society', and that the alternatives are 'far more mired in contradiction' than is the meritocratic ideal. Horowitz is right. There will be no anti-meritocratic populist revolt, because there is in modern Britain a widespread and deeply held commitment to the ideal of an open society in which people compete to make their talents marketable, and in which they are well rewarded when they succeed.

Nor is this just an ideal. It is, to a large extent, a reality.

The Future

The New Assets Agenda

ANDREW GAMBLE and RAJIV PRABHAKAR

Introduction

THE role of assets in promoting greater equality has received new attention in recent years.[1] Asset-based welfare has created a new agenda, but draws on some old ideas about equality and justice.[2] In doing so, it provides a different way of meeting some of the main objectives of the modern welfare state, and a different way of achieving equality of opportunity. The traditional programmes of the welfare state provide income support and services in kind. The former have often employed means testing, so that help can be targeted on those who need it most, while the latter have often been universal services, such as health and education, provided for all citizens. These two pillars of the postwar welfare state were designed to provide a social minimum, a basic level of security for all citizens, and at the same time a more level starting point for everyone. This did involve some redistribution; however, the aim was not a strict equality of outcome, but greater equality of opportunity, which politicians from all parts of the political spectrum supported.

Equality of opportunity meant that some of the advantages, such as social status and wealth, that individuals derived from being members of particular families should be minimised or removed altogether in deciding who was best qualified to perform the various roles that a society required. If birth or wealth were not to be used, however, then some other criterion was necessary, and various measures of intelligence, knowledge and capacity came to fill that role. Substituting merit for wealth or status did not abolish hierarchy, inequality and authority. It changed their forms, and created a different kind of ruling class, meritocrats rather than aristocrats, but it was still rule by a minority, and society was still conceived as a pyramid with only a few coveted places at the top.

Opening up all posts to competition was a fundamental demand of the liberal, democratic and socialist movements in the nineteenth and twentieth centuries. But their critics, such as Gaetano Mosca, Vilfredo Pareto and Joseph Schumpeter, always doubted that equality of opportunity could be achieved under socialism. All that would happen, they suggested, is that one elite would displace another. The old aristocracy of birth and wealth would give way to a new elite chosen because of their professional and educational qualifications. But it would still be an elite, and as keen on maintaining hierarchy and justifying its rule as natural and commonsense. The great struggle between capitalism and socialism was seen, by these theorists, as a battle between rival elites to control the modern state, rather than one between alternative visions of social and economic order. Some liberal critics

Published by Blackwell Publishing Ltd, 9600 Garsington Road, Oxford OX4 2DQ, UK and 350 Main Street, Malden, MA 02148, USA 197

of socialism, such as Ludwig von Mises and Friedrich von Hayek, went even further. The problem with socialism was that once this meritocratic elite had taken possession of the levers of the modern state and had begun to interfere in the economy, it would soon become entrenched, and would use its position to acquire wealth and status, and become a new self-perpetuating elite.

One of the great problems in modern political thought has been how this problem might be averted, and how a more egalitarian social order can be created that does not benefit a new class of highly educated professionals. The concept of the new class became popular with American conservatives in the 1960s, because it was a way of attacking the liberal establishment and claiming that the public sector was expanding to find highly paid and unnecessary jobs for the meritocracy itself, at the expense of old wealth, and the self-employed. The conflict between these two coalitions was played out in different ways in many countries, and the balance between them meant that meritocracy was only partially successful in any state. But the struggle between conservatives and liberals, or conservatives and social democrats, seemed to be less and less about the creation of a classless society, and more about which elite should rule it. For both conservative and liberal elites, the reward for being an elite was expressed in the acquisition of assets and of status.

A pure meritocracy of the kind that Plato imagined would possess no property and no assets, and its members would be separated from their families, because otherwise they could not be expected to devote themselves to the public good. They would be corrupted and diverted from their high calling to be rulers and administer society according to the rules of justice. But with very few exceptions, no state has been organised in this way, so elites have never been divorced from the acquisition and ownership of assets; indeed, the popular perception of elites is that their members enjoy opportunities to acquire wealth and assets that other members of the society do not have, or only to a much more limited extent. Members of liberal meritocratic elites often have a guilty conscience about the advantages and privileges they have acquired, but seldom are prepared to give them up.

Asset egalitarianism

Despite the displacement of old elites by new ones, social mobility remains low, and in Britain the progress towards a more equal distribution of wealth and income has been reversed in the past twenty-five years. The new inequality is particular marked in the ownership of assets. Between 1979 and 1997, the percentage of households with no assets of any kind rose from 5 per cent to 10 per cent. For those aged between 20 and 34, it rose from 10 per cent to 20 per cent. For those with no financial assets, the percentages were even higher. By contrast, the top 1 per cent had 20 per cent of all personal wealth.[3]

The inequalities in the distribution of wealth and of assets have always been more marked than those of income, and much less easy to reduce by public policy. The rich have always found ways to avoid paying taxes, which leads to the paradoxical recommendation from some economists that reducing taxes on the rich can increase the tax take, because it makes tax avoidance more costly than paying taxes. Many economic liberals have long argued that inequality is necessary for economic progress, and if societies are forced to be equal there will be no growth or economic success. On this argument, the distribution of income and wealth should not be a concern of public policy.

It still is quite troubling, however, even to economic liberals, if there are large numbers of citizens who earn low wages or are unemployed, and who have no assets at all, and never accumulate any throughout their lives. This can be reconciled with older conservative notions of a just hierarchy of social status, but it is harder to do so with any version of liberalism, since such weight is placed on the notion of equality of opportunity, and on the idea of every individual being given the chance to make the most of his or her potential. The disadvantages under which individuals labour if they have no assets are obvious, and although some exceptional or lucky individuals do overcome them, many more do not.

That is why there is an old debate about assets and how to ensure that everyone has access to them. This often involves some redistribution, but it may not. Many contributors to the debate have only been concerned to ensure that every member of the society should have access to assets, and an opportunity to acquire them. There are quite large differences over how this should be done, and particularly over how it should be financed. Once the issue of the distribution of income and wealth was taken up by socialists, the conservative wing of liberalism emphasised that property rights were natural and inviolable. Taxation was bad enough, but taxation to redistribute wealth and income was regarded as an infringement of property rights that threatened liberty, and therefore that could not be justified. A wide dispersal of property rights among citizens is generally considered desirable, but this should be promoted through the spontaneous working of markets and competition, in a framework of law. It cannot be engineered by the state. Property will be dispersed naturally if there is competition. These pillars of the market order—the rule of law, competitive markets and inheritance through families—will gradually spread wealth and assets through the society. Any attempt to speed it up, or to control it, will end in making inequality worse rather than better, by frustrating the forces that alone can moderate it.[4]

On the other side of the debate have always been those who take a more radical approach to the market economy, arguing that market institutions, if not designed by human beings, can at least be modified by them. The processes of market competition and family inheritance have over time entrenched advantage and privilege in contemporary societies, rather than eroding them. Numerous proposals have been produced for the redistribution of assets, or to ensure at the very least that everyone has a chance of acquiring them. Such ideas resonate in many traditions of political thought, from the republican arguments of Paine and Jefferson to the romantic Toryism of G. K. Chesterton and Hilaire Belloc. Although there are many differences between them, a common strand is that a healthy polity requires limits to be set to inequality in the ownership of property. All wanted a society that was self-governing, composed of citizens who were also owners, and therefore independent from government. Only in this way could there be a self-governing society in which extremes of wealth and monopoly of power could be avoided. Many economic liberals also believed that a wide dispersion of property was essential for a healthy market order, and for keeping government limited. On the left, the theme of dispersing the ownership of assets, rather than concentrating them either in the hands of the individuals or of the state, was stressed by G. D. H. Cole and R. H. Tawney. Assets did not have to be individually owned; they could be held by cooperatives and collectives. The important point was that they were not held by the state.

These republican, liberal, conservative and socialist traditions were rather eclipsed in the twentieth century by the turn to collectivist solutions, and the central role assumed by the state in sustaining the market economy and moderating some of its effects through welfare programmes. But they never died out completely, and in recent decades there has been a revival, particularly on the centre left, through the market socialism of James Meade, Tony Atkinson and Julian Le Grand, and the market egalitarianism of Michael Sherradan, Samuel Bowles, Herbert Gintis, Richard Freeman and Bruce Ackerman. There are also close links with theories of stakeholding and ideas about citizens' income. All are seeking ways in which overcentralised bureaucratic welfare states can be decentralised, and new ways found of addressing the inequalities in the distribution of assets and wealth.

Asset egalitarianism is therefore a broad programme that tackles both the social democratic concern with inequality and the civic republican concern with self-government. It argues that apart from considerations of fairness, there are wider social benefits from having a society in which wealth and assets are not concentrated but widely distributed. If all citizens have a property stake, they have a reason to be both independent and self-reliant and able to contribute to the self-government of their community. A wider distribution of assets creates greater opportunity, choice, diversity and self-fulfilment for all citizens, and in doing so it moderates the tendency for either a meritocracy or an aristocracy to emerge. It contributes to a society of greater pluralism, by facilitating a number of different pathways by which individuals can excel, and avoids status being defined by a single criterion. Equality of opportunity is thereby reinterpreted. By enabling all citizens to acquire assets, the society becomes more open, and individuals more in control of the choices they make. New energy is injected from below.

The conservative liberal argument that redistributing assets is an infringement of liberty is countered by the claim that individuals are only able to acquire personal wealth as part of a community, and that all individuals therefore have a right to a fair share in the initial distribution of resources and

200

assets. The community has a right to take back part of the wealth that citizens earn in their lives, to give opportunities to other citizens and to ensure that property does not become too concentrated, threatening democracy with the rise of a privileged and self-perpetuating elite.

Redistributing assets

One of the main ideas in the new assets agenda in recent years is to give all citizens, either at birth or in early adulthood, a capital grant. At first, the idea was closely tied to the ownership of the land and the ability of citizens to be self-supporting. In 1795, Tom Paine proposed the establishment of a fund to provide a capital grant to all citizens, in his pamphlet *Agrarian Justice*. Paine argued that every individual had a right to a share in the natural inheritance represented by the Earth:[5]

When a young couple begin in the world, the difference is exceedingly great whether they begin with nothing or with fifteen pounds apiece. With this aid they could buy a cow and implements to cultivate a few acres of land; and instead of becoming burdens upon society . . . would be put in the way of becoming useful and profitable citizens.

The assertion that free citizens should be given stakes that would enable them to be independent both economically and politically was a key part of the Jeffersonian tradition in the United States, and lay behind the nineteenth-century Homestead Acts. In Britain, some of the early ideas for redistributing assets also emphasised land reform, such as the radical Liberals' demand for 'three acres and a cow' in the last decades of the nineteenth century. They wanted to break up the big estates, and ensure that as many citizens as possible were enabled to acquire independence through ownership of small parcels of land.

Many of these ideas were, however, only practical in societies that had an abundance of land and in which the main occupation was agriculture. Making it possible for the landless to acquire land, as was done in the US in the nineteenth century, gave stakeholding a very tangible meaning. Even in countries where all the land was already owned, there were still often opportunities for land reform. But the meaning of stakeholding in the complex industrial urban societies of the twentieth century presented a different set of problems. Reconciling stakeholding in particular with a developed market economy and an advanced division of labour poses a significant challenge. One strand of egalitarian thought argued for the complete abolition of the market, and for the distribution of resources on the basis of need. But serious drawbacks to such proposals appeared whenever there were attempts to put them into practice. A second strand has sought alternatives to state socialism, and these have been explored by a variety of social democrats, market socialists and market egalitarians. They have been critical of markets, but wished to reform them rather abolish them. James Meade, for example, argued that markets are generally desirable on efficiency grounds, but have consequences for distribution that are often undesirable.[6] The task as he saw it was to find policy instruments that work with markets rather than against them, but that counter their harmful distributive effects and so contribute to a more equal society.

Asset egalitarianism in this sense has developed as one means of moderating the powerful pressures towards ever greater inequality in contemporary capitalist societies, and seeks to give citizens a greater measure of independence, giving them more chance to pursue the lifestyle or career they choose. In this way, the new assets agenda seeks to promote equality of opportunity, but without promoting a meritocracy. Asset egalitarians are not interested in creating any particular kind of elite, or in prescribing any particular content for the good society. Rather, they seek to make a wide range of lifestyles viable, by ensuring that individuals have the resources to choose them. Nevertheless, asset egalitarians are divided as to how much choice individuals should be allowed, and the extent to which citizens should be expected to acknowledge their obligation to their society.

Much of the energy of supporters of the new assets agenda has gone into the idea of capital grants. There has been an increasing amount of social science research into the advantages that possession of assets confers at particular points in the life-cycle—early adulthood, parenthood and retirement. The rationale for an active assets policy is to do something about the large minority of citizens who lack assets at all three stages of the life-cycle, and who are as a result much less able to cope with economic misfortunes, and much more dependent on the safety net of the welfare state.

The most ambitious of the capital grant schemes have sought ways in which all citizens might be provided with a stake. Since, in practice, it would be very hard to determine which citizens should be helped and which not, the emphasis has been placed upon designing a new universal welfare benefit, which all citizens would receive regardless of their income. In that sense, as with other universal benefits, the aim is not to target resources on the most deserving, but to establish a basic minimum. The receipt of a capital grant becomes a right of citizenship, not a function of need. Everyone born into a community acquires the right to receive one. Three main questions arise: How large should the grants be? Should restrictions be placed on their use? And how should they be funded?

How large should the grants be?

If the grants are small as in the Labour Government's Child Trust Fund, announced in 2003, some of the issues about funding and restrictions are easier to handle, but then the effectiveness of the scheme in achieving the objectives of providing everyone with assets is also in doubt. Will relatively small sums make much of a dent in the huge inequalities in the distribution of assets? Proposals for much larger grants, however, raise problems of political and fiscal feasibility. The most ambitious of these plans is that put forward by

Bruce Ackerman and Anne Alstott in their book *The Stakeholder Society*. They propose a capital grant of $80,000 (£45,000) to be paid at age 21 to every citizen, except for those serving prison sentences or who did not complete high school. Individuals have to demonstrate that they are good citizens before they are eligible for the grant, by becoming educated and not being involved in crime. £45,000 is a large capital grant, which would be paid as of right to every eligible citizen.[7] By contrast, the Child Trust Fund, initially developed by the Institute for Public Policy Research, gives a capital grant of £250 (£500 for families below the poverty threshold) to every new baby in Britain. With further top-up payments at age seven, and with the permitted amounts that family and friends may pay into the fund, the Child Trust Fund when it matures at age 18 could be worth £30,000.[8] But this top amount would only be available to those families able to use the fund to save for their child, and the funds of the poorest children would be worth much less, although they would receive twice the initial payment from the state. A different model has been proposed by Julian Le Grand and David Nissan.[9] They suggest a capital grant at age 18 of £10,000. This would be less than the fully matured Child Trust Fund, and much less than the Ackerman and Alstott proposal, but like the latter it would be paid to everyone, with no restrictions on eligibility.

Should restrictions be placed on their use?

The case for restrictions has been trenchantly put by Le Grand and Nissan. Recipients of the grants should be stakeholders and not stakeblowers. Accordingly, the grant should only be used for certain approved uses, such as education and training, buying a home and starting a business. If young people were given a large capital grant and spent it on alcohol, drugs, holidays and other transient pleasures instead of building up long-term assets, gaining political support for the idea of capital grants would be very difficult. Many of those concerned with the design of the Child Trust Fund also initially favoured restrictions, but were persuaded that the administrative and practical difficulties of policing how each generation of 18 year olds spent their grant were too great, particularly when some of the sums involved were expected to be quite small. As a result, there will be no restrictions when the first Child Trust Funds mature in 2020. Ackerman and Alstott go further, objecting to any restrictions on use, on libertarian grounds: 'Stakeholders are free. They may use their money for any purpose they choose: to start a business or pay for more education, to buy a house or raise a family or save for the future. But they must take responsibility for their choices. Their triumphs and their blunders are their own.'[10] With universal capital grants, all citizens gain the kind of financial assets that wealthy families have always provided for their children. They provide autonomy, but they also make citizens responsible for their own choices, which has to include the possibility that they squander the grant.

How should grants be funded?

The Child Trust Fund is being financed out of general taxation, and in that sense is being treated as another welfare programme. Both the other two proposals, however, wish to see the provision of these capital grants funded by inheritance tax. The details differ, but the principle is the same. Existing holders of assets would not have to hand over all their assets to be redistributed on their death, but they would be expected to contribute a proportion, sufficient to fund the capital grants paid to young adults. The justification would be that in this way those who had amassed assets would help to create opportunities for the next generation. In the Ackerman and Alstott plan, the fund would become self-financing. Such proposals, although logical, encounter a quite strong popular resistance to the very idea of inheritance tax. In the US, an unlikely coalition has recently succeeded in abolishing all inheritance taxes, at least until 2010.[11] If this part of the new assets agenda is to work, then new ways of justifying inheritance taxes will have to be found.

The future of the assets agenda

The new assets agenda has been criticised for proposing to divert resources that can better be spent elsewhere on supporting children and families, although for any new proposal there is always this kind of opportunity cost. The commitment to an assets programme only makes sense if it is part of a much broader consideration of welfare and the purposes of welfare, which goes beyond simply providing people with a national minimum, and also addresses the bigger question of how opportunities can be broadened for all individuals. Other critics allege that, like the idea of the social investment state, the assets agenda subordinates welfare policy to the demands of the global market. Instead of welfare being understood as a universal entitlement of citizenship, it becomes a means to fit individuals to the requirements of work in flexible labour markets, and to compensate in part for declining collective provision for higher education and for pensions.

But it is not clear that they have an alternative. Certainly, if the assets agenda were to be treated as a replacement for all other forms of welfare, rather than a supplement to them, it would be both ineffective and undesirable. But if it is used in addition to other forms of welfare provision, and if the element of universality is retained, then there are prospects for deepening assets programmes in the future that make them a real tool of redistribution—not just of assets but, more importantly, of opportunities.[12] And what makes a well-designed assets policy worth pursuing is the range of different lifestyles and different statuses that it could help to promote.

New Labour and the Withering Away of the Working Class?

JON CRUDDAS

Introduction

MANY working-class people feel disenfranchised by the Labour Government: disproportionately they don't vote; many are developing a relationship with the BNP.[1] Discussion of class remains deeply unfashionable within the Labour Party. In contrast, in popular culture the working class is everywhere, albeit successively demonised in comedy or in debate around fear, crime and antisocial behaviour; seen through caricature whilst patronised by reality TV. Arguably, the cumulative effect of this is that the working class itself has been dehumanised—now to be feared and simultaneously served up as entertainment.

The consequences of mass unemployment and failings in the education system have led to generations without work, structured training or even a basic education. Alternatively, they remain trapped in low-wage, unskilled employment. Yet rather than locate contemporary cultural developments within a wider material analysis of economic and social change, the media and our political elites brutally stigmatise the victims. Arguably, the Labour Party itself has colluded in this process through its own retreat from class, given the political imperatives of Middle England. Yet this process of disengagement is hardly ever dissected or even discussed in the party itself. This is an extraordinary state of affairs, given the historic role of the party as the emancipatory vehicle for the self-same working class. In *The Rise of the Meritocracy*, the Labour Movement loses its force, as intelligent members of the working class become drawn into higher social positions within the increasingly individualised society based on education. In real life, though, this is not what is happening. It is almost as if New Labour, in a bid to avoid this fate, has repositioned itself instead: leaving the working class behind.

The question remains: Is what is offered up by New Labour—in its retreat from class—a necessary prerequisite for a modern social democratic revisionism? The benign interpretation of New Labour positioning considers it a systemic product of our electoral system. However—and this is obviously a heretical viewpoint—would a return to consideration of contemporary class relations and inequality provide for a more durable Labour Government?

Published by Blackwell Publishing Ltd, 9600 Garsington Road, Oxford OX4 2DQ, UK and 350 Main Street, Malden, MA 02148, USA 205

Jon Cruddas

The genius of New Labour

The common criticism of New Labour from the left is that it is too conservative. In essence, New Labour is no different from, and therefore part of, the neo-liberal right. This thesis assumes that New Labour has accepted the neo-liberal framework and, indeed, developed this project through the commodification of the public services, the renunciation of redistribution as an act of public policy, its deference to corporate power, its privatisations and the rest. In effect, this form of critique assumes that these orthodox political positions are deductively produced out of a neo-liberal philosophical disposition.

Yet arguably this form of critique is at odds with the practicalities of New Labour. For example, the cornerstone of neo-liberal political economy remains the principle of state withdrawal; its basic assumption is that the state cannot be trusted to do better than the market. As such, government itself is not benign—rather, it is economically and socially destructive.[2] This is *not* the hallmark of New Labour. New Labour does actually support the role of the state and retains a core belief in the efficacy of state intervention and action.

An alternative take on New Labour is *not* to assume that it is the product of a body of ideas as such. This alternative approach is to see it as singularly driven by the imperatives of retention of power; that is, to see it as the pure logical manifestation of Schumpeter's famous dictum that the core of democracy lies in the 'competitive struggle for the people's vote', similar to the way in which the capitalist seeks to exchange commodities in the marketplace.[3] In this model, votes are the form of exchange, policies are the commodities themselves and elected office is the derived profit. If we return to our earlier example, there is therefore no *a priori* hostility to the state; rather, action is considered legitimate through its derived benefit to the political party in reproducing its political power *ceteris paribus*. We do not, therefore, see New Labour as a consequential product of a series of philosophical positions but, rather, as a scientifically pure form of political organisation calibrated for the purpose of winning the votes of the people that matter. Ideas or traditions of thought are only introduced to render intelligible this exercise in political positioning.

Under this approach, the originality—indeed, the genius—of New Labour rests in the method by which policy is scientifically constructed out of the preferences and prejudices of the swing voter in the swing seat in order to reproduce itself through dominating Middle England—New Labour's marketplace. Policy is the product of positioning; devised through the rigour of polling rather than the rigour of thought. Two questions follow. First, what ideas are used to control Middle England? Second, does this produce a policy programme at odds with the needs of those outside of the tight confines of Middle England swing voters? By considering these issues we can isolate tensions between New Labour policy-making and the realities of modern Britain. What emerges is a disturbing picture of how, for the purposes of

206

political positioning, our policy framework is moving further towards an orthodox neo-classical political economy.

Class and New Labour

Throughout the 1980s and 1990s, Labour's problems were seen as being associated with failed periods of economic intervention, tax-and-spend welfarism and union militancy. The defeat of 1992 pushed policy further towards an active 'supply side socialism' so as to deal with these polling negatives. This trend intensified with the election of Tony Blair in 1994. Polling increasingly determined policy; and policy became an exercise in abstract political positioning driven by the demands of swing voters.

A few key ideologists rose to the task and sought to make sense of Blairite repositioning with reference to a supposed revolution in economic relations that was luckily occurring just as Blair came to the leadership.[4] Most important in the 1994–7 period was the introduction of a new economic and social world view based around the notion of the 'new knowledge based economy'.[5] This body of ideas became the axis for New Labour repositioning from 1994, and can still be detected today in the core wiring of the whole New Labour project.

New Labour and the knowledge economy

Within this framework, globalisation and new information technologies are widely cited as the key contemporary levers of change in work and employment relations. Some analysts conjure up a haunting spectre of disappearing employment opportunities in the traditional sectors of the economy, and point to growing insecurities, widening social divisions and mass unemployment.[6]

In contrast, from a British perspective, Charles Leadbeater is optimistic about the prospects for working life in the twenty-first century. Echoing earlier accounts,[7] he argues that the wider application of 'smart' technologies and the forces of globalisation are inducing the emergence of a knowledge-driven economy centred on the exploitation of intangible assets. 'The real wealth creating economy is de-materialising,' he writes: 'The private and public sectors are increasingly using the same sorts of intangible assets— people, knowledge, ideas, information—to generate intangible outputs, services and know how.' The hierarchical structures and internal labour markets that characterised large public- and private-sector organisations are being supplanted in the new economy by networks of independent, small-scale companies based on cellular, self-managed teams.

Leadbeater's vision, dismissive of established employment patterns, is controversial. Trade unions and other allegedly rigid institutions must adapt or die, for there is no place in the 'new economy' for traditional,

adversarial industrial relations. With networks supplanting hierarchy, conflicts between workers and bosses will become a distant memory. Future
economic prosperity will be driven by the expanding production of knowledge and intangible assets, set against the steady erosion of traditional
manufacturing and heavy industry. These commentators assume a rapid
growth in scientific, technical, managerial and professional employment and
a corresponding decline in traditional manual work. Economic policy shifts to
the supply side to help these self-actualising entrepreneurs develop their
portable skills. The distinction between worker and employer is withering
away as the wage-labour system is consigned to history.

For elements within the Labour Party, this ideological analysis of the world
of work functionally resolves the historic dilemma inherent in previous
Labour Governments' support for manufacturing, as supporting this sector
offers diminishing returns. It reinforces, intellectually, an in-built hostility to
organised labour and labour market regulation from within the Labour
Government. Economic policy becomes re-focused on market (and government) failure in the provision of human capital—captured in the famous focus
on 'education, education, education'. Concessions to labour market regulation
have to be forced out of the government and are seen as residual trade-offs to
appease 'Old Labour'—an outdated hangover from the 'old economy'.

In a stunning and quite brilliant political move, these ideas legitimised the
repositioning of New Labour. At a stroke, the old negatives were dealt with,
as they belonged to a previous epoch of industrial work organisation and to a
Labour Party that belonged in that era. As such, New Labour is free from a
working class that is literally withering away. Class, inequality and issues of
power can be overcome by individual self-actualisation once we overcome the
only inequality that matters—access to human capital. What occurs—for the
sake of political positioning—is that the fundamental economic issues that
have preoccupied the left for generations are reduced to issues of deficient
information and orthodox human capital theory.

A withering away of the working class?

For the architects of the 'new knowledge economy', there remains one basic
problem—empirical evidence for the withering away of the working class.
According to successive Labour Force Surveys, over the past ten to fifteen
years there has been a slight rise in those jobs that can be considered white
collar and above—up from some 35 per cent to 37 per cent of the total stock of
directly employed and self-employed occupations in the British labour
market since 1992. Yet on the same statistical series, manual workers still
account for a relatively stable 10.5 million workers—approaching 40 per cent
of total employment. If you were to add in clerical and secretarial work, then
the traditional labour force would stand at some 15 million—approaching two
in three jobs.

Where are the growth areas in the economy? There has been a slight rise in computer managers, software engineers and programmers. Yet the real growth has been in the long-established services of sales assistants, data input clerks, storekeepers, receptionists, security guards and the like. Alongside this has been a massive expansion in cleaning and support workers in the health and education services and beyond, and increased work amongst the caring occupations—for example, care assistants, welfare and community workers and nursery nurses. In short, throughout the past fifteen years there has been no revolution in the demand for labour—rather, the key growth areas have been in traditional, often low-paid jobs, most of which are undertaken by women.

What stands out is the emergence of an 'hourglass' economy in Britain.[8] On the top half of the hourglass there has been an increase in highly paid jobs, performed by those with significant discretion over their hours and patterns of work—in a generalised sense these might be described as knowledge workers. However, in Britain, of more empirical significance has been the growth trend in low-paid, routine and largely unskilled work, in occupations that were pre-eminent fifty years ago.

The future demand for labour

Despite the empirical realities of the past fifteen years—and, indeed, the experience of corporations such as Enron and Worldcom—ministerial speeches are still littered with references to the 'new knowledge economy', and much government analysis presumes that future demand for labour is almost entirely driven by high-wage, highly skilled, knowledge labour. A body of ideas initially used to justify a straightforward political repositioning is now a key template for *actual* policy-making. For example, former Education Secretary Charles Clarke stated: 'demand for graduates is very strong, and research shows that 80% of the 1.7 million new jobs which are expected to be created by the end of the decade will be in occupations which normally recruit those with higher education qualifications'.

Yet this ignores the fact that a high proportion of this relates to NVQ Level 3 and not higher-education qualifications. Once this extra growth is taken out, then the figure for new jobs by 2010 requiring a degree drops to 55 per cent. Moreover, this does not include demand for so-called replacement jobs— which are five times as numerous as new jobs.[9] Overall, when the government's own statistics are broken down, they actually reveal that by 2010 the figure for those in employment required to be first degree graduates or postgraduates will be 22.1 per cent. In other words, by 2010, 77.9 per cent of jobs will not require a degree.

As such, based on empirical changes over the past fifteen years and the best projections for the future, we are witnessing an ever clearer polarisation within the labour market—the hourglass economy. On the one hand, there is a primary labour market—the knowledge-based economy—that is covering about 21 per cent of jobs. On the other hand, there is an expanding secondary labour market, which is where the largest growth is occurring—in service-related elementary occupations, administrative and clerical occupations, sales occupations, caring personal service occupations and the like.

Policy formation and rational economic man

The preceding analysis exposes a real problem for the architects of New Labour, which is increasingly being played out in terms of contemporary policy conflicts within the party. On the one hand, we see a policy-making process that is driven by the preferences and prejudices of swing voters, codified increasingly with reference to conservative intellectual traditions; and, on the other, the empirical realities of modern Britain, which demand an alternative set of policies in order to confront inequality. For example, take the issue of differential top-up fees. The original problematic was a structural funding one for higher education, the solution being one of levering in more contributions from those who derive an economic benefit from participation.

Options were then systematically polled amongst key voters. It was agreed that a system of differential top-up fees polled better than a graduate tax. That is because the case could be presented more effectively in terms of a rigidly individual, utilitarian economic argument that—in the context of an explosion in the demand for graduates—prospective students should discount for the future and borrow more, as the future-derived yield would expand in the new, knowledge-driven, classless world of New Labour. It is a rational economic move for a rational economic man or woman to borrow to accumulate greater reward financially.

Yet empirically, if you start with a different proposition—that there will be a limited demand for graduates—then your solution to the funding gap is different: you would tax the job that requires the degree rather than the person who seeks to participate in higher education, as there will be an excess supply of graduates. However, this rests on a different point of departure—not rational economic man, but the liberating potential of education and human knowledge, driven by concerns over and above the cash nexus and rational, individual economic exchange.

Arguably, this example exposes a critical modern fault line within the party. The economic framework that was incorporated to make sense of the repositioning of the party, but which is at best empirically questionable, is now used to actually forge the policy agenda itself. While this may play well for pivotal elements within the electorate, it further dislocates the policy process from the empirical realities of modern Britain. Critically, the way this process rolls out pushes us into an ever more elaborate framework of rational choice economics which, paradoxically, is the hallmark of right-wing economics dating back to the 1870s.

Neo-classical economics and New Labour

Since the latter decades of the nineteenth century, the dominant economic orthodoxy has set itself the task of providing a rigorous model of resource allocation in the pure exchange process. This project has rested on a view that sees the economy in terms of the aggregation of individual acts of exchange within the marketplace. What emerged is a general equilibrium approach to exchange, determined by crude psychological assumptions about the formation and impact of subjective preferences in the pursuit of maximum utility. There are obvious similarities here when considering current debates around secondary and higher education. This so-called marginalist revolution—the onset of the dominance of the neo-classical paradigm—can be seen partly as an attempt to define systematically the limits of state intervention within the economy, set against the backdrop of growing pressures for social reform— especially developing working-class organisation and the declining relevance of strict *laissez-faire* political economy. Again, what is striking is how contemporary this debate sounds when considering the language used by New Labour to confront its internal critics.

This attempt to provide a coherent theory of price begins with individual economic agents entering the marketplace, equipped with their own subjective preferences in terms of consumption and the allocation of time—precisely the assumptions we detected in the recent debate on top-up fees. The next step is to assume that all economic agents obtain maximum utility within the context of scarcity. The project then aims to determine prices by aggregating the numerous acts of individual economic exchange. Yet goods do not just appear in the marketplace. Therefore, the analysis of the efficient properties of individual choice is simply extended to introduce into the framework a theory of production, specifying the purely technical relationship between factors of production and outputs. Labour is treated as one of these fixed technical inputs into production. Assumptions of perfect information and rational activity ensure technically efficient outcomes.

The whole framework is dependent on a pure theory of what rational economic agents actually are, from which is deduced a pure theory of the technical constructs that collectively form the economy. On the supply side, labour market participation is seen as purely voluntary, dependent on the way in which individuals resolve the trade-off between wages and the marginal disutility of work. This dovetails with the hiring policies of the firm in terms of examining the prospective employee's marginal productivity. The necessary prerequisite for such fluid market transactions is perfect information on the part of both of the parties into the workings of the labour market and, indeed, any other form of economic exchange. As such, some 130 years later, we are right back to where we started when we discussed the 'new knowledge economy'—the classless world of individual, rational economic exchange and mutual benefit.

The onward march of neo-classical labour

Just as the neo-classical takeover of modern economics removed any political insights supplied by Marx, Smith, Mill and Ricardo, so have 'new economy' theorists performed an equivalent political exercise for New Labour. In both instances, the consequence has been the removal of class as an economic or political category. Instead, the dominant paradigm is one based around rational, atomised economic exchange. This process began with an attempt intellectually to codify a straightforward move to the political centre. Since then, however, these self-same ideas have had an ever more systematic influence over public policy-making.

The most obvious example of this process is the current debate around the efficient allocative properties of markets and the reform of health and education policy. Once again, the language of choice is used because of the traction it creates amongst ruthlessly polled swing voters. Policy is then built around these buzz phrases, with reference to rational choice analysis developed by marginalist theories of efficient exchange—in education around the form of parent power, in health around patient choice. In order to placate internal concerns, this deeply ideological agenda is disguised as a progressive devolution of power down to the working class. This is an exact replica of the form in which neo-classical economics scientifically defines the brilliance of the market.

Space does not permit greater elaboration, but in essence these policies contain the same fundamental weaknesses as the neo-classical framework that has produced them—assumptions of perfect information, the psychology of rational choice and the way an economic subject discounts for the future, the empirical realities of class, race and inequality, the role of intermediary institutions and market imperfection, and so on.[10] This reflects an increasingly ideological project born out of the exercise of political positioning at the expense of an evidence-based, rational form of public policy-making. Recent criticisms of policy on the basis of a lack of evidence are a reflection of this.[11]

Further tensions emerge when we try to make sense of people's involuntary inactivity, or indeed their lack of opportunity. Within the neo-classical frame of reference, these remain elusive concepts—beyond the explanatory power of the framework. Either they do not understand their own preferences or they fall foul due to imperfect information. We tend to reduce our approach to one of loading fresh incentives/compulsions on to those who are often the victims of broader economic and political forces. It is a short hop to actually blaming the victim for his or her own predicament—again an element in current debate around work, leisure and welfare. These people, in turn, can then be served up on the altar of Middle England. Indeed, we can stray into all sorts of interesting territory in terms of crime and antisocial behaviour that plays to the prejudices of the voters who really matter, and reinforces a condescension for working-class lifestyles that is dominant in public debate.

The notion of a lawless, modern ASBO nation reinforces our political bona fides with regard to our core Middle England constituency.

Concluding remarks

It is a common observation that New Labour is efficient at winning elections due to its ruthless scientific analysis of the preferences and prejudices of the swing voter in the swing seat and its key seat organisation. It is another common observation that many working-class people are rendered invisible by the current political system—they appear to have no voice.[12] When we even acknowledge the existence of a working class, it tends to be demonised—in almost the exact parallel to that of the migrant—so as to reproduce the political power of New Labour within its Middle England marketplace.

Since the 1997 election, two responses can be identified within New Labour to legitimise itself. The first is empirically to restate that there is no alternative to the further development of the New Labour strategy.[13] The other is to seek to rewrite the whole genealogy of New Labour and see it anchored within the revisionist traditions of democratic socialism and the Labour Party.[14] The former simply argues for an ever more elaborate versions of the familiar New Labour architecture. The latter is a more interesting contribution because of its focus on equality. Yet this approach fails to comprehend how the evolution of New Labour is fundamentally at odds with this tradition of thought; the revisionist tradition of democratic socialism was actually constructed as a critique of neo-classical political economy. In stark contrast, core elements within New Labour have actually built a neo-classical Labour project.

The objective now is to build a modern New Labour project grounded in the empirical realities of the modern world, and not some stylised construction of modernity that scientifically seeks to entrench class and income inequality with recourse to some spurious heuristic device known as 'rational economic man'. Unless this is done—and done quickly—the failure to represent working-class interests leaves the door wide open for parties such as the BNP, which do appear to understand the collectivist nature of their orientations.

A Delay on the Road to Meritocracy

PETER WILBY

The comprehensive moment

THE turning point on the road to Michael Young's dystopia in *The Rise of the Meritocracy* was the failure to establish comprehensive schools.[1] As Young, writing in 1958, tells it, only 'a small wave of them' was started in the 1960s and even these were streamed so that the more able children were taught separately:

Socialists who wanted all children, regardless of their ability, educated as in America and Russia, commanded enough popular support for a time . . . Yet they were bound to fail. To succeed . . . they needed a social revolution which would overthrow the established hierarchy, values and all. But with the masses dormant and their potential leaders diverted into self-advancement, what hope was there? Grammar schools remained. Comprehensive schools withered.[2]

In fact, as we now know, the momentum behind the introduction of comprehensives proved so strong that even Margaret Thatcher, as Secretary of State for Education in the early 1970s, was unable to resist it. Although the Labour governments of 1974–9 failed to complete the revolution, they removed another layer of selection in the form of the direct grant grammar schools. Tory governments from 1979 made tentative and largely stealthy attempts to re-establish selection—for example, ministers and their advisers encouraged the West Midlands borough of Solihull to propose a scheme to restore grammar schools in the 1980s—but they were largely frustrated. Although they brought back something similar to the old direct grant in the form of the Assisted Places Scheme, it was later abolished by New Labour, and even Tories never regarded it as a very efficient way of helping bright children from poor homes to get a better education.

Except in their very early days, comprehensives had rarely received a good press, and their reputation declined further as more comparative information on examination results became publicly available. (Even those few numerate journalists who understood that the apparently inferior performance of comprehensives was almost wholly attributable to their intake had no idea how to explain the figures to their readers.) But the difficulty of abolishing them in favour of grammar schools was that the majority of parents would have to accept their children going to secondary moderns, or to some equivalent of them. The Tories already faced parental unrest in the 1980s as a result of the widespread closures and mergers of schools that were necessitated by falling rolls. An open return to selection, with all the upheaval it entailed, was a vote-loser.

 Published by Blackwell Publishing Ltd, 9600 Garsington Road, Oxford OX4 2DQ, UK and 350 Main Street, Malden, MA 02148, USA

Instead, the Tories introduced more 'diversity' and 'parental choice' within the comprehensive system, mainly through the opening of city technology colleges and the introduction of a scheme that allowed schools to opt out of local authority control and become self-governing recipients of grants direct from Whitehall (grant-maintained schools). In effect, they introduced new classes of schools, which might satisfy those parents who would otherwise have aspired to grammar schools for their children, while leaving other schools in a condition that might still plausibly be described as comprehensive. Officially, neither the colleges nor the grant-maintained schools were allowed to select. But Labour critics were in no doubt that they were designed to undermine the comprehensive system, not least because they had more favourable funding, and that middle-class parents—better informed, more mobile, more aspirational—were most likely to take advantage.

Comprehensives, indeed, had become one of the articles of the Labour faith, to which most party activists, backbench MPs and trade unionists held undying allegiance. No matter how many other sacred cows they slaughtered, it was politically unthinkable for Labour leaders openly to embrace selection. What little Labour had done to achieve equality of income and capital was brutally reversed by the Tories in the 1980s. But comprehensives, like the National Health Service (NHS), remained as monuments to the principles of egalitarianism and social solidarity. 'Read my lips. No selection by examination or interview,' David Blunkett, the Shadow Education Secretary, told the Labour Party conference in 1995. From Blunkett, a member of the Labour left and former leader of Sheffield City Council, that seemed as good a guarantee as you could get.

The reality has proved different. Although new grammar schools remain off the agenda ('there will be no return to the divisive 11-plus', the 2005 White Paper stated categorically and prominently), the end of the 'bog-standard comprehensive' was announced by Alastair Campbell, the Prime Minister's press secretary, towards the end of New Labour's first term of office. It could well be argued that Michael Young got his predictions broadly right after all and that, after a couple of decades in the sun, comprehensives have indeed started to wither. If Britain fails to achieve a meritocracy, it may be only because the Labour policies designed to bring it about suffer from incoherence and may prove to be deeply flawed.

Drawn towards selection

That ministers aspire to meritocracy is surely beyond dispute. 'The government's fight is on behalf of hard-earned merit, not easy prizes,' said David Miliband, then schools minister, in August 2004.[3] In a speech on 'education and social progress' to the IPPR think tank on 26 July 2005, Ruth Kelly, Secretary of State for Education, said she wanted a society 'where people don't have their life chances predominantly determined by their background, rather than their own ability and efforts'—a distinct echo of

Michael Young's famous equation I + E = M (intelligence plus effort equals merit). 'We don't yet have a Britain where merit is the key to success,' Tony Blair told Labour's 2001 spring conference, 'where the only thing that counts is not where you come from but what you are, and where everyone, not just the privileged few, get the chance to succeed.' Blair acknowledged, as a brief aside, that 'of course we should value all our citizens, not just those who rise to the top. But I say: we have still not achieved even a meritocracy.'

The education system, at all levels, is the key to Blair's meritocracy. Education is repeatedly described in ministerial speeches as 'a driver of social mobility' or, sometimes, as 'a locomotive'. 'I see my department as the department for life chances,' said Kelly. 'We must create a society . . . where ability flows to the top irrespective of an individual's background.' Schools, ministers say, must 'add value' to children. They must not 'coast along'; they must aim to improve year by year, as must the nation as a whole. Ministers have set their faces firmly against mixed-ability teaching, and have all but ordered secondary schools to sort children into ability sets for each major subject. There must, they say, always be 'stretch for the most able' and, in a rather chilling echo of Young's dystopia (in which details of everyone's IQ were held centrally), the 2005 White Paper proposes a 'national register of gifted and talented pupils'. 'This will allow us,' the White Paper continues, 'to invite all who fall within the top 5%' to join the National Academy for Gifted and Talented Youth—a body set up in 2002 to organise various programmes for the gifted and talented (or g&ts, as they are racily called) including residential summer schools and sponsorship for those from deprived backgrounds.[4]

New Labour is in no doubt of the role of universities in supporting meritocracy. Despite the recommendations of official committees over more than twenty years, it insists that A-levels must stay because, as Ruth Kelly put it in April 2005, they are 'a ticket to further learning'. To increase 'stretch for the most able', and to help the universities select more efficiently, it proposes Advanced Extension Award questions in all subjects, and to make grades in individual modules available to universities as well as the overall grades. 'It is essential,' said the schools minister, Lord (Andrew) Adonis, in August 2005, 'that the most able continue to be stretched to the full—and that leading universities, whose places are limited, can differentiate properly in awarding them on merit.' Obstacles to full meritocracy in the universities are to be eliminated and New Labour has determinedly identified social biases in entry to the leading universities such as Oxford, Cambridge and Bristol, and appointed a regulator to reduce them. Although critics argue that student fees, and particularly top-up fees, discourage entrants from poor homes, ministers see them as a blow for meritocracy. The fees, they point out, are means tested and incentives for less affluent students to attend are therefore increased.

Michael Young pointed out that the chief interest of the comprehensive pioneers 'was not . . . so much educational as social'.[5] Professor Robin Pedley, one of the most prominent early campaigners, defined the comprehensives' purpose as 'the forging of a richly diverse communal culture by the pursuit of quality with equality, by the education of pupils in and for democracy, and by the creation of happy, vigorous, local communities in which the school is the focus of social and educational life'.[6] It would be hard to imagine anything further away from New Labour's conception of education. For New Labour, the purpose of education is almost entirely instrumental. It is about individual ambition and aspiration—and, through that, national economic competitiveness—not about 'communal culture' and social solidarity. Higher education was 'the best investment' for a prospective student, argued Ruth Kelly in her speech to the all-party group. The universities' role was to boost 'economic performance, innovation and higher level skills'.

Yet at the heart of New Labour's education policy—at least as it applies to schools—there lies a profound ambiguity. On the one hand, as repeatedly proclaimed in ministerial speeches, New Labour is committed to the achievement of a pure meritocracy. On the other, New Labour is also determined to protect and strengthen the defining principle of public services such as education and health: that they should be free at the point of use.

At first sight, there may seem to be no conflict between these aims; on the contrary, they may seem complementary, in so far as equal access to schooling depends on its being free of charge. But when New Labour took power in 1997, its leaders believed that the biggest threat to public services was the desertion of the middle classes. If the middle classes abandoned the NHS and state schools for the private sector in large numbers, they would eventually resist paying taxes for services that were used only by other people. And the only way to persuade the middle classes to stay with the public sector, ministers reasoned, was to offer them the same quality of personal service and the same choice as they would find in the private sector. The Tories, probably through voucher schemes, would assist the middle classes in opting out; Labour would make it far more attractive for them to opt in.

Securing political support

New Labour's aspiration to meritocracy, therefore, is constrained by the need to placate two constituencies. The first is the party itself, with its deep commitment to the more egalitarian version of comprehensive education and its suspicion of the very idea of sorting sheep from goats. The second is the middle class, which—much as it may pay lip service to meritocracy—cannot bear the idea that its own children may fail. If the first constraint seems likely to weaken in future—as the importance of Labour activists and trade unions declines and 'old Labourites' gradually drift away from the party—the second will surely grow. Some academic studies have suggested that, in the recent past, social mobility in Britain has declined: a child born into the working classes in the 1960s or 1970s was more likely to stay there than one born in the 1940s or early 1950s.[7] Many critics have blamed the decline of the grammar schools. A more plausible explanation is that the enormous postwar expansion of middle-class jobs has slowed. Once, a bright child from a poor family could move up without any need for a dull child from a rich family to move down and make way. (I use the terms 'bright' and 'dull' as meritocrats tend to use them, without necessarily endorsing them myself.) Increasingly, that is not the case. If we are to have a true meritocracy, upward social mobility needs to be matched by downward mobility. It is hard to see how any politician could sell that message to middle-class voters.

Selection has flourished under New Labour, despite ministerial protestations. Hopes that a Labour Government would quietly strangle the 164 remaining grammar schools in England and Wales have been disappointed. Although legislation provides for parents to call ballots in areas where the schools survive, the rules are so framed that an attempt to close a grammar school is almost certain to fail, if a vote is held at all. Although no new grammar schools have opened, the existing ones have been allowed to expand—often 'creaming off' children from comprehensives in neighbouring areas—and the number of children attending them is higher than when New Labour came to power. The newly created specialist schools are allowed to select 10 per cent of their intake by 'aptitude', though few have taken advantage of that provision.

But the more important influence has been New Labour's constant attempts to differentiate between comprehensives, with voluntary-aided schools, foundation schools, city academies and, in the 2006 Education Bill, a proposed new category of 'trust schools', which may include some independent schools wooed into the state system. Officially, none of these schools is allowed to select on academic grounds and, under the government's code of practice for admissions, even parental interviews are frowned upon. But in reality, selection still takes place in all kinds of subtle ways.

The Office of the Schools Adjudicator, in its annual report for 2004–5, states that 'we are . . . still receiving cases where schools are accused of selecting children by ability and social group'.[8] The Catholic Education Service acknowledges that 'dozens' of Roman Catholic schools continue to interview parents, despite the admissions code (to which schools are merely required to 'have regard').[9] Other schools seek reports from primary schools on a child's conduct, motivation, attendance and home background. Church schools can seek evidence of family religious commitment (which is likely to be a proxy for, at the very least, strong parental support for education): stories of 'midnight conversions' as sons and daughters approach secondary school age are legion. Department for Education figures show that, in both the primary and secondary sectors, faith schools have significantly lower proportions of pupils with special needs than do secular schools.[10]

As a last resort, a favoured school, with a surplus of applicants over places, can remove a 'difficult' pupil. The nuclear weapon of expulsion, which is subject to appeal, is rarely necessary; it is usually enough gently to persuade parents to withdraw their child before sanctions go on his or her record. That child will often find its way to an under-subscribed school, which may already have an above-average number of poorly behaved children with little motivation for academic work.

The effect of all this is best illustrated by a report from the Sutton Trust, a private charity.[11] This found that, at the 200 top-performing state schools (as measured by their exam results), only 3 per cent of the pupils were eligible for free meals (the most convenient proxy for low family income), against a national average of 14.3 per cent. That would come as no surprise to those who criticise the 'postcode lottery', whereby house prices rise within the catchment areas of 'good' schools, thus putting them beyond the reach of poor families. But the Sutton Trust shows that location is only part of the story, and not even the major part. 'The postcode sectors in which the top 200 schools are situated,' said the report, 'are . . . only marginally more affluent than average, with 12.3% of pupils eligible for FSM.'

Nor did the well-known social bias of grammar schools tell the full story. Among the top 200 were thirty-nine comprehensives and, though they had more children on free meals than the grammars (6 per cent against 2.1 per cent), the disparity with their local areas was just as great.

The problem of parental choice

This takes us to the heart of New Labour's dilemma. In the 2005 election campaign, it promised, as in the previous campaign, to extend parental choice. This is ground it dare not concede to the Tories because, as we have seen, the middle classes' support for state education (and for New Labour itself) depends on the kind of 'consumer power' they would get in the private sector. But the parental choice policy runs directly counter to New Labour's goal of developing meritocracy. The ambition to find the 'best' school, the knowledge to make a judgement, the money to travel to distant schools, the confidence to tackle the often complex admission processes, the persistence to go through appeals, the willingness to 'play' the system (by, for example, taking temporary 'accommodation addresses' within a school's catchment area)—all these are more likely to be found among the more affluent families. Moreover, where schools are over-subscribed, it becomes the schools that exercise choice between families, not the other way round. When test results and truancy rates are so important to a school's reputation and its teachers' careers, and when fund-raising may be crucial for a school's hopes of development, the temptation to cherry-pick children from 'good' families, with supportive, reasonably affluent parents is almost irresistible.

New Labour acknowledges that the attainment gap between children from deprived backgrounds and those from more affluent homes has not narrowed—if anything, it has widened since the mid-1990s. Ministers also acknowledge, though more grudgingly, that this problem may be partly related to their policies on school admissions. One, advocated by the Social Market Foundation, is to allocate all places in over-subscribed schools by lottery—or 'ballot', to use a less contentious term.[12] All kinds of selection would be banned (except in the remaining grammar schools), as would priority for parents who live near the school. This would bring all schools closer to 'a balanced intake' (in which the proportions of rich and poor, bright and dull roughly match those in the general population) and, according to educational research quoted by the foundation, would thus raise standards at all levels. Another idea is to give all children an ability test at age eleven. This would not, as Young envisaged, be used to select the most able for better treatment; rather, it would be used to place children in bands to ensure that each school took its 'fair' share from each ability level. The point of both these proposals is to avoid schools that have a preponderance of low-ability and unmotivated children, dragging down the few bright classmates they have as well as depressing their own ambitions. Educational research suggests that the peer group is at least as important as family background in determining attainment. In that sense, these proposals are consistent with New Labour's aspirations to meritocracy.

Though ministers were too fearful of alienating the middle classes to embrace either solution in its entirety, Labour backbench pressure during the passage of the 2006 Education Bill—supported by Lord (Neil) Kinnock, a former Labour leader and shadow Education Secretary—did persuade them to draft proposals for tightening the admissions code significantly. Secondary schools were to be banned from interviewing parents and pupils before entry, and from setting written tests. Even primary and nursery school reports would no longer be used to take account of 'past behaviour, attitude or achievement'. The Church of England was persuaded that at least a quarter of the places in all its new schools should go to non-churchgoers. Moreover, ministers planned to offer subsidies for children from poor homes who have to travel long distances to 'good' schools and to make 'choice advisers' available to help parents seek out such schools. How well these devices work remains to be seen.

Comprehensive schools flourished more than Young expected partly because their supporters managed to make the case that they offered a more efficient route to meritocracy than the grammar schools. Eleven-plus selection, it was argued, was too blunt an instrument and too socially biased to identify the most able with any confidence.

That argument has been undermined, partly by the neighbourhood social bias of comprehensives ('the postcode lottery'), partly by the effects of parental choice. Some Labour-supporting commentators—and even, in private, some ministers and advisers—now believe that we would be better off with a return to the grammar schools, which—for all their imperfections—would come closer to meritocracy than what we have now. The defeat of the comprehensives that Young envisaged may, after all, only have been delayed.

220

Putting Social Contribution back into Merit

GEOFF DENCH

The British disease

LABOUR's pursuit of the opportunity society has put the concept of meritocracy right at the centre of our political agenda. But we cannot assume that the original ideas and argument are directly applicable any more. British society—as indeed the Labour Movement—has not developed along the lines suggested by Michael Young in *The Rise of the Meritocracy*. So although several features of contemporary Britain, notably growing social polarisation and alienation of the lower orders, bear some resemblance to the future predicted in the novel, we should not take it for granted that the processes underlying this are those that figure in Michael's story.

On the contrary, I would argue that in so far as contemporary Britain does constitute a meritocracy, it takes a rather unusual form. Its social problems may be more to do with its peculiarities than with meritocracy itself, and may be resolvable without turning our backs on the concept in general. What distinguishes contemporary Britain from that of the 1950s, indeed from every other society that I can think of, is the extent to which it formally embraces a cult of individualism. In the 1950s—and the Britain that runs on through *Meritocracy* to 2034—things were very different, with patriotism and service to the nation emphasised. Michael wrote at a time when individual endeavours and aspirations were contained within a collective project to make the nation strong and competitive. The story only works in that context.

Placed in modern Britain, it would not make any sense at all. In fact, it would be considered laughable by most people below a certain age. For what our new, libertarian culture tells us is that society (mediated by the caring state) is there for us, to underwrite our personal security. We don't even need to behave prudently in order to expect a life of happiness and fulfilment. Part of this birthright is the chance to get on, have a career and be successful, and if this does not work out then it is society that is at fault. The moral order of the 1950s has thus been reversed. Instead of people serving society, and being rewarded for their efforts, now it is society that serves individuals and is judged by them for its ability to meet their needs.

At this point some readers will be protesting, and pointing out that if this is true of Britain, then it is also true of many other Western societies, and certainly those with welfare regimes that encourage individual dependency on a generalised collectivity. Up to a point, I accept this. But I would argue that the culture is far more embracing in Britain, and that there is a further

Published by Blackwell Publishing Ltd, 9600 Garsington Road, Oxford OX4 2DQ, UK and 350 Main Street, Malden, MA 02148, USA

dimension to it here that does *not* figure elsewhere. This is the absence of overt patriotism and attachment to Britain (or its constituent parts, especially England) among the influential and respectable classes.[1] This phenomenon is something that you may find temporarily in other societies, but that in the strength, conviction and durability with which it has been manifest in Britain since the 1960s surely has no parallel.

This has enormous implications for the working of Michael's famous formula regarding effort and merit. It is implicit in this equation that 'effort' entails some useful contribution to society. Otherwise, no transaction is taking place from citizen and community that merits rewarding; no social value is created. This did not need spelling out in the 1950s because it was so obvious. But our society is now so highly individualised that such connections are no longer made publicly by the ruling class; and as the notion of social value withers, so the social contract itself may start to unravel.

The particular problem in Britain, I suggest, is that our imperial history—or, more to the point, the way in which we have tried but failed to detach ourselves from it and our guilt—now makes it extremely hard to give positive, open recognition to patriotism or service to the community. This does not simply make it difficult to define success other than in largely individualistic terms. It also makes it very hard to give respect to the efforts and labours of ordinary, *un*successful people, who in normal circumstances would be able to find satisfactions, in spite of personal failure and low status, through contributing to the common good. Even Michael's fictional Britain, contemptuous as it was of 'stupid' losers, did not deprive them of their chance to participate in the collective effort.

Merit in Britain's internal empire

This shift in values is rooted in changes in Britain's global role, which *Meritocracy* addressed but did not fully anticipate. When Michael was writing about the 'meritocracy of talent', the Labour Party was embroiled in bitter internal wrangling over its future direction. The debate went right to the heart of Britain's mission and identity. As the postwar government, Labour had had to confront the reduced position of the nation in the world. Most senior party members were hostile to Empire, and welcomed international (and United Nations) pressures to decolonise. But the loss of imperial trading preferences threatened industrial profitability, and it was clear that a massive programme of modernisation was needed before Britain could survive as a properly competitive manufacturing nation. Attlee's route of nationalisation of key sectors proved slow and unpopular, and led to loss of power in 1951. After that defeat there was a virtual civil war in the party. Advocates of further state ownership and control were gradually worn down by economic liberals. Similarly, working-class warriors were edged aside by political modernisers, who argued that the future lay not with traditional heavy industries but through scientific enterprise, in which the most valuable labour would be performed by highly educated workers with advanced technological training. The germ of New Labour was already forming.

However, what is most striking in retrospect about this debate is the level of consensus underlying it, concerning what it was all ultimately about—that is, transformation of Britain from complacent and inefficient metropolitan power into a well-oiled and profitable industrial machine. This mercantilist impulse, and yardstick, was moreover shared with the Conservatives (and had moved the bipartisan 1944 Education Act) and was being vigorously implemented by Harold Macmillan when *Meritocracy* was published. It provided the guiding spirit for Harold Wilson's modernising regime after Labour regained power in 1964. Significantly, Michael was himself clearly concerned about the national economy during this period. One of his lesser-known creations was Bethnal Green Exports Ltd ('Bethex'), formed in 1964 to help local businesses to boost their exports—as part of a popular, patriotic drive to ease Britain's balance-of-payments deficit.

The reservations that some party members had about prioritising economic competitiveness, and that Michael expressed in *Meritocracy*, were less to do with this objective itself than with the means being considered to achieve it. An efficient industrial society obviously required cultivation of available talents. That in itself was fine. But how to achieve this without abandoning equality? For Labour, education was traditionally a means of liberating individuals, and promoting social justice, through the creation of a more open society. What, though, if giving greater importance to education facilitated the formation of a new class system? Egalitarians in the 1950s became increasingly concerned about how to serve the national good by identifying and encouraging able students *without* sowing the seeds for a self-serving educated elite.

In the event, though, Britain's development was not down an industrial road—largely, I think, because the unravelling of Empire took unexpected turns. When Michael was imagining the implications of meritocratic selection, Britain had no viable alternative to wholesale industrial modernisation. Suez had signalled the end of an imperial role, and confirmed the global dominance of the United States. Other European economies were already rebuilding from the ground up, and for the next few decades British governments would be chasing them. But over this period the withdrawal from Empire also created a different type of society in Britain, around priorities other than maximisation of production.

The crucial period in this transformation was from the mid-1950s to the early 1970s. Attempts to make industry profitable—or even capable of surviving while investments in new plant or techniques were made— pulled in economic migrants from former imperial territories, and stimulated emigration pressures in those countries. The need for immigrants fell off as some industries collapsed altogether. But the flow of migrants increased, leading to growing conflicts of interest between indigenous citizens and newcomers. At the same time, the running down of imperial institutions and administrations brought families who had lived abroad in the service of British interests—sometimes over several generations—home to stay, together with deep concern for the colonial territories in which they had served, and many personal ties with their citizens. The stage was set for a reworking of British identity and social structure.

This remixing of the components of the old British Empire, inside the metropolis, subsequently created a sort of internal empire within Britain itself. As factory jobs dried up, many immigrants decided to stay here, and draw support from the welfare state, rather than go back to their countries of origin. This was facilitated by a remarkable (and little-analysed) alliance among those indigenous Britons who recognised the need to reshape British society (and the structure of welfare) to help this new sector of needy citizens. New Left critics of Empire joined with old imperial hands—who retained a Whig pride in Britain's imperial legacy of tolerance and respect for other cultures—to rewrite Britain's world role.[2] National economic goals, failing anyway, became subordinated to the creation of a fair, cohesive multicultural nation. Thus a new British Empire and source of (unspoken) national pride was reborn inside Britain, and a new patriotic ideology fostered. Empire imposed on other nations had been wrong. But Britons could still (dammit) show the world how to run a peaceful, multicultural and open metropolitan society. A progressive mission was drafted around a new sort of empire that would atone for the old.

By itself, this vision might easily have been very short-lived. It did little to solve Britain's balance-of-payments problems, beyond promoting a positive national image to smooth the reshaping of trade links within the new Commonwealth. However, it was reinforced by a fortuitous twist of events that gave it economic value. Margaret Thatcher's deregulation of financial services allowed the City to build on its former role as the financial hub of British imperial trading, and grab a lucrative share in running America's blossoming global empire. Experience gained over centuries of administering the most diverse empire in history had allowed movement towards a multicultural society at home, especially in London. This in turn enabled the City to sell itself as a uniquely progressive environment for the global financial elite to live and work. The income derived from this activity has cushioned the British economy from the effects of meltdown in the manufacturing sector, thereby protecting the ongoing multicultural experiment itself. The national importance of multiculturalism is reflected in the image of London as the cosmopolitan capital of Cool Britannia, energetically manipulated by leaders such as Mayor Ken Livingstone to drum up further business.[3]

Sovereignty of the individual

Transformation into an internalised empire has produced a new type of social structure in Britain, in which the task of the national elite revolves around managing a diverse and potentially conflictual population rather than

224

maximising industrial production.[4] The key to social balance and stability lies in the formal emphasis, which has been evolving since the 1960s, on individual needs and rights, rather than on family, community or nation. For in such a diverse and fast-changing society, group ties and loyalties can be divisive. What, by contrast, is highly integrative is the chance for everyone to 'do well'. So this is what the new elite exists to promote and, to a large extent, itself symbolises. This task requires a strong state, and so during the half-century since Suez, in which the British Empire has turned in on itself, we have seen the emergence of a highly centralised state machine—very novel on the British scene, and against the trend among our neighbours—dedicated to weakening all groups standing between it and the citizens whose main protector it has become.

Controlling this machine is a political class that seeks to de-communalise the content of state policies and detach itself from any ethnic or national identity that might be seen as partisan—including British (and even more so English) patriotism. It upholds a political creed asserting that all individuals, whatever their provenance, should enjoy equal rights and respect and opportunities. In practice, this elite does need to give greater weight to the rights of certain groups—particularly newcomers and the most needy—if the integrative image of a fair and open society is to be upheld. And there can be little doubt, given levels of ethnic monitoring and official targets relating to group parity, that the state does (discreetly) sponsor opportunities and mobility among poorly placed minorities.[5] It will, however, deny engaging in affirmative action in favour of those groups, which it acknowledges can be divisive, and insist that it is guided simply by the pursuit of substantive equality to focus on the requirements of the most needy individuals. This is what modern British meritocracy stands for.

Under this formula, children of immigrants have enjoyed extra help and resources at school, and have achieved a larger share of recent social mobility. Critics of state policies claim that this represents covert sponsorship, and that the effect is not merely divisive, but also potentially devalues such mobility as well as damaging the motivation of children in the white working class, who can see that their own success is less socially desirable than that of minorities.[6] But so long as there is official emphasis on *individual* needs, such views are easily dismissed as racist, and as imagining communalist plots and plans where there are none.

Thus the emphasis on rights and needs has shunted priorities in the state education system away from education as such towards the notion of providing fair opportunities.[7] This has been accompanied in urban schools, especially in London, by an explicit promotion of behaviour deemed appropriate in a cosmopolitan, globally oriented society. Whereas these schools formerly set great store by sports, and learning to handle competition, it is now skills in conflict resolution and conciliation that are highly regarded. It is this shift, I suspect, that has sustained comprehensive schools in spite of their manifest failures to impart skills. For what they can do rather well is to respond to the diversity agenda and encourage a sense of common citizenship among pupils from different backgrounds. In the same way, modern universities teach social more than mechanical engineering, and it is in social administration (and especially the management of diversity) that the greater number of new jobs for graduates now lies.

Here, we should note in passing that Michael Young, the author and real-life activist, may have missed the point when he advocated comprehensive schools as a means of *promoting* diversity of values and thereby greater respect between citizens in different classes. There are inconsistencies in Michael's own thinking here. In an article written with Peter Willmott, a few years before the publication of *Meritocracy*, he demonstrated how social isolation of Bethnal Greeners permitted them to hold a schema of occupational valuation, at odds with conventional rankings, in which they gave an especially honourable position to their own jobs. Local autonomy enabled them to see themselves as playing useful and valued roles.[8] So it was optimistic of Michael to assume that more inclusive schooling during the years when young people start to differentiate themselves occupationally would result in greater flexibility and diversity in social evaluations. It would be equally likely—or to be honest rather *more* likely—to encourage *uniformity* of ranking, with greater *competition* for high-status positions.

Similar contradictory impulses may have lain behind the introduction of comprehensives. At first blush, non-selective, mixed-ability teaching appears to ensure a greater level of civic equality between people entering different occupational classes than would be possible if they remained segregated at school. But on reflection it also evidently serves the goal of *selectivity*. For by delaying selection, and giving teachers longer to sort out able children, more accurately, it renders that selection more legitimate.[9] Many opponents of the eleven-plus have not been against selection *per se*, but simply against it taking place before schools have had a chance to overcome the effects of different social backgrounds and tease out 'hidden talent'.

In this sense, comprehensives can be seen as a particular expression of meritocracy that extends the period before children are required to specialise (which for the majority entails relinquishing the notion that they may be destined for academic success). This new formulation of meritocracy may be linked with some enduring weaknesses of comprehensive schools. The generality and woolliness of syllabi and teaching; the reluctance to rank and grade and criticise pupils; the steady decline of vocational subjects in favour of keeping academic options open, lest talent or greater potential be overlooked, discouraged or wasted—all these relate to extended selection, intensifying pressure on top prizes, and prolongation rather than diminution of competitiveness.

Against these drawbacks, delayed selection does have the great advantage of allowing schools to overcome cultural differences. This helped prompt adoption of comprehensives in the emerging multicultural society of the 1960s. It has protected them since in spite of their limited success in imparting skills. British state schooling has thus been heavily co-opted to the causes of social and political integration, by being used to symbolise the chance that citizens from all cultural backgrounds can have, in a fair, open society, to write their own destinies and climb to the station in life they deserve, rather than being banished early into mediocrity.

Ironically, given its ideological attachment to it, something that this state education system does not seem generally good at is producing social mobility. But this may be as much a result of the wider shift in values and objectives as of movement away from selectivity itself. The influence of political objectives has created a dual education system. It was the careful attention given in grammar schools to science and technology that allowed the working class many of its best opportunities. But subjects such as these are now taught much more efficiently within the private sector, which has remained more responsive to the industrial (and financial sector) job market. Private schools, along with immigration from countries where state education systems are geared to actual achievement, produce a dispropor-tionate share of the highly qualified workforce in Britain. Their striving towards traditional meritocracy has made them increasingly popular among parents—even those on limited incomes—while less so with many Labour politicians, who consider that by giving priority to educational goals these schools are in some way cheating.

A further irony in this is that even the newly valued skills of human management, which the internal empire has made more salient, and which are central to the 'new' meritocratic rationale of state education itself, confer advantages on middle-class children at the expense of the working class. Jobs where conflict management and fostering of social integration are central rely heavily on old-fashioned leadership qualities, which come much more readily to confident, middle-class children. They tend to be acquired outside of formal educational settings, and depend a lot on the security of people's status—which has been affected in divergent ways by recent social changes. Within the internal empire, middle-class families have found an expansion of interesting work, promoting rights and diversity. But white working-class families have lost out heavily, as they now have to compete with needy newcomers for menial jobs, scarce public resources and state support. This underlies much of the polarisation that is taking place in British society. The *déclassé* position of the indigenous working class, and the resentful attitudes that come with this—which are sharpened by perceptions that the elite is actively sponsoring social mobility of newcomers—make it harder for them to take on integrative leadership roles and create serious obstacles to the movement of their children into a higher class.

In various ways, the public emphasis on individual rights has clearly had an enormous impact on British society. This is not, of course, a unique situation. There is always some tension between the imperatives of group need and individual social justice—as shown elsewhere in this collection; for example, in the chapter on Japan. But in the British case the value given to individual rights seems to have totally eclipsed that of collectivism—certainly at the public level. And this generates a paradox, or perverse loop, whereby the ostensible purpose of our new meritocratic elite appears simply to be the promotion of yet more social mobility. Much attention is given to achieving elite status, and very little to what the occupants are expected to *do* when installed, apart from smoothing the way for more of their kind.[10] This is both detrimental to essential social processes and, I believe, misses the point of what most ordinary people actually want out of life.

Service as its own reward

Michael's fictional meritocracy foundered because of its ruthless efficiency in dividing winners from losers. This is unlikely to happen in contemporary Britain. Our opportunity society is more likely to prove unsustainable because in according such priority to encouraging people to fulfil their potential, it fails to see that this is not what many people want or society needs. In any durable social system, a structure of public rewards needs to be joined to explicit recognition of public *service.* In most societies, the primary reward for service is the acknowledgement by others that one has made a valuable contribution to the group. Other rewards are usually justified on this basis, and are in a sense symbolic of it.

There is an even more fundamental corollary to this, which is crucial here. This is that the 'intrinsic' reward for service to others, of *knowing* that you have been useful, is available to some extent to any member of a group, not just to leaders. For most ordinary people, this is precisely where their main motivations and satisfactions in life arise. Social mobility into positions carrying greater status and rewards is not so valued by many people as New Labour imagine, not least because of its negative effect on families.[11] As noted elsewhere in this collection, by Belinda Brown, family ties are in practice what give individuals the incentive and encouragement to compete and succeed. By the same token, it is the knowledge that they are being useful to their families and communities that assures ordinary people of the self-respect they need to carry on leading productive lives even when this does *not* result in great success and public recognition. In both types of situation, it is being of use to others that is the source of appropriate motivations, and this give and take in the private realm comes before public rewards and status. Without these patterns of modest reciprocity, there would be no societies in which elites could occupy leading roles.

The great danger of New Labour's opportunity society may be that it places so much stress on public success unrelated to direct social inputs that it ends up devaluing the language of ordinary social contributions. The promise of social mobility has become a new opiate, handed out indiscriminately by our leaders, which interferes with our ability to cope with everyday business. Many people in Britain are aware of a serious dissonance between practices in the public realm and the moral economy of private life. In the latter they understand that self-respect comes from helping others, and that equality of esteem requires give and take with some mutual dependency. But this does not match what they see in the public realm. Not only are many of the most successful and rewarded people ones who do not appear to give anything (back) to society, but the ruling ethic invites all citizens to behave in exactly this way. Opportunity is not tempered with responsibility. At the same time, they see a growing underclass of people who are prevented from developing self-respect through contribution to the common good by the low (even negative) value attached to ordinary jobs and by the counter-incentives set up by the welfare system to remain dependent on public charity.

It is surely time to revive the notion that opportunities for advancement presented by the state should not be geared to gratification of ambition *per se*. They need to be qualified by an appreciation that ambition is most satisfying when it is harnessed to service, and also that you do not have to be a high-flyer in order to make *some* contribution. Social mobility in itself is not that important. Lower-class communities in the past have been able to build satisfying lives for their members around modest inputs to wider society. Mobility does have a place, for individuals as a vehicle for self-expression or escape from a group experienced as oppressive, and for groups as a means of recruiting people to do especially demanding or important jobs. But when promoting mobility for its own sake becomes a state objective, then this seems likely to produce a profoundly discontented and unstable society, with a demoralised underclass at its heart. When New Labour figures such as David Lammy start haranguing parents for 'not being ambitious enough for their children', then the political class has clearly lost touch with common sense.[12] This is alarming, and also coincides ominously with what Michael foretold in *Meritocracy*:

Everyone had to be imbued with eagerness to rise as high as his abilities justified. Before modern society could reach maturity, ambition had to be forced ever upwards, and the ideology of the people brought into conformity with the needs of the new scientific age.[13]

Paradoxically, the success of the *Meritocracy* book may itself have helped to feed the obsession with mobility, even though Michael the author was clearly sympathetic to the Chelsea Manifesto declaring that what needed distributing more equally was not access to *top* jobs, but respect for the contribution to society that *all* jobs make. Belief in the value of *all* work still survives in many quarters of Britain. And believers can perhaps take heart from the fact that as the idea of fully developing all talents becomes intensified, our government has increasing difficulty in finding people (other than recent migrants) willing to take on less prestigious work. This itself points to a weakness in any pro-meritocracy argument. In most societies, the *hardest* jobs to fill are probably the menial and boring positions right at the bottom of the occupational hierarchy. In many societies, these are given to slaves, serfs and unfree labourers, such as convicts and prisoners of war; and in virtually all societies, to new migrants. A state genuinely aiming at a fair and efficient economy would do well to cultivate greater rewards for *this* work, rather than courting ambition.

Where people have family and small-community responsibilities to meet, as most new migrants do now and workers did generally in the 1950s, then even these menial jobs can be satisfying and valued. But they hold little attraction for locally born people who have been brought up in a culture that insists on the right of everyone to develop their capacities to the full, and dismisses traditional awareness that self-respect derives in the end from doing things for others—even though this sentiment clearly helps motivate the ruling elite itself. The whole idea that extensive social mobility is important to society may be flawed. By assuming that talent is a scarce resource, possessed only by the few, it may generate more competition than is needed or can be contained. Many languishing in the underclass are not there because of lack of ability, or perverse incentives, or laziness. They are there precisely because the rhetoric of the 'opportunity society' makes them *so* ambitious that they cannot handle not being winners. They prefer to fail completely (and blame the system) than to set their sights lower—hence the stampede away from humble but essential labour. This is the other side of contemporary meritocracy, which we must start to confront and redress.

What we need now is not to be pushed into being more ambitious. This is not necessary. There will always be people who want to get more rewards than others. The priority should be to ensure that there are enough who are not too ambitious to be able to find satisfaction in making an ordinary-size contribution to society, in return for an ordinary reward.

The enabling state

The way to achieve this lies in re-creating a society that makes it possible for people to progress to more important positions if they have both aptitude and motivation, without in the process devaluing those who do not. It may be worth adding here, for those who take rates of social mobility as measures of the health of a society, that this need not work against it. Restoring value to social contribution, and stemming the power of the central state to sponsor mobility, might well boost levels of mobility, as it will remove current obstacles to motivation. Not least, by putting more control in the hands of people themselves, any withdrawal from sponsored meritocracy is likely to restore 'effort' as a key factor determining 'success'.

Any way forward involves reducing the *political* demands on the education system. While most educationalists are trying to respond to requests from parents, employers and communities to teach useful skills, the political class seems bent on manipulating outcomes in order to engineer social balance and stability. This is an unsustainable system. But instead of admitting that it has failed to understand what makes people and society tick, the state is now cranking up the opportunity rhetoric by blaming parents (even children themselves) for not having the sort of motivations that the state plan assumes and requires them to have. The price of this failure is that state education is becoming ever further divorced from the practical needs of the country. If we are to stand any chance of flourishing in the future, especially when—as must happen one day—we lose our privileged position helping to manage the global economy, then a change of direction is needed.

The fundamental principle that needs to be restored here is that rewards to individuals should reflect not just 'effort' and individual needs but service to a group. Some may object to this principle on the grounds that in a plural society it may be divisive to celebrate the idea of service to community. But this is surely based on a misconception, and always was. Any national society has many levels of group identity and shared interests, excluding some people and including others, all of which are compatible with an overall inclusive citizenship. In the British context, there need be no problem—apart from in the minds of the most fanatical statists or nationalists—in allowing communities of all sorts and sizes to enjoy their own cultures, internal loyalties and shared assets so long as they recognise an overarching British-ness. This has become better understood in recent years, so that the urge towards radical individualism may already be waning.

It follows from this that the state education system should itself be allowed to be more directly responsive to 'local' influences. I do not think that this would make it less attentive to the interests of parents, children and students engaged in the system. Indeed, in practice a state education service that was more able to listen to what its users actually wanted would soon become much more geared to practical imparting of skills and knowledge—as this is what private schools, which have to survive in the marketplace, do so well.[14] Many of the problems of state schools, including classrooms full of bored and disruptive pupils, might abate if they were able to respond more to what parents and children wanted and were less obliged to hold forcibly on to children in the name of maximising their opportunities.

One of the things that Michael often talked about in his later years was how *custodial* schools seemed to have become, and how counter-productive this was. There is little virtue in keeping adolescents at schools until an official leaving age if this just increases their resistance and prevents them from learning. Far better to allow them to leave years earlier, if they have achieved reasonable levels in literacy and numeracy. Those children eager to leave school would then have a real incentive to apply themselves. This would surely then uncover far more 'hidden talent' than the present regime. And if it were combined with greater supports for the return to education of adults who had acquired social responsibilities—and, with those responsibilities, good reasons to get qualifications—then the system could become structured efficiently around social needs rather than wasted on obstructive teenagers. In that way, movement through the upper reaches of the education system would be solely according to performance and desire. Michael remained ambivalent to the end about the idea of meritocracy. But reforms such as this might lead to a version of which he could have approved.

Ladder of Opportunity or Engine of Inequality?

RUTH LISTER

Introduction

IT has been suggested that meritocracy would be New Labour's 'big idea' for a third term.[1] In the run-up to the 2005 election, senior Labour politician Alan Milburn argued for Britain to become 'a nation based on merit, not class' and that promoting social mobility (as an expression of meritocracy) 'must be at the core of our ambitions for a Labour third term'.[2] In response, the central argument of this chapter is that if our goal is a more socially just society, meritocracy does not offer the way forward for a third term.

Meritocracy tends to be used in political debate as a synonym for equality of opportunity. As such, it is a principle of allocation of people to positions in the socio-economic hierarchy, typically jobs. From a social justice perspective, the principle is preferable to allocation of positions on the basis of inherited endowments, be they of social class, gender or 'race'/ethnicity. Here, equality of opportunity shades in to what are popularly called equal opportunities policies. The theory is that meritocracy offers a 'ladder of opportunity', on which everyone has an equal chance to climb as far as their 'merit' permits.

There is, though, as Adam Swift has argued, another meaning of meritocracy, which tends to be conflated with and elided by its 'equality of opportunity' meaning. Here it is a principle of distribution of rewards. It is, in his words, the claim that 'social justice demands that people's rewards should reflect their merit—with "merit" understood as some combination of their ability and commitment'[3] (IQ + effort, in Michael Young's original formulation). But, Swift warns, this is not a just principle of distribution at all.

I do not want to argue against the principle of equality of opportunity as an allocative mechanism. Instead, my argument is that when we move on to the territory of distributive mechanisms, the ideal of a meritocratic society offers us not the ladder of opportunity held out by its proponents but an engine of inequality. This was in effect the warning contained in Michael Young's satirical exposition, as he reminded us in a *Guardian* article in response to Tony Blair's espousal of the meritocratic ideal in the run-up to the 2001 election.[4]

 Published by Blackwell Publishing Ltd, 9600 Garsington Road, Oxford OX4 2DQ, UK and 350 Main Street, Malden, MA 02148, USA

The case against meritocracy

I will make four points in support of my argument:

- The economic inequality underpinned by a meritocratic distributive mechanism undermines meritocracy as an allocative mechanism of equality of opportunity.
- Moreover, meritocracy is likely to exacerbate socio-economic inequality both directly through, for example, 'winner takes all' tendencies and indirectly through its legitimisation of wide inequality.
- The meritocratic distributive principle tends to be based on narrow definitions of merit and of what is of value to society, which are insufficiently questioned but which have implications for social justice from the perspective of recognition as well as of redistribution, applying Nancy Fraser's formulation.[5]
- New Labour tends to bracket the principle of meritocracy with that of equal worth. Yet meritocracy and extreme inequality undermine recognition of equal worth, and therefore we should not abandon more egalitarian distributional principles.

Let me expand on each of these briefly.

Inequality undermines meritocracy

Ultimately, meritocracy is self-defeating in that the inequality associated with it as a distributional principle undermines it as an allocative principle. As Anthony Giddens, a proponent of the redistribution of opportunities over resources, acknowledges, in the kind of social order created by meritocracy 'the privileged are bound to be able to confer advantages on their children— thus destroying meritocracy'.[6] More recently, with Patrick Diamond he has strengthened the message: 'pure meritocracy is incoherent because, without redistribution, one generation's successful individuals would become the next generation's embedded caste, hoarding the wealth they had accumulated'.[7]

At the other end of the ladder, the evidence suggests that poverty makes it difficult for some children to get beyond the bottom rungs. A study by the Centre for Economic Performance a few years ago found that social and economic disadvantage was the most important factor hindering basic skills development.[8] It concluded that arguably the most powerful educational policy would be to tackle child poverty directly. At its most basic, hungry children cannot learn. Part of the policy agenda therefore has to be to ensure that all parents, regardless of their employment status, have adequate resources to enable their children to benefit from the educational opportunities available and to have a decent childhood.

This is very much the message of the Fabian Commission on Life Chances and Child Poverty. In its interim report, it argues as follows:[9]

What concerns us . . . is not merely the fact that talented children from income-poor backgrounds are less likely to realise their potential than those from affluent families, but that all children from income-poor backgrounds are less likely to realise their potential and to live in meaningful and rewarding ways than children from affluent families. The goal is therefore to improve the experiences and outcomes of all children and not merely to increase social mobility amongst the most able children, according to a meritocratic view of social justice.[10]

Meritocracy likely to exacerbate socio-economic inequality

A Performance and Innovation Unit (PIU) discussion paper on social mobility observes that 'a highly meritocratic society characterised by high rates of social mobility might have significant income inequalities and social tensions . . . The winners or upwardly mobile could scoop all the rewards leaving little for the rest'.[11] This is in part a reflection of the 'winner-takes-all' mentality that allows the meritorious few to streak ahead, accumulating huge material rewards of various kinds, leaving the rest of the field behind.[12] The enormity of these rewards cannot, however, be justified with reference to the merit of those to whom they accrue.[13] This is particularly so given that 'the opportunities to achieve "merit" are so unequal'.[14]

The tendency observed by the PIU may also be an indirect result of the legitimisation of inequality that meritocracy provides. As Michael Young argued, 'If meritocrats believe, as more and more of them are encouraged to, that their advancement comes from their own merits, they can feel that they deserve whatever they can get . . . So assured have the elite become that there is almost no block on the rewards they arrogate to themselves'.[15] R. H. Tawney characterised it beautifully in his parable of the tadpoles and frogs:

intelligent tadpoles reconcile themselves to the inconvenience of their position by reflecting that though most of them will live to be tadpoles and nothing more, the more fortunate of the species will one day shed their tails, distend their mouths and stomachs, hop nimbly onto dry land and croak addresses to their former friends on the virtues by means of which tadpoles of character and capacity can rise to be frogs.[16]

The flip side is that those who remain tadpoles or who slide back down into the swamp are likely to be branded as failures, deserving of their fate. As the PIU paper put it, 'the losers or downward mobile in a meritocracy would have no one to blame for their circumstances but their own lack of ability and commitment'.[17]

Narrow definitions of merit

The phrase 'their own lack of ability and commitment' raises another important issue: that of how ability and commitment—or merit—are defined and measured in a meritocratic, or would-be meritocratic, society. It is a question

234

that Barbara Wootton raised in a different context half a century ago, in her classic book *The Social Foundations of Wages Policy*. The equivalence between her own earnings in the 1930s and those of the elephant that gave children rides at Whipsnade Zoo contributed to Wootton's 'fundamental reflections about the social and economic forces which determine the valuations which our society sets upon different kinds of work'.[18]

It could be argued, for instance, that the childcare worker who is skilled at working with children and who gives herself 100 per cent to the job of childcare does not 'lack ability or commitment'. Yet childcare workers are paid a pittance. It cannot be argued that their work is not of value to society. Indeed, there are fears that the government's childcare strategy could be undermined by the lack of an adequate supply of childcare workers. In a series of studies, childcare workers 'said repeatedly that low pay encouraged society to afford low value to the work, which in turn affected recruitment and retention'.[19] So we have a vicious circle—the low value attached to care work means that it is low paid, which in turn encourages it to be lowly valued. There is a strong gender dimension to this.

A related point is made by Geoff Dench when he criticises New Labour for its lack of interest in 'providing proper rewards for menial or low-skill workers'. He observes that 'such quaint notions as the dignity of all labour, or importance of interdependence and value to all of the part played by the smallest cog in the machine—which were the essence of Old Labour—have long since disappeared from party manifestos'.[20]

One of the few public commentators to raise such issues regularly today is Polly Toynbee. Reflecting on her stint as a low-paid worker, she observes that 'what a person is paid signifies their worth and it is of primary emotional and social importance'.[21] 'Low pay is low status . . . Just as pay is a cause for boasting among the fat cats, it is equally a source of daily humiliation for the low paid, seeing how little one hour of their hard work is valued at'.[22]

Her remarks open up a perspective on social justice that tends to be overlooked or discounted when social justice is defined in purely distributional terms. It is emphasised by recognition theorists such as Alex Honneth, who argues that 'the core of all experiences of injustice [lies] in the withdrawal of social recognition, in the phenomena of humiliation and disrespect'.[23] I would not go quite that far but would, rather, apply Nancy Fraser's 'perspectival dualism', which looks at social justice through the bifocal lens of recognition and redistribution.[24] Low pay—particularly in a meritocratic, or would-be meritocratic, society—offends social justice principles of both distribution and recognition.

We therefore need: to do more about low pay; question the overall distribution of pay and in particular the huge salaries received by some; and, more generally, open up the whole issue of how different kinds of work are rewarded.

Equal worth

This leads to my last point, which concerns the tendency, most notably by Tony Blair, to bracket the principle of equal worth with that of meritocracy. This appears to provide a softening egalitarian gloss to the harsh edges of meritocracy—padding for those on the bottom rungs of the ladder. But the kind of extreme inequalities that are associated with meritocracy are likely to undermine equal worth in its more meaningful 'thick' sense, which goes beyond its 'thin' sense of simple equality before the law. It embraces what David Miller terms 'social equality': 'the idea of a society in which people regard and treat one another as equals, and together form a single community without divisions of social class'.[25]

It is difficult, though, for people to 'regard and treat one another as equals' in the context of a meritocratic ethos, which in effect is telling them they are not equals at all. The person at the top of the ladder is more meritorious than the person at the bottom. Meritocracy solidifies the structure of social hierarchy, which is in tension with the idea of social equality, even if it allows individuals to move up and down the structure more easily.

Moreover, if the gap between rich and poor is very wide, as it is likely to be in a meritocracy, then those at the top are too far removed geographically, socially and/or culturally from those at the bottom to feel that the latter are their equals or to recognise the bonds of common citizenship. Respect does not easily transcend 'the boundaries of inequality'.[26] This, in turn, is damaging for political equality and political citizenship.[27]

Conclusion

So, for all these reasons I would argue that while the allocative principle of equality of opportunity is in itself a fair one, it is not in itself sufficient to achieve social justice. Moreover, as a distributional principle, meritocracy acts not as a ladder of opportunity but as an engine of injustice. Thus, if we genuinely believe in recognition of equal worth, it is necessary to return to more egalitarian principles of distribution to guide policy, including policy on taxation of income and wealth.

The Future of Meritocracy

DAVID WILLETTS

Merit, worth and success

THE idea of a public intellectual is in vogue. Last year, *Prospect* magazine listed our top 100 'public intellectuals'. Stephan Collini's recent book, just like *Prospect*'s recent list, has created a fluttering in the dovecotes about who is in and who is out, who is up and who is down. High on anyone's list of great postwar public intellectuals would be Michael Young. He had a deep understanding and interest in social and economic change. But he wasn't a detached observer; he had a powerful moral vision too about how society could be better. As the author of Labour's 1945 manifesto, his was in many ways an egalitarian vision, though it was not narrow or mean-spirited; instead, it was what we would now call a commitment to widening participation in society.

Michael Young spent most of his life trying to pursue his vision in a way that Conservatives can understand and value. He did not try to pass laws to make us good. He tried to create institutions that would embody that vision. Whereas in theory he may have believed in the power of the state, in practice he worked through civil society. That is one reason why his influence lives on so strongly.

Michael Young didn't just create institutions, he also created concepts and words. Notably, he coined the term 'meritocracy' in his famous book *The Rise of the Meritocracy*, published in 1958. It is a fascinating, odd and deeply ambiguous book. Although some people in America have read it as a paean of praise for meritocracy, it is really a deeply ironic critique of the whole idea. He argues that to lose out in a society because of bad luck is painful enough, but to lose out because you are assessed as being without merit is far worse. In fact, it is a vision of a kind of dystopia that must have been influenced by other examples of the genre earlier in the century, such as Huxley's *Brave New World* and Orwell's *Nineteen Eighty-Four*. The debate over opportunity and social mobility is as lively today as it was then, so his heretical challenge to the conventional wisdom is as striking as ever.

Young's central argument is that in a meritocracy worldly success, and indeed moral worth, are all judged by the single benchmark of merit, defined as IQ plus effort. IQ is just a matter of being a member of the 'lucky sperm club', although effort does add a moral dimension. One of Michael Young's last writings before he died was an attack on Tony Blair for his worship of success. He thought the New Labour faith in creating opportunities for everybody to move up and move on showed a moral blindness to people who just couldn't make it in a modern mobile economy. It is the theme of

Published by Blackwell Publishing Ltd, 9600 Garsington Road, Oxford OX4 2DQ, UK and 350 Main Street, Malden, MA 02148, USA 237

Richard Sennett's recent book *Respect*. The argument coming from the left is that we are failing to show respect to people who have had a tough deal from life and are not going to be conventional successes.

Oddly enough, this is a strand in conservatism too, though it is all too easily submerged within a caricature of us worshipping personal success and regarding it as always coming with its own automatic justification. Friedrich von Hayek, in his great book *The Constitution of Liberty*, sets out a position that is both more compassionate and also shows a much deeper understanding of a market economy. He argues that in a free market economy prices work to signal demand and match it with supply. The overall system of ordered liberty may have a moral justification, but that does not mean that the individual outcomes represent moral worth or personal merit:

Most people will object not to the bare fact of inequality but to the fact that differences in reward do not correspond to any recognisable differences in the merits of those who receive them. The answer commonly given to this is that a free society on the whole achieves this kind of justice. This, however, is an indefensible contention if by justice it is meant proportionality of reward to moral merit. Any attempt to found the case of freedom on this argument is very damaging to it, since it concedes that material rewards ought to be made to correspond to recognisable merit, and then opposes the conclusion that most people draw from this by an assertion which is untrue. The proper answer is that in a free system it is neither desirable nor practicable that material rewards should be made generally to correspond to what men recognise as merit, and that it is an essential characteristic of a free society that an individual's position should not necessarily depend on the views that his fellows hold on the merit he has acquired.[1]

He carries on:

A society in which it was generally presumed that a high income was proof of merit and a low income of the lack of it, in which it was universally believed that position and remuneration corresponded to merit, in which there was no other road to success than the approval of one's conduct by the majority of one's fellows, would probably be much more unbearable to the unsuccessful ones than the one in which it was frankly recognised that there was no necessary connection between merit and success.

It would probably contribute more to human happiness if, instead of trying to make remuneration correspond to merit, we made clearer how uncertain is the connection between value and merit. We are probably all much too ready to ascribe personal merit where there is, in fact, only superior value.[2]

Indeed, Hayek cautiously welcomes Young's book in a footnote to this passage.

By civil society we mean not just a diversity of institutions, we mean a diversity of measures of moral worth. That then opens up deep questions about the shared principles on which we are to be governed. The American commentator, Nicholas Lemann, has observed that the debate on meritocracy is 'all prefix and no suffix'. There are deep questions here about the legitimacy and respect that needs to be earned by the people governing us. Michael Young has been absorbed by the sociologists. But perhaps because of his

238

rather old-fashioned faith in the Civil Service and government, less attention has been paid to some of the questions about the legitimacy of government that the book opens up. I am no exception to that rule. Instead, I want to focus here on the links between Michael Young's work and our current preoccupation with social mobility.

The decline in social mobility

Social mobility is now conventionally measured by transition matrices, in which 'perfect' mobility is taken to mean that your eventual income or social class are completely uncorrelated with those of your parents. This immediately raises key questions about the legitimate role and power of the family. We celebrate the success of those who move up and move out from poor families and deprived backgrounds, but we shouldn't forget those left behind, nor the reasons why. Inherited poverty, which we all wish to eradicate, is very closely linked to something we deeply value—the family. One recent study, for example, by the Institute of Social and Economic Research at Essex, showed that if you are brought up in a deprived area, your earnings are 10 per cent higher if you have a sibling than if you are an only child. The explanation for this striking difference was fascinating. The researchers argued that the obligation to help care for parents is greater if one is an only child. Hence an only child is more likely to stay in the area where he or she has been brought up, and perhaps sacrifice some of the time and effort needed to earn more. If, however, you shared these responsibilities with other siblings, then you have greater opportunities to work and train more, and indeed to move away.

People often ask why it is so hard to abolish child poverty in practice, although it is obviously an admirable aspiration in theory. The answer is that it requires a level of intervention in the family that would be unacceptable in a modern liberal society. That is why we can't suddenly create a meritocratic society. In his book Michael Young recognises this, comparing a meritocratic society to the Mohicans, 'who took away the best young men and women from a conquered tribe and reared them as members of their own families'. Even if a modern bureaucratic state could do the job as well as the Mohicans, which I rather doubt, we would still find it deeply objectionable. Indeed, John Goldthorpe has argued that if you want an example of a society that efficiently matches ability with occupation, using the state to do so, then the model is probably the postwar Soviet Union. This is not exactly a shining example for us to follow in twenty-first-century Britain.

Meritocracy and social mobility are both therefore very problematic once we think carefully about what achieving them would really involve. But they do both capture a crucial feature of modern capitalism—it doesn't like waste. It may not reward merit, but it certainly hates unused talent. That key feature of capitalism is ironically most famously captured in Thomas Gray's beautiful, melancholy poem *Elegy Written in a Country Church-Yard*:

Full many a gem of purest ray serene,
The dark unfathom'd caves of ocean bear:
Full many a flower is born to blush unseen,
And waste its sweetness on the desert air.

Some village-Hampden, that with dauntless breast
The little tyrant of his fields withstood,
Some mute inglorious Milton here may rest,
Some Cromwell, guiltless of his country's blood.

Michael Young conveys the same thought. He can't really have been mocking the idea of meritocracy where he describes the existing unmeritocratic system as follows:

Education was very far from proportioned to merit. Some children of an ability which would have qualified them as assistant secretaries were forced to leave school at 15 and become postmen. Assistant Secretaries delivering letters!—it is almost incredible. Other children with poor ability and rich connections, pressed through Eton and Balliol, eventually found themselves in mature years high officers in the Foreign Service. Postmen delivering demarches—what a tragic farce.[3]

Education, above all, is the key for opening up opportunities and ensuring that talents are not wasted. Let's now turn to what is actually happening to social mobility in Britain today, and why.

It is now generally accepted that social mobility in Britain is actually declining. This is particularly shocking because we are so used to thinking of social trends inexorably pushing us to become a more open and mobile society—'classless', with 'opportunities for all', as we politicians like to say. What is going on?

The main evidence comes from two longitudinal studies of people born in either 1958 or 1970. Researchers use the two databases to compare outcomes. The traditional matrices that measure mobility show that the outcomes of the 1970 cohort were more influenced by parents than for the 1958 cohort. The figures show that someone born in the poorest income quartile in 1958 had a 31 per cent chance of himself (this is sons only) being in the bottom quartile at age 33 and a 17 per cent chance of being in the top quartile. Someone whose parental income was in the highest quartile had a 17 per cent chance of ending up in the bottom quartile and a 35 per cent chance of being in the top quartile. In a world of frictionless social mobility, these figures would of course all be 25 per cent. If you then look at the cohort of sons born in 1970, for those born into the bottom income quartile, the son had a 38 per cent chance of remaining in the bottom quartile and a 16 per cent chance of moving into the top quartile. If your parental earnings were in the top quartile, then you only had an 11 per cent chance of yourself going down to the bottom income quartile, as against a 42 per cent chance of remaining in the top quartile yourself.

The deterioration in the trend is clearly taking us in the wrong direction. However, there are some who challenge the evidence. It is a long and technical debate. On balance, however, I think the case made by experts

240

such as Paul Gregg, Steve Machin and Jo Blanden is persuasive.[4] Britain is indeed becoming less socially mobile.

Michael Young seems to have assumed that meritocracy could be delivered, but that people would revolt against the very idea when they saw what it meant in practice. In reality, the opposite has happened. The idea of meritocracy and mobility is still very potent as an objective, but achieving it is proving much harder than people thought.

If social mobility is declining, and that appears to be the evidence from comparisons between the 1958 and 1970 cohorts, then many people assume that education must be the culprit.

The role of education

We can track the debate about education's failure to deliver increased mobility through the different stages of the system. Gordon Brown focused attention on universities with his notorious intervention in the Laura Spence affair. Higher education is very important. There has been a dramatic increase in the economic returns to education and this comes almost entirely from higher education. Over the past twenty years, Britain has seen a big increase in the earnings of graduates relative to non-graduates. It does indeed look as though the expansion in higher education has meant, above all, more places for students from more affluent backgrounds rather than students from poorer backgrounds. So the chances of a child from a high-income family getting a degree are still much greater than those for a child from a low-income background. This means that the expansion of higher education has not increased social mobility but, if anything, has contributed to its decline.

The universities were blamed for failing to reach out to potential students from more modest backgrounds, and we now have the useful Aim Higher Scheme. The trouble is that the scheme focuses very much on outreach to school students in their late teens, whereas raising awareness of the university option needs to start much earlier in a child's school career. That is why David Cameron and I have said there is a very strong case for strengthening the Aim Higher Scheme so that it reaches out to children at an earlier stage of their school careers—Aim Higher Sooner.

Universities, however, argue very powerfully that they can't be expected to correct for all the failings in the school system. If schools in deprived areas are not performing well, then there is a limit to what universities can do to adjust for this. Ultimately, they have to look not only at the potential but also the attainments of candidates coming before them. So the attention moved on to schools, and here the Sutton Trust has assembled some powerful evidence of the social background of children at our 200 best schools. It does look, sadly, as though these schools are not socially representative of the country as a whole, or even of the areas in which they are located. They have a lower than average proportion of pupils on free school meals than the areas in which they are located. One solution to this problem is to try to impose ever stricter controls over admissions. But it is just not possible to impose central controls that deliver equitable access. There are just far too many mechanisms whereby parents are going to be able to play the system. Instead, we need to take a very different approach, moving away from the dismal zero-sum game of deciding how a fixed number of places should be allocated at good schools. What we need is more good schools in total. That is the argument for reforms to open up the delivery of schooling to make it easier to create a greater diversity of schools, and to make it easier for schools to expand and link up with others.

Even this, however, isn't the end of the story. There is worrying evidence that measured cognitive ability does, if anything, decline for some groups of children during their infancy. There is a very lively debate now about the role of early years in providing intellectual and social stimulus for young children. I am sure there is much to be achieved here, but we need to be wary of what has been rightly criticised as 'infant determinism'. As Jerome Kagan argues in his fascinating book *Three Seductive Ideas*, some child development experts are beginning to match physicists and cosmologists in so confidently attributing so much explanatory power to initial events in the distant past. John Brewer has warned us in his challenging book *The Myth of the First Three Years* that we mustn't get carried away by such theories.

There is clearly much that education can do. It is incredibly frustrating that despite the best efforts of successive governments to try to improve educational standards, the contribution of education towards social mobility is, if anything, going backwards. Can we offer any further explanation of all this, beyond the continuing failings of our education system? There is one powerful explanation. The enormous expansion of education, especially higher education, must by definition have succeeded in bringing extra opportunities to many more to gain university qualifications than ever before. The assumption was that this would mean more students from modest backgrounds. But in reality the main beneficiaries have been a different, though equally meritorious, group. Only a generation ago, middle-class families attached much more significance to the education of sons than of daughters. The biggest single group of beneficiaries from the expansion of higher education have been young women, often from higher-income family backgrounds— even if ones that would not previously have sent daughters into higher education. Research by Galindo-Rueda and Vignoles bears this out. In the 1958 cohort, high-ability boys from high-income backgrounds were 1.7 times more likely to get a degree than high-ability boys from low-income backgrounds. For the 1970 cohort, this had increased to 1.8.

For girls, the figures are far more dramatic. A 1958 cohort girl from a high-ability/high-income background was 1.6 times more likely to get a degree than a girl from a high-ability/low-income background. A 1970 cohort girl from a high-ability/high-income background was 2.7 times more likely to get a degree than a girl from a high-ability/low-income background. So what has really happened is that daughters from high-income backgrounds have poured into higher education as never before. But there hasn't been a similar opening up of opportunities for girls from more modest backgrounds, and when it comes to boys the gap has barely shifted.

The crude figures reveal the scale of what has been going on. Back in 1974, 145,000 men and 75,000 women went to university. So there was a total of 220,000 university students, with almost twice as many men as women. Since then, of course, polytechnics have become universities, increasing the number of university students at a stroke by several hundred thousand. But the trend has carried on upwards as well. Thirty years later in 2004, the number of male university students more than quadrupled to 650,000. But the number of female university students increased twelve-fold to 950,000. Back in 1974, there were half as many female students as men. Now there are one and a half times as many female students as men. The expansion of education has helped both men and women—but it has had a far greater impact on women than men.

No one can be against this expansion of opportunities for young women. What we must hope is that after the big increase in participation by women from more affluent backgrounds in education, we can now once more turn our attention to the group that has benefited surprisingly little from the education expansion of the past thirty years—boys and girls from more modest backgrounds.

This is just one example of a wider phenomenon. I don't believe we pay enough attention to the changing role of women as a driver of social trends in Britain. We worry not just about mobility, but about the growing inequality of incomes between households. Again, you have to understand the trans-formation of opportunities for women to make sense of this phenomenon. As these competent women emerge from higher education, they are very likely to marry men from a similar background—so-called assortative mating. Most measures of inequality focus on household incomes, not individual incomes. A household with two highly paid earners separates itself even further from other households.

Perhaps in the spirit of Michael Young, I could be so brave as to formulate a proposition that summarises these changes as well as anything. Increasing equality between the sexes has meant increasing inequality between social classes. Feminism has trumped socialism.

Notes

Introduction: Reviewing Meritocracy (pp. 1–14)

1 See page 281 of Peter Hennessy, 'Michael Young and the Labour Party', *Contemporary British History*, vol. 19, no. 3, 2005, pp. 281–4.
2 Geoff Dench, 'Tracking the Demeter tie', in Geoff Dench, Tony Flower and Kate Gavron, eds, *Young at Eighty: the Prolific Public Life of Michael Young*, Manchester, Carcanet, 1995.
3 Michael Young, *The Rise of the Meritocracy*, New Brunswick, Transaction, 1994, p. 123.
4 See, for example, Geoff Dench, Kate Gavron and Michael Young, *The New East End*, London, Profile, 2006, chapters 5 and 6.
5 See, for example, Tom Sefton, 'Give and take: attitudes to redistribution', in Alison Park et al., eds, *British Social Attitudes, the 22nd Report*, London, Sage, 2005.
6 Edward Shils and Michael Young, 'The meaning of the coronation', *The Sociological Review*, new series, vol. 1, no. 2, December 1953.
7 In this respect, it is interesting that the sponsorship of social mobility within relatively deprived groups is seen in Britain as part of the normal practice of running an effective meritocracy. In many countries there is a sharp distinction made between meritocracy—where educational and occupational progression is based strictly on performance—and affirmative action—where preference is shown to members of under-achieving groups, and which is usually regarded as hostile to meritocracy. The Labour Government does not deny promoting the social mobility of under-performing groups, in the interests of social harmony and stability, and overall social justice. But it generally claims that this does not constitute affirmative action, on the grounds that no specific quotas are set!
8 See my chapter below.
9 'Social justice demands [*sic*] that a person's life chances should not depend on those of their parents. In a socially just society, the daughter of a Hartlepool shop assistant would have the same chance of becoming a high court judge as the daughter of a Harley Street doctor. It may never be possible to attain that ideal of social mobility, but we should strain every ounce of our political energy to get nearer it and make it the animating theme of New Labour.' (*The Guardian*, 10 January 2002.)
10 W. G. Runciman, *Relative Deprivation and Social Justice: a Study of Attitudes to Inequality in Twentieth Century England*, London, Routledge, 1966.
11 Adam Swift, 'Would perfect mobility be perfect?' *European Sociological Review*, vol. 20, no. 1, 2004, pp. 1–11.

The Labour Party as Crucible (pp. 17–26)

1 A fuller account and discussion of this subject can be found in chapters 3 and 5 of Asa Briggs' biography of Michael: *Michael Young: Social Entrepreneur*, Basingstoke, Palgrave, 2001.
2 See I. Zweiniger-Bargielowska, 'Rationing, austerity and the Conservative Party recovery after 1945', *Historical Journal*, vol. 37, no. 1, 1994.

Published by Blackwell Publishing Ltd, 9600 Garsington Road, Oxford OX4 2DQ, UK and 350 Main Street, Malden, MA 02148, USA

3 See Bernard Donoughue and George W. Jones, *Herbert Morrison: Portrait of a Politician*, London, Weidenfeld & Nicholson, 1973; and K. Middlemas, *Power, Competition and the State, vol. 1: Britain in Search of Balance, 1940–1961*, Basingstoke, Macmillan, 1986, pp. 61 and 185.

4 For an early discussion of the subject, see P. A. A. Rogow and P. Shore, *The Labour Government and British Industry*, Oxford, Blackwell, 1955.

5 Donoughue and Jones, *Herbert Morrison*, p. 355.

6 For a near-contemporary analysis, see N. Dennis, F. Henriques and C. Slaughter, *Coal is Our Life*, London, Routledge, 1956.

7 Michael Young, *Labour's Plan for Plenty*, London, Gollancz, 1947, p. 11.

8 Ibid., p. 56.

9 See Margaret Cole, *The Life of G. D. H. Cole*, London, Macmillan, 1971. G. D. H. Cole had written *Guild Socialism* in 1920.

10 Alan Bullock, *The Life and Times of Ernest Bevin, vol. II*, London, Heinemann, 1967, p. 338.

11 Michael Young, *Small Man, Big World: a Discussion of Socialist Democracy, Towards Tomorrow*, no. 4, 1948.

12 William Temple, 'The state', quoted in C. I. Schottland, ed., *The Welfare State: Selected Essays*, New York, Harper & Row, 1967, p. 23.

13 H. G. Nicholas, *The British General Election of 1950*, London, Macmillan, 1951, p. 51.

14 See, for example, R. F. McKenzie, a professor at LSE (R. F. McKenzie and A. Silver, *Angels in Marble: Working Class Conservatives in Urban England*, London, Heinemann Educational, 1968).

15 See Asa Briggs, *A Study of the Work of Seebohm Rowntree, 1871–1954*, London, Greenwood, 1961.

16 Roy Jenkins, *A Life at the Centre*, London, Macmillan, 1991. See also Stephen Haseler, *The Gaitskellites*, London, Macmillan, 1969, pp. 141–58.

Meritocracy in the Civil Service, 1853–1970 (pp. 27–35)

1 Michael Young explained that although *The Rise of the Meritocracy* was published in 1958, it was written over five years between 1952 and 1957, with eleven publishers rejecting it. One thought it would be better if it was turned into a novel *à la* Aldous Huxley's *Brave New World* (interview, August 2001, and Michael Young, *The Rise of the Meritocracy*, New Brunswick, Transaction, 1994, p. 9).

2 The Northcote–Trevelyan Report can be found in the Fulton Report; see Committee on the Civil Service, *The Civil Service*, Cmnd 3638, 1968, vol. 1, Appendix B.

3 Peter Hennessy, *Whitehall*, London, Secker & Warburg, 1989, pp. 41–2.

4 House of Commons, *Official Report*, 15 June 1855, col. 2043.

5 Ibid., col. 2099.

6 Ibid., col. 2106.

7 Ibid., col. 2109.

8 Ibid., col. 2094.

9 Ibid., 9 April 1869, col. 483.

10 Ibid., 2 April 1869, col. 31.

11 Hennessy, *Whitehall*, pp. 114–15.

12 Phillip Gummett, *Scientists in Whitehall*, Manchester, Manchester University Press, 1980, pp. 22–8.

13 Hennessy, *Whitehall*, pp. 90–114.

14 Roy Jenkins, *Asquith*, London, Collins, 1964, pp. 413–15.

15 Hennessy, *Whitehall*, pp. 120–68.
16 Ibid., p. 127.
17 Harold Laski's most famous works include *Authority in the Modern State* (Yale University Press, 1919), *Parliamentary Government in Britain* (George Allen & Unwin, 1938) and *A Grammar of Politics* (George Allen & Unwin, 1948).
18 *Social Insurance and Allied Services*, Cmnd 6404, London, HMSO, 1942.
19 Interview with Sir Frank Cooper, 13 June 2001.
20 Armstrong was interviewed for BBC2's *Man Alive*. The transcript was published in *The Listener* on 28 March 1974.
21 Hennessy, *Whitehall*, p. 165.
22 Leo Pliatzky, *Getting and Spending*, Oxford, Basil Blackwell, 1982, p. 27.
23 Anthony Sampson, *Anatomy of Britain*, London, Hodder & Stoughton, 1962, p. 620.
24 Hugo Young, *This Blessed Plot*, London, Macmillan, 1998, p. 106.
25 *Employment Policy*, Cmnd 6527, London, HMSO, 1944.
26 Edmund Dell, *The Chancellors*, London, HarperCollins, 1997, p. 266.
27 See pages 83–5 of Thomas Balogh, 'The apotheosis of the dilettante: the establishment of mandarins', in Hugh Thomas, ed., *The Establishment*, London, Blond, 1959, pp. 83–126.
28 Tony Benn, *Out of the Wilderness: Diaries 1963–67*, London, Hutchinson, p. 25; diary entry for 25 May 1963.
29 Balogh, 'The apotheosis of the dilettante', p. 111.
30 Ibid., p. 84.
31 Ibid., p. 88.
32 Ibid., p. 91.
33 Ibid., p. 84.
34 Ibid., p. 117.
35 Ibid., p. 110.
36 Fabian Society, *The Administrators*, Fabian Tract No. 355, London, Fabian Society, 1964, p. 17.
37 Ibid., p. 15.
38 Ibid., p. 1.
39 Hennessy, *Whitehall*, p. 190.
40 Interview with Michael Young, August 2001.

A Tract for the Times (pp. 36–44)

1 This is an updated version of my chapter 'The ups and downs of the meritocracy', which first appeared in Geoff Dench, Tony Flower and Kate Gavron, eds, *Young at Eighty: the Prolific Public Life of Michael Young*, Manchester, Carcanet, 1995.
2 Robert Hewison, *Too Much: Art and Society in the Sixties, 1960–75*, London, Methuen, 1988.
3 Paul Barker, 'Michael Young', *New Society*, vol. 12, no. 304, 8 August 1968 (reprinted from *Interplay*, New York).
4 At Thames & Hudson, Helen Scott-Lidgett kindly gave access to the publisher file of newspaper and magazine reviews of the first British and US editions of *The Rise of the Meritocracy*.
5 Edward Shils and Michael Young, 'The meaning of the Coronation', *The Sociological Review*, new series, vol. 1, no. 2, December 1953.
6 See Central Advisory Council for Education—England, *15 to 18, vol. 1: Report* (the Crowther Report), London, HMSO, 1959.

7 Richard Herrnstein and Charles Murray, *The Bell Curve: Intelligence and Class Structure in American Life*, New York, The Free Press, 1994.

8 Nicholas Lemann, '2034' (review of new American edition of *The Rise of the Meritocracy*), *The Atlantic Monthly*, vol. 273, no. 6, June 1994.

9 Richard Hoggart, *The Uses of Literacy*, London, Chatto & Windus, 1957.

10 Raymond Williams, *Culture and Society*, London, Chatto & Windus, 1958.

11 Jonathan Swift, *A Modest Proposal for Preventing the Children of Poor People from Becoming a Burthen to their Parents or Country; and for Making Them Beneficial to the Publick*, Dublin, S. Harding, 1729 (reprinted in Ian MacGowen, ed., *The Restoration and 18th Century London*, Macmillan Anthologies of English Literature, vol. 3, London, Macmillan, 1989).

12 Raphael Samuel, *Theatres of Memory*, London, Verso, 1994.

13 Paul Rock and Stanley Cohen, 'The Teddy Boy', in Vernon Bogdanor and Robert Skidelsky, eds, *The Age of Affluence, 1951–64*, London, Macmillan, 1970.

14 Una McGovern, ed., *Chambers Biographical Dictionary*, 7th edn, Edinburgh, Chambers Harrap, 2002.

15 Herbert Spencer, *The Principles of Biology*, London, Williams & Norgate, 1864–7.

16 H. C. Dent, *Growth in English Education, 1946–52*, London, Routledge & Kegan Paul, 1954; cited in Peter Hennessy, *Never Again: Britain 1945–51*, London, Jonathan Cape, 1992.

17 Susan Crosland, *Tony Crosland*, London, Jonathan Cape, 1982.

18 David Donnison, 'Education and opinion', *New Society*, vol. 10, no. 265, 26 October 1967.

19 Anonymous, 'Education: exam pass', *The Economist*, 23 October 2004.

20 Ferdinand Mount, *Mind the Gap: the New Class Divide in Britain*, London, Short Books, 2004; see also his chapter in this present collection.

21 Colin MacInnes, *Absolute Beginners*, London, MacGibbon & Kee, 1959.

22 Iona and Peter Opie, *The Lore and Language of Schoolchildren*, Oxford, The Clarendon Press, 1959.

23 Zelda Cheatle and Michael Mack, eds, *The Street Photographs of Roger Mayne*, London, Zelda Cheatle Press, 1993.

24 Bernard Crick, *George Orwell: a Life*, London, Secker & Warburg, 1980.

25 Margaret Drabble, ed., *The Oxford Companion to English Literature*, 6th edn, Oxford, Oxford University Press, 2000.

We Sat Down at the Table of Privilege . . . (pp. 45–60)

1 The title of this chapter is attributed to Angela Carter, as quoted by Ali Smith in 'Renaissance woman: the passionate legacy of Angela Carter', *Guardian Review*, 15 May 2004, p. 4.

2 Michael Young, *The Rise of the Meritocracy*, Harmondsworth, Penguin, 1961, p. 169.

3 Ibid., p. 171.

4 Ibid., p. 122.

5 Ibid., p. 172.

6 John Bowlby, 'Maternal care and mental health', *WHO Paper No. 14*, World Health Organisation, 1951 (second edition published as *Child Care and the Growth of Love*, Harmondsworth, Penguin, 1953).

7 Michael Young, 'The future of the family', the first *ESRC Annual Lecture*, Swindon, ESRC, 1990, p. 16. Michael Young was the first chairman, in 1965, of what was then called the Social Science Research Council.

8 Young, *The Rise of the Meritocracy* (1961 edn), p. 94.

9 Shulamith Firestone, *The Dialectic of Sex: the Case for Feminist Revolution*, New York, Morrow, 1970.

10 See page 414 of K. Kiernan and J. Eldridge, 'Inter and intra-cohort variation in the timing of first marriage', *British Journal of Sociology*, vol. 48, no. 3, 1987, pp. 406–28.

11 Committee on Higher Education (the Robbins Committee), *Higher Education, Report*, Cmnd 2154, London, HMSO, 1963, p. 100.

12 See chapter 6 of K. Kiernan, H. Land and J. Lewis, *Lone Motherhood in Twentieth Century Britain*, Oxford, Oxford University Press, 1998.

13 Ibid., chapter 2.

14 Committee on Higher Education (the Robbins Committee), *Higher Education, Appendix One*, Cmnd 2154–1, London, HMSO, 1963, p. 224.

15 Alison Hennegan, 'And battles long ago', in L. Heron, ed., *Truth, Dare or Promise. Girls Growing Up in the Fifties*, London, Virago, 1985, p. 148.

16 Kiernan et al., *Lone Motherhood*, chapter 8.

17 See Lesley Doyal et al., 'Your life in their hands: migrant workers in the National Health Service', *Critical Social Policy*, vol. 1, no. 2, 1981.

18 Committee on Higher Education (the Robbins Committee), *Higher Education*, p. 168.

19 See Central Advisory Council for Education—England, *15 to 18, vol. 1: Report* (the Crowther Report), London, HMSO, 1959, p. 453.

20 Committee on Higher Education (the Robbins Committee), *Higher Education, Appendix One*, p. 82.

21 Committee on Higher Education (the Robbins Committee), *Higher Education*, p. 168.

22 For a full account of the origins of the Open University, see P. Hall, 'Creating the Open University', in P. Hall, H. Land, R. Parker and A. Webb, *Change, Choice and Conflict in Social Policy*, London, Heinemann, 1975.

23 Committee on Higher Education, p. 211.

24 Ibid., p. 127.

25 Ibid., p. 168.

26 Crowther Report, p. 33.

27 Ibid., p. 34.

28 Ibid., p. 36.

29 Central Advisory Council for Education—England, *Half Our Future* (the Newsom Report), London, HMSO, 1963, introduction, p. xiii, emphasis added.

30 Ibid., p. 137.

31 Ibid., p. 135.

32 Ibid., p. 137.

33 Cited in Hannah Gavron, *The Captive Wife*, London, Routledge, 1968, p. 142.

34 A. Hunt, *A Survey of Women's Employment*, London, HMSO, 1968, p. 185.

35 *The Observer*, 1964; cited by Gavron, *The Captive Wife*, p. 108.

36 C. Steadman, 'Landscape for a good woman', in Heron, *Truth, Dare or Promise*.

37 Heron, *Truth, Dare or Promise*, p. 7.

38 Eleanor Rathbone, *The Disinherited Family*, London, George Allen & Unwin, 1924, p. 217.

39 A. Marshall, *Elements of Economics of Industry*, 3rd edn, London, Macmillan, 1901, p. 342.

40 Audrey Wise, interviewed in M. Wandor, *Once a Feminist: Stories of a Generation*, London, Virago, 1990, p. 203.

41 Irene Breugel, 'Women's employment, legislation and the labour market', in Jane

Lewis, ed., *Women's Welfare, Women's Rights*, London, Croom Helm, 1983, p. 138; see also Sheila Rowbotham, *Women's Consciousness, Man's World*, Harmondsworth, Penguin, 1973 and Wise, in Wandor, *Once a Feminist*.

42 Wise, in Wandor, *Once a Feminist*, p. 223.

43 See, for example, Ellen Malos, ed., *The Politics of Housework*, London, Alison & Busby, 1980. See also Anne Phillips, *Divided Loyalties: Dilemmas of Sex and Class*, London, Virago, 1987; and Sheila Rowbotham, *Dreams and Dilemmas: Collected Writings*, London, Virago, 1983.

44 Young, *The Rise of the Meritocracy* (1961 edn), p. 173, emphasis in the original.

45 Rathbone, *The Disinherited Family*; and H. Land, 'The family wage', *Feminist Review*, vol. 6, 1980, pp. 55–78.

46 See, for example, C. Cockburn, *The Machinery of Dominance: Women, Men and Technical Know-how*, London, Pluto, 1985.

47 Anne Phillips and B. Taylor, 'Sex and skills: notes towards a feminist economics', *Feminist Review*, vol. 6, 1980, pp. 56–79. For an overview of feminist debates on women and employment in the 1970s, see the collection of articles in *Feminist Review*, ed., *Waged Work: a Reader*, London, Virago, 1986.

48 The title of this section comes from a 1970 Women's Liberation Workshop.

49 Sheila Rowbotham, *Threads through Time: Writings on History and Autobiography*, Harmondsworth, Penguin, 1999, p. 78.

50 Steadman, 'Landscape for a good woman', p. 119.

51 Gavron, *The Captive Wife*, p. 132.

52 See page 276 of M. Nicol, 'You opened the door', in Helene Curtis and Mimi Sanderson, eds, *The Unsung Sixties: Memoirs of Social Innovation*, London, Whiting & Birch, 2004, pp. 268–83.

53 See page 296 of Ellen Malos, 'He always says he's sorry afterwards: Bristol Women's Aid', in Curtis and Sanderson, *The Unsung Sixties*, pp. 284–97.

54 See page 382 of J. Faux, 'A learning experience for us all: pre-school playgroups', in Curtis and Sanderson, *The Unsung Sixties*, pp. 381–93.

55 Ibid., p. 385.

56 Ibid., p. 389.

57 Curtis and Sanderson, *The Unsung Sixties*, p. xi.

58 Rowbotham, *Threads through Time*, p. 77.

59 Ibid., p. 76.

60 Heron, *Truth, Dare or Promise*.

61 J. McCrindle and S. Rowbotham, eds, *Dutiful Daughters*, Harmondsworth, Penguin, 1977.

62 M. Ingham, *Now we are Thirty: Women of the Breakthrough Generation*, London, Eyre Methuen, 1981.

63 Valerie Walkerdine, 'Dreams from an ordinary childhood', in Heron, *Truth, Dare or Promise*, p. 74.

64 See, for example, Peter Marris, *Loss and Change*, London, Routledge, 1974.

65 B. Martin, 'Post-war austerity to postmodern carnival: culture in Britain from 1945', in A. Roberink and H. Righart, eds, *The Great, the New and the British*, Utrecht, Institut voor Geschredenis, 2000, p. 40.

66 McCrindle and Rowbotham, *Dutiful Daughters*, p. 9.

67 Walkerdine, 'Dreams from an ordinary childhood', p. 76.

68 M. Rendall and S. Smallwood, 'Higher qualifications, first-birth timing, and further childbearing in England and Wales', *Population Trends*, 111, Spring 2003, p. 18.

69 Malos, *The Politics of Housework*.
70 Leonora Davidoff, 'Regarding some "old husbands' tales": public and private in feminist history', in *Worlds Between: Historical Perspectives on Gender and Class*, Cambridge, Polity, 1995, p. 227.

The Chequered Career of a Cryptic Concept (pp. 61–72)

1 Thanks are due to Anne Hill, Research Assistant in REPP, for her efforts to collate data used in this chapter, and for the legwork involved in locating various elderly journal papers in the 'creepy basements' of libraries at ANU; and to Barry Hindess, for helpful observations on the inherent ambiguities of studying a dual narrative and interpreting the changing role of authorial voice over time. An earlier version of this paper was presented at The Australasian Political Studies Association Conference, Adelaide, 29 September–1 October 2004.
2 'Blair leads tributes to OU founder', BBC News Online, 16 January 2002; http://news.bbc.co.uk/1/hi/uk/1762699.stm
3 Michael Young, 'Down with meritocracy', *The Guardian*, 29 June 2001.
4 Michael Young, *The Rise of the Meritocracy*, New Brunswick, Transaction, 1994, p. xv.
5 This chapter does not insist that there is a 'right' reading of Young's text or that there can only be one meaning of 'meritocracy', particularly when it is difficult to decode which early sections of the book are advocacy and which are ironic, when the real or fictional Michael Young is speaking, or even if any true words are spoken in jest. It does, however, review the political science literature with the aim of understanding the 'misunderstanding' in Young's terms as his views on the text remained consistent throughout his lifetime.
6 This chapter refers to the 1994 Transaction edition, which includes a valuable new introduction by the author, reflecting upon the reception of 'meritocracy'.
7 Michael Young, *The Rise of the Meritocracy, 1870–2033: an Essay on Education and Equality*, London, Thames & Hudson, 1958.
8 Young, *The Rise of the Meritocracy* (1994 edn), p. xi.
9 Ibid., p. 1.
10 Ibid., p. 180.
11 Ibid., p. 84.
12 Ibid., p. 100.
13 Young did not go on to publish this *BJS* paper in 1967, which is a pity—if only on the grounds that if he had done so, this really would have confused the historians.
14 Young, *The Rise of the Meritocracy* (1994 edn), p. 11.
15 Young, 'Down with meritocracy'.
16 Young, *The Rise of the Meritocracy* (1994 edn), pp. xiv–xv; Daniel Bell, 'The meritocracy and equality', *The Public Interest*, vol. 29, 1972, pp. 9–68; and Daniel Bell, *The Coming of the Post-industrial Society*, New York, Basic Books, 1973.
17 Young, *The Rise of the Meritocracy* (1994 edn), p. xv.
18 Ibid., p. xv.
19 Ibid., p. xvii.
20 John Rawls, *A Theory of Justice*, Oxford, The Clarendon Press, 1972, pp. 100–7.
21 Young, *The Rise of the Meritocracy* (1994 edn), p. xvii.
22 Ibid., pp. xv–xvi.
23 Ibid., p. xvii.
24 See Jennifer Platt, 'The affluent worker revisited', in Colin Bell and Helen Roberts,

eds, *Social Researching: Politics, Problems, Practice*, London/Boston, Routledge & Kegan Paul, 1984; Anthony J. Chapman, 'Assessing research: citation-count shortcomings', *The Psychologist*, vol. 8, 1989, pp. 336–44; and Sara Delamont, 'Citation and social mobility research: self-defeating behaviour?', *Sociological Review*, vol. 37, no. 2, 1989, pp. 322–37.

25 Young, *The Rise of the Meritocracy* (1994 edn), p. xv.

26 Ibid., p. xii.

27 Ibid., p. xvi.

28 This chapter was originally conceived of as a paper for a political science audience; hence the orientation of the sample. The sample papers were taken from ISI Web of Science in September 2004 and updated in March 2005, and are as follows (the papers are analysed as a group and not identified individually): Perry Anderson, 'Left and right', *New Left Review*, vol. 231, 1998, pp. 73–81; Bruce Baum, 'Millian radical democracy: education for freedom and dilemmas of liberal equality', *Political Studies*, vol. 51, 2003, pp. 404–28; Claudia Buchmann, 'The state and schooling in Kenya: historical developments and current challenges', *Africa Today*, vol. 46, 1999, pp. 95–117; Thomas R. Conrad, 'Debate about quota systems—analysis', *American Journal of Political Science*, vol. 20, 1976, pp. 135–49; P. H. Coombs, 'Elitism and meritocracy in developing countries: selection policies for higher education—R. Klitgaard', *Annals of the American Academy of Political and Social Science*, vol. 494, 1987, pp. 201–3; John W. Danford, 'Adam Smith, equality and the wealth of sympathy', *American Journal of Political Science*, vol. 24, 1980, pp. 674–95; D. B. Davis, 'American Jews and the meritocratic experiment: the other Zion', *New Republic*, vol. 208, 1993, p. 29; Heinz Eulau, 'ASDA Presidential Address, 1972: skill revolution and consultative commonwealth', *American Political Science Review*, vol. 67, 1973, pp. 169–91; C. E. Finn, 'The big test: the secret history of the American meritocracy—N. Lemann', *Commentary*, vol. 108, 1999, pp. 57–60; Franklin Foer, 'After meritocracy: toward a sociology of the Bushies', *New Republic*, vol. 224, 2001, pp. 20–3; Nathan Glazer, 'The end of meritocracy: Should the SAT account for race?', *New Republic*, vol. 221, 1999, p. 26; P. Green, 'IQ and future of equality', *Dissent*, vols 23–4, 1976, pp. 398–414; R. Gross, 'The rise of the meritocracy—Young, M.', *Commentary*, vol. 28, 1959, pp. 458–60; D. Jones, 'The lot of black professionals: meritocracy proves elusive in New York', *Dissent*, vol. 34, 1987, pp. 530–5; D. Karen, 'The big test: the secret history of the American meritocracy—N. Lemann', *Nation*, vol. 269, 1999, pp. 40–4; R. W. Krouse, 'Polyarchy and participation: the changing democratic theory of Robert Dahl', *Polity*, vol. 14, 1982, pp. 441–63; Seymour M. Lipset, 'Trade-union exceptionalism: the United States and Canada', *Annals of the American Academy of Political and Social Science*, vol. 538, 1995, pp. 115–30; Richard M. Merelman, 'Public education and social structure, 3: modes of adjustment', *Journal of Politics*, vol. 35, 1973, pp. 798–829; Richard M. Merelman, 'Social mobility and equal opportunity', *American Journal of Political Science*, vol. 17, 1973, pp. 213–36; Gregory Mitchell, Philip E. Tetlock, Daniel G. Newman and Jennifer S. Lerner, 'Experiments behind the veil: structural influences on judgments of social justice', *Political Psychology*, vol. 24, 2003, pp. 519–47; Kim Phillips-Fein, 'The big test: the secret history of the American meritocracy—N. Lemann', *Dissent*, vol. 47, 2000, pp. 113–6; R. Rabkin, 'The big test: the secret history of the American meritocracy—N. Lemann', *Policy Review*, vol. 101, 2000, pp. 67–71; Douglas Rae, 'Maximum justice and an alternative principle of general advantage,' *American Political Science Review*, vol.

69, 1975, pp. 630–47; John Stanley, 'Equality of opportunity as philosophy and ideology', *Political Theory*, vol. 5, 1977, pp. 61–74; P. Starr, 'The big test: the secret history of the American meritocracy—N. Lemann', *New Republic*, vol. 221, 1999, pp. 36–9; Abigail Thernstrom, 'The end of meritocracy: should the SAT account for race?', *New Republic*, vol. 221, 1999, p. 27; Michael Walzer, 'Exclusion, injustice, and the democratic state', *Dissent*, vol. 40, 1993, pp. 55–64; W. A. Weisskop, 'Dialectics of equality', *Annals of the American Academy of Political and Social Science*, vol. 409, 1973, pp. 163–73; Dennis H. Wrong, 'The rise of the meritocracy—Young, M.', *Dissent*, vol. 7, 1960, pp. 207–10.

29 See http://isi6.isiknowledge.com/

30 The ISI Subject Categories include some multiple counting, as journals may be assigned to more than one area.

31 It is interesting to note the dominance of American political scientists to date in both citing Young's original work and discussing meritocracy. The present volume (a book) was earlier conceived of as a special journal-based edition of *The Political Quarterly* and would have been the first foray into this territory within the British political science serial literature, veering neither sharply towards the utopian or dystopian versions, but reclaiming the concept in the search for a workable middle ground: a positive take on Young's ambivalence.

32 Young, *The Rise of the Meritocracy* (1994 edn), p. xvii.

Looking Back on *Meritocracy* (pp. 73–7)

1 This is a transcript of a filmed interview with Michael and it is reproduced here by kind permission of Jane Gabriel, Gabriel Productions Ltd.

A Brief Profile of the New British Establishment (pp. 81–9)

1 M. Bils and P. J. Klenow, 'Does schooling cause growth or the other way around?', *NBER Working Paper 6393*, Cambridge, Mass., National Bureau of Economic Research, Inc., 1998.

2 In 1973, there were 453,000 students in higher education, in 1997–8 1.2 million and in 2002–3 2.4 million; see National Statistics, *Social Trends*, nos. 30 and 35.

3 National Statistics, *Social Trends*, no. 35, 2005.

4 From 1998, public-sector employment rose every year, to stand at 5,882,000 in December 2005. This was 719,000 higher than in June 1998, but still below the levels of 1991 and 1992 (National Statistics, 'Public sector employment: growth slows in 2005', published online, 7 April 2006; http://www.statistics.gov.uk/CCI/nugget.asp?ID=407&Pos=1&ColRank=1&Rank=374).

5 See, for example, Pierre Bourdieu, *The State Nobility: Elite Schools in the Field of Power*, trans. Lauretta C. Clough, Stanford, Stanford University Press, 1996.

Face, Race and Place (pp. 90–6)

1 Sandra Sanglin-Grant, *Widening the Talent Pool: Racial Equality in FTSE 100 Companies*, London, Runnymede Trust, 2002; Sandra Sanglin-Grant, *Divided by the Same Language? Equal Opportunities and Diversity Translated*, London, Runnymede Trust, 2003.

2 Sandra Sanglin-Grant and Robin Schneider, *Moving On Up: Racial Equality and the Corporate Agenda. A Study of FTSE 100 Companies*, London, Runnymede Trust, 2000.

3 Sandra Sanglin-Grant, *The Space Between: Bridging the Gap between Policy and Practice on Race Equality*, London, Runnymede Trust, 2005.

4 Runnymede Trust, *This is Where I Live: the Past, Present and Future of Multi-ethnic Britain* (CD-ROM and notes for teachers), London, Runnymede Trust, 2005.
5 Runnymede's official response to the Government's White Paper on establishing a single equalities body is entitled 'Runnymede's response to "Fairness for All"', and can be read in its entirety on the Runnymede website (http://www.runnymedetrust.org).
6 Geoff Dench, *Minorities in the Open Society*, New Brunswick, Transaction, 2003, p. xxix.

Marginalised Young Men (pp. 97–104)

1 Paul Willis, *Learning to Labour: How Working Class Kids Get Working Class Jobs*, Farnborough, Hants, Avebury, 1977.
2 Finnola Farrant, *Out for Good*, London, Howard League for Penal Reform, 2006.
3 John H. Laub and Robert J. Sampson, *Divergent Lives: Delinquent Boys to Age 70*, Boston, Mass., Harvard University Press, 2003.

The Unmaking of the English Working Class (pp. 105–8)

1 Michael Young, *The Rise of the Meritocracy, 1870–2033: An Essay on Education and Equality*, London, Thames & Hudson, 1958, p. 106.
2 Ibid., p. 107.
3 Ibid., pp. 107–8.
4 Ibid., pp. 189–90.
5 Ibid., p. 190.
6 An extended version of these arguments is to be found in Ferdinand Mount, *Mind the Gap: the New Class Divide in Britain*, London, Short Books, 2004.
7 Michael Young and Peter Willmott, *Family and Kinship in East London*, London, Routledge & Kegan Paul, 1957.

Age and Inequality (pp. 109–15)

1 J. Steintrager, *Bentham*, London, George Allen & Unwin, 1977.
2 P. Thane, *The Foundations of the Welfare State*, London, Longman, 1982.
3 N. Isles, *Life at the Top: the Labour Market for FTSE 250 Chief Executives*, London, The Work Foundation, 2003.
4 C. Trinder, G. Hulme and U. McCarthy, *Employment: the Role of Work in the Third Age*, Dunfermline, Carnegie United Kingdom Trust for Carnegie Inquiry into the Third Age, 1992.
5 R. H. Tawney, *Equality*, 4th edn, London, George Allen & Unwin, 1952.
6 David Donnison, *The Politics of Poverty*, Oxford, Blackwell, 1982.
7 Peter Laslett, *A Fresh Map of Life: the Emergence of the Third Age*, London, Weidenfeld & Nicholson, 1989.

The Moral Economy of Meritocracy (pp. 127–33)

1 New introduction to Michael Young, *The Rise of the Meritocracy*, New Brunswick, Transaction, 1994.
2 *The Economist*, 29 December 2004.
3 The *Times Literary Supplement*, 24 June 2005.
4 Suggested further readings: Kenneth Arrow, Samuel Bowles and Steven Durlauf, eds, *Meritocracy and Economic Inequality*, Princeton, Princeton University Press,

2005; Daniel Bell, *The Cultural Contradictions of Capitalism*, New York, Basic Books, 1996 [1976]; Geoff Dench, Tony Flower and Kate Gavron, eds, *Young at Eighty: the Prolific Public Life of Michael Young*, Manchester, Carcanet, 1995; and Thomas Nagel, *Equality and Partiality*, Oxford, Oxford University Press, 1991.

Japan at the Meritocracy Frontier (pp. 134–56)

1 See Makoto Aso, *Eriito to kyoiku* (*Education and the Elite*), Tokyo, 1968; and R. V. Clements, *Managers: a study of their careers in industry*, London, 1968.

2 Hiroshi Ishida, *Social Mobility in Contemporary Japan*, Stanford, Stanford University Press, 1993, p. 70.

3 Takehiko Kariya, paper in preparation.

4 Ibid.

5 Sorifu survey, 1968; Naikakufu survey, 2000.

6 Takehiko Kariya, paper in preparation.

7 Takehiko Kariya and James Rosenbaum, 'Bright flight: unintended consequences of detracking policy in Japan', *American Journal of Education*, vol. 107, no. iii, May 1999.

8 Takehiko Kariya, *Kaisoka nihon to kyoiku kiki* (*Increasingly Stratified Japan and the Educational Crisis*), Tokyo, Yushindo, 2001.

9 Takehiko Kariya, 'Towards a "learning capitalist" society: expanding inequality in Japanese education and Japan's knowledge-based economy', paper presented at Nissan Institute seminar, Oxford, 28 November 2005. The 'family cultural environment score' was calculated by means of a factor analysis, which produced a single factor.

10 Naikakufu, *Kokumin seikatsu ni kansuru yoron chosa* (*An Opinion Survey on National Living Conditions*), quoted in Yoshiki Honda, 'Ruten no churyuron' ('Volatile notions of the middle class'), *Shinjoho*, 92, March 2005.

11 *Asahi Shimbun*, 3 January 2006.

12 Ministry of Health, Labour and Welfare, *Shugyo kozo kihon chosa* (*Annual Wage Census*), Tokyo, 2002.

13 *Nihon Keizai Shinbun*, 27 December 2005.

14 Toshaki Tachibanaki, ed., *Fuin sareta fubyodo* (*Inequality Signed and Sealed*), Tokyo, 2004; Kariya, *Kaisoka nihon to kyoiku kiki*; Toshiki Sato, *Fubyodo shakai Nihon* (*Japan: the Unequal Society*), Tokyo, Chuko Shinso, 2000; Masahiro Yamada, *Kibo kakusa shakai* (*Society of Stratified Hopes*), Tokyo, Chuo Koron Shinsha, 2005; Yoshio Higuchi and Zaimusho, Zaimu sogo seisaku kenkyujo (Ministry of Finance Policy Research Institute), eds, *Nihon no shotoku-kakusa to shakai kaiso* (*Income Differentials and Social Stratification in Japan*), Tokyo, Nihon Hyoronsha, 2003.

15 Higuchi, *Nihon no shotoku-kakusa to shakai kaiso*.

16 Jouni Valijarvi, paper presented at seminar on Education and Reform in a Global Age, University of Tokyo, December 2004.

Just Rewards (pp. 157–62)

1 Katharine Newman, *No Shame in My Game*, New York, Knopf and The Russell Sage Foundation, 1999.

2 Michael Young, *The Rise of the Meritocracy*, Harmondsworth, Penguin, 1961.

3 John Rawls, *A Theory of Justice*, Oxford, The Clarendon Press, 1972.

Resolving the Conflict between the Family and Meritocracy (pp. 168–82)

1 Michael Young, 'Is inequality inevitable?' First *Rita Hinden Memorial Lecture*, Bedford College, London, 18 November 1972, p. 4.
2 Ibid., p. 10.
3 Ibid., p. 5.
4 Ibid., p. 159.
5 India Knight, 'Sucks to Cinderella syndrome', *The Sunday Times*, 31 October 2004.
6 Michael Young, *The Rise of the Meritocracy*, New Brunswick, Transaction, 1994, p. 122.
7 Ibid., p. 44.
8 Ibid., p. 176.
9 Ibid., p. 13.
10 Peregrine Worsthorne, *In Defence of Aristocracy*, London, HarperCollins, 2004.
11 Young, *The Rise of the Meritocracy* (1994 edn), p. 157.
12 Ibid., p. 130.
13 Ibid., pp. 19–20.
14 Ibid., p. 64.
15 Ibid.
16 Ibid., p. 158.
17 Ibid., pp. 161–2.
18 Ibid., p. 94.
19 Ibid., p. 21.
20 Ibid., p. 167.
21 David Miliband, 'Opportunity for all: targeting disadvantage through personalized learning', *New Economy*, vol. 10, no. 4, 2003.
22 Harry Brighouse, 'Learning by example? Replicating the success of exemplary schools is no simple task', *New Economy*, vol. 10, no. 4, 2003.
23 Neil McIntosh, 'Promoting a pro-education culture', *New Economy*, vol. 10, no. 4, 2003.
24 Adam Swift, 'Justice, luck and the family', in Samuel Bowles, Herbert Gintis and Melissa Osborne Groves, eds, *Unequal Chances: Family Background and Economic Success*, Princeton, Princeton University Press, 2005.
25 Ibid.
26 Ibid.
27 Ibid.
28 Young, *The Rise of the Meritocracy* (1994 edn), pp. 13–14.
29 Stephen Aldridge, 'Social mobility: a discussion paper', Performance & Innovation Unit (PIU), London, DfES, 2001, point 55.
30 Nick Cohen, 'How our schools are failing the poor', *Evening Standard*, 17 January 2005.

Meritocracy and Popular Legitimacy (pp. 183–94)

1 Richard Herrnstein and Charles Murray, *The Bell Curve: Intelligence and Class Structure in American Life*, New York, The Free Press, 1994.
2 P. Bauer, *Equality, the Third World and Economic Disillusion*, London, Weidenfeld & Nicolson, 1981, chapter 2.

3 A. H. Halsey, *A History of Sociology in Britain*, Oxford, Oxford University Press, 2004.

4 Peter Saunders, *Unequal but Fair? A Study of Class Barriers in Britain*, London, Institute of Economic Affairs, 1996.

5 G. Payne, *Mobility and Change in British Society*, Basingstoke, Macmillan, 1987.

6 John Goldthorpe, *Social Mobility and Class Structure in Modern Britain*, 2nd edn, Oxford, The Clarendon Press, 1987; Gordon Marshall, Harold Newby, David Rose and Carol Vogler, *Social Class in Modern Britain*, London, Routledge & Kegan Paul, 1987; R. Erikson and J. Goldthorpe, *The Constant Flux: a Study of Class Mobility in Industrial Societies*, Oxford, The Clarendon Press, 1992.

7 Saunders, *Unequal but Fair?*, chapter 6; and Peter Saunders, 'Might Britain be a meritocracy?', *Sociology*, vol. 29, no. 1, 1995, pp. 34–41.

8 Saunders, *Unequal but Fair?*, chapters 7 and 8; Peter Saunders, 'Social mobility in Britain: an empirical evaluation of two competing explanations', *Sociology*, vol. 31, no. 2, pp. 261–88; R. Bond and P. Saunders, 'Routes of success: influences on the occupational attainments of young British males', *British Journal of Sociology*, vol. 50, no. 2, 1999, pp. 217–50; Peter Saunders, 'Reflections on the meritocracy debate in Britain', *British Journal of Sociology*, vol. 53, no. 4, 2002, pp. 559–74; D. Nettle, 'Intelligence and class mobility in the British population', *British Journal of Psychology*, vol. 94, 2003, pp. 551–61.

9 Emile Durkheim, *The Division of Labour in Society*, London, Macmillan, 1933, pp. 375–7.

10 K. Davis and W. Moore, 'Some principles of stratification', *American Sociological Review*, vol. 10, 1945, pp. 242–9.

11 Frank Field, *Neighbours from Hell*, London, Politico's Publishing, 2003. See also J. Bartholomew, *The Welfare State We're In*, London, Politico's Publishing, 2004; Theodore Dalrymple, 'The frivolity of evil', *City Journal*, Autumn 2004, pp. 113–19.

12 Robert K. Merton, 'Contributions to the theory of reference group behaviour', in his *Social Theory and Social Structure*, New York, The Free Press, 1957.

13 Quoted in Ronald Dore, 'Man of merit', in Geoff Dench, Tony Flower and Kate Gavron, eds, *Young at Eighty: the Prolific Public Life of Michael Young*, Manchester, Carcanet, 1995, p. 173. See also Gordon Marshall and Adam Swift, 'Merit and mobility', *Sociology*, vol. 30, 1996, pp. 375–86.

14 Hans Eysenck versus L. Kamin, *Intelligence: the Battle for the Mind*, London, Pan, 1981.

15 Peter Saunders and Colin Harris, *Privatization and Popular Capitalism*, Buckingham, Open University Press, 1994, Table 7.2; and Peter Saunders, 'What is fair about a "Fair Go"?', *Policy*, vol. 20, no. 1, Autumn 2004, pp. 3–10.

The New Assets Agenda (pp. 197–204)

1 Keith Dowding, Jurgen de Wispelaere and Stuart White, eds, *The Ethics of Stakeholding*, London, Palgrave Macmillan, 2003.

2 Stuart White, *The Civic Minimum: on the Rights and Obligations of Economic Citizenship*, Oxford, Oxford University Press, 2002.

3 Will Paxton, ed., *Equal Shares? Building a Progressive and Coherent Asset-based Welfare Policy*, London, IPPR, 2003, p. 3; Will Paxton and Mike Dixon, *The State of the Nation: an Audit of Injustice in the UK*, London, IPPR, 2004.

4 F. A. von Hayek, *The Constitution of Liberty*, London, Routledge & Kegan Paul, 1960.

5 Thomas Paine, 'Agrarian justice', in Michael Foot and Isaac Kramnick, eds, *The Thomas Paine Reader*, Harmondsworth, Penguin, 1987, p. 483.

6 James Meade, *Efficiency, Equality and the Ownership of Property*, London, George Allen & Unwin, 1964.

7 Bruce Ackerman and Anne Alstott, *The Stakeholder Society*, New Haven, Conn., Yale University Press, 1999.

8 Gavin Kelly and Rachel Lissauer, *Ownership for All*, London, IPPR, 2000.

9 Julian Le Grand and David Nissan, *A Capital Idea: Start-up Grants for Young People*, London, Fabian Society, 2000.

10 Ackerman and Alstott, *The Stakeholder Society*, p. 5.

11 Michael Graetz and Ian Shapiro, *Death by a Thousand Cuts: the Fight over Taxing Inherited Wealth*, Princeton, Princeton University Press, 2005.

12 Will Paxton and Stuart White, eds, *The Citizen's Stake*, Bristol, Policy Press, 2006.

New Labour and the Withering Away of the Working Class? (pp. 205–13)

1 This chapter is a revised version of an article that appeared as 'Neo-classical Labour', in *Renewal*, vol. 14, no. 1, 2006.

2 See David Marquand, *The Unprincipled Society: New Demands and Old Politics*, London, Jonathan Cape, 1988.

3 Jospeh Schumpeter, *Capitalism, Socialism and Democracy*, London, George Allen & Unwin, 1979.

4 Nick Cohen, *Pretty Straight Guys*, London, Faber & Faber, 2003, pp. 223–47.

5 See C. Leadbeater, *Living on Thin Air: the New Economy*, London, Viking, 2000.

6 See, for example, M. Bridges, *Job Shift: How to Prosper in a Workplace without Jobs*, London, Nicolas Brealey, 1995; and R. Rifkin, *The End of Work: the Decline of the Global Labour Force and the Dawn of the Post Market Era*, New York, G. P. Putnam & Sons, 1995.

7 See, for example, R. Reich, *The Work of Nations*, London, Simon & Schuster, 1993.

8 See J. Cruddas, P. Nolan and G. Slater, 'The real economy not the new economy: the case for labour market regulation', in K. D. Ewing and J. Hendy, eds, *A Charter of Workers' Rights*, London, Institute of Employment Rights, 2002; and D. Coates, *Raising Lazarus: the Future of Organized Labour*, London, Fabian Society, 2005.

9 M. Campbell, S. Baldwin, S. Johnson, R. Chapman, A. Upton and F. Walton, *Skills in England 2001—Research Report*, Nottingham, DfES, 2001, p. 9.

10 See, for example, D. Lipsey, 'Too much choice', *Prospect*, December 2005.

11 John Denham, 'The rigid market model won't survive the real world', *The Guardian* 21 December 2005.

12 See Polly Toynbee, *Hard Work: Life in Low-pay Britain*, London, Bloomsbury, 2003.

13 L. Byrne, *Why Labour Won: Lessons from 2005*, London, Fabian Society, 2005.

14 Patrick Diamond, *Equality Now: the Future of Revisionism*, London, Fabian Society, 2005.

A Delay on the Road to Meritocracy (pp. 214–20)

1 An adaptation of this piece, addressing issues behind the 2006 Education Bill, was published in the *New Statesman* on 6 March 2006, as 'Where did it all go wrong?'

2 Michael Young, *The Rise of the Meritocracy*, Harmondsworth, Penguin, 1961, pp. 55–6.

3 This and other ministerial speeches can be found on the Department for Education and Skills website; see http://www.dfes.gov.uk

4 Department for Education and Skills (DfES), *Higher Standards: Better Schools for All*, Cmd 6677, October 2005, paragraph 4.24.

5 Young, *The Rise of the Meritocracy* (1961 edn), p. 41.

6 Robin Pedley, *The Comprehensive School*, 3rd edn, Harmondsworth, Penguin, 1978, p. 173.

7 See, for example, Jo Blanden, Paul Gregg and Stephen Machin, *Intergenerational Mobility in Europe and North America*, London, LSE Centre for Economic Performance, 2005; and Performance & Innovation Unit (PIU), *Social Mobility: a Discussion Paper*, London, HMSO, 2001.

8 Office of the Schools Adjudicator, *Annual Report*, September 2004 to August 2005.

9 The *Times Educational Supplement*, 4 November 2005.

10 The *Times Educational Supplement*, 11 November 2005.

11 Sutton Trust, *Rates of Eligibility for Free School Meals*, London, Sutton Trust, 2005.

12 Social Market Foundation, *School Admissions: a Report of the Social Market Foundation Commission*, London, SMF, 2004.

Putting Social Contribution back into Merit (pp. 221–31)

1 See, for example, Jeremy Paxman, *The English: a Portrait of a People*, London, Michael Joseph, 1998.

2 These were sometimes the same people. A number of the key figures in the emerging social sciences who carried out the necessary revolution in social administration were people such as David Donnison and Eileen Younghusband, who had grown up in the colonies.

3 Ken Livingstone, 'A City for the Asian century', *The Guardian*, 7 April 2006; though he conspicuously fails to note the City's dependence on the US global capitalist empire.

4 Geoff Dench, 'The new mysteries of class', *Prospect*, December 2004.

5 Cabinet Office, *Ethnic Minorities and the Labour Market*, London, HMSO, 2002.

6 Geoff Dench, 'The new meritocracy', *New Statesman*, 24 March 2003.

7 Minette Marin, 'Do-gooding schools that do everything but teach', *The Sunday Times*, 9 March 2003.

8 Michael Young and Peter Willmott, 'Social grading by manual workers', *British Journal of Sociology*, vol. 7, no. 4, 1956, pp. 337–45.

9 Peter Sacks, 'Pseudo-meritocracy', *Boston Review*, December/January 2000.

10 Adam Swift, 'Seizing the opportunity', *New Economy*, vol. 10, no. 4, 2003, pp. 208–9.

11 This is not a new point: for example, see Peter Marris, 'Individual achievement and family ties: some international comparisons', *Journal of Marriage and the Family*, November 1967.

12 David Lammy, 'I know too many grieving families', *Evening Standard*, 20 September 2004.

13 Michael Young, *The Rise of the Meritocracy*, New Brunswick, Transaction, 1994, p. 117.

14 Dennis O'Keeffe, *Political Correctness and Public Finances*, London, Institute of Economic Affairs, 1999.

Ladder of Opportunity or Engine of Inequality? (pp. 232–6)

1 Richard Reeves, 'The belief that more education will create more equal opportunities has been proved wrong', *New Statesman*, 24 May 2004, pp. 29–31.
2 Alan Milburn, 'Labour values', in *Fabian Commission on Life Chances and Child Poverty*, London, Fabian Society, 2005, pp. 77 and 80.
3 Adam Swift, 'Seizing the opportunity', *New Economy*, vol. 10, no. 4, 2003, pp. 208–9.
4 Michael Young, 'Down with meritocracy', *The Guardian*, 29 June 2001.
5 Nancy Fraser, *Justice Interruptus*, London, Routledge, 1997; Nancy Fraser, 'Social justice in an age of identity politics; redistribution, recognition and participation', in Nancy Fraser and Alex Honneth, *Redistribution or Recognition? A Political–Philosophical Exchange*, London, Verso, 2003.
6 Anthony Giddens, *The Third Way*, Cambridge, Polity, 1998, p. 102.
7 Patrick Diamond and Anthony Giddens, 'The new egalitarianism: economic inequality in the UK', in Anthony Giddens and Patrick Diamond, eds, *The New Egalitarianism*, Cambridge, Polity, 2005, p. 108.
8 Peter Robinson, *Literacy, Numeracy and Economic Performance*, London, LSE Centre for Economic Performance, 1997.
9 Fabian Commission on Life Chances and Child Poverty, *Why Life Chances Matter*, London, Fabian Society, 2005, p. 47. See also its final report, *Narrowing the Gap* (2006).
10 See also Edward Miliband, 'Does inequality matter?' in Giddens and Diamond, *The New Egalitarianism*.
11 Stephen Aldridge, 'Social mobility: a discussion paper', Performance & Innovation Unit (PIU), London, DfES, 2001, paragraphs 69 and 71.
12 R. D. Atkinson, 'Inequality in the new knowledge economy', in Giddens and Diamond, *The New Egalitarianism*.
13 Ben Jackson and Paul Segal, *Why Inequality Matters*, London, Catalyst, 2004.
14 Brian Barry, *Why Social Justice Matters*, Cambridge, Polity, 2005, p. 110.
15 Aldridge, 'Social mobility: a discussion paper'.
16 R. H. Tawney, *Equality*, 4th edn, London, George Allen & Unwin, 1952, p. 108.
17 Aldridge, 'Social mobility: a discussion paper', paragraph 71.
18 Barbara Wootton, *The Social Foundations of a Wages Policy*, London, George Allen & Unwin, 1955, p. 9.
19 C. Cameron, A. Mooney and P. Moss, 'The child care workforce', *Critical Social Policy*, vol. 22, no. 4, 2002, p. 578.
20 Geoff Dench, *Minorities in the Open Society*, New Brunswick, Transaction, 2003, p. xxiii.
21 Polly Toynbee, *Hard Work: a Challenge to Low Pay*, London, The Smith Institute, 2002, p. 35.
22 Ibid., p. 14; see also Polly Toynbee, *Hard Work: Life in Low-pay Britain*, London, Bloomsbury, 2003.
23 Alex Honneth, 'Redistribution as recognition: a response to Nancy Fraser', in Fraser and Honneth, *Redistribution or Recognition?*, p. 134.
24 Fraser, 'Social justice in an age of identity politics', p. 63.
25 David Miller, 'What kind of equality should the Left pursue?', in Jane Franklin, ed., *Equality*, London, IPPR, 1997, p. 83.
26 Richard Sennett, *Respect*, London, Allen Lane, 2003, p. 23.
27 Anne Phillips, *Which Equalities Matter?* Cambridge, Polity, 1999.

The Future of Meritocracy (pp. 237–43)

1 F. A. von Hayek, *The Constitution of Liberty*, London, Routledge & Kegan Paul, 1960, pp. 93–4.
2 Ibid., pp. 98–9.
3 Michael Young, *The Rise of the Meritocracy*, Harmondsworth, Penguin, 1961, p. 10.
4 See, for example, Jo Blanden, Paul Gregg and Stephen Machin, *Intergenerational Mobility in Europe and North America*, London, LSE Centre for Economic Performance, 2005.

Index

Editorial organisation © 2006 The Political Quarterly Publishing Co. Ltd

Editorial organisation © 2006 The Political Quarterly Publishing Co. Ltd